To
Grace, Caleb, and Sutton

FOREWORD

When you're taking a trip to an exotic or alien place, you want an experienced tour guide—one who has been there before, knows the terrain well, can help you find the best places to see and knows the pitfalls to avoid. Whether you're an experienced follower of Jesus or a relatively new Christian, you *want* Debbie Johnson as your guide through the New Testament. She tells us what to expect and what we will need to make the most of our journey through this life—and into the next. She uses humor to great effect. She is vulnerable, no arm-chair observer who seems immune to the struggles of the journey. Her prescriptions are realistic and connected to real life. She writes in plain, accessible language—with ample examples at every turn. With the New Testament in one hand and Debbie's guidebook in the other, you will experience the Christian journey to be an exciting venture—though not one for the fainthearted.

William W. Klein, PhD
Professor of New Testament
Denver Seminary

ENDORSEMENTS

Deep, messy, humorous, fun, enlightening, and refreshing is Debbie's journey through the New Testament. Although a familiar hike, Debbie's lead into the scriptures makes the ancient wisdom blossom with fresh and sudden "aha applications" at every turn. I felt wrapped in my Savior's love, new and remarkable! Debbie's words are creatively genuine making for a rigorous hike, not a simple "postcard" destination. I absolutely loved the experience! A real masterpiece!

—Luis Villarreal, Founder, Save Our Youth Mentoring

Debbie is skilled not only in understanding the scriptures but traveling along as a compassionate friend. You will not experience a sense that the journey is only for professionals, but with a bit of coaching, you might discover that the scriptures seem to be written for the joy and benefit of all. Happy adventures!

—Karl Wheeler,
Manager of Stuck in the Middle, a conversation place for those wanting to navigate the fractures between left and right Christianity,
Littleton, Colorado

An enduring challenge for evangelism is making God's timeless and holy word fresh, informative, and accessible for Christians and non-Christians alike. With *The Journey*, Debbie Johnson aptly meets that challenge with a creative "backpack tour" through the New Testament. I don't even like to hike, and I was captivated by Johnson's engaging voice and interesting analysis. The book will be very useful to anyone seeking to revitalize their ministry.

—Adrian Miller,
James Beard Award-winning author and Executive Director of the Colorado Council of Churches

Taking this journey through the New Testament with Debbie is like traveling with a wise good friend. She brings fresh insights into familiar passages and new clarity for more difficult to understand passages. At the end of each reading, Debbie offers a word or a phrase to place in our "backpacks." I want to encourage you to take Debbie's suggestion and meditate on that word of truth… it provides a sweet reflection to savor throughout the day. You are going to love this journey! I'm ready to take it all over again.

—Cindy Smith, LCSW

PRETRIP INTRODUCTION

Years ago I took a six-week backpacking trip to Europe. It was glorious...so worth the blisters and weariness and surprises.

We camped a lot since we went on the cheap, so my backpack contained everything I needed. It was heavy but a good fit. A week or so into the trip I actually preferred having it on. It balanced me. I got to visit some of the world's most amazing places with my trusty backpack.

For the most part I knew where items were in my pack (like my toothbrush!), but every now and then I had to dig for something. I discarded a few things along the way. And of course, I picked up new treasures.

I loved that journey, so I've decided to call our trek through the New Testament (what else but) *The Journey*. Our backpack contains items for nearly a year. Frankly, you just need one item—trusting belief—but the whole pack-full makes for the trip of a lifetime.

Some people will start the journey already sold on it. Some may have an a-ha moment along the way. Some may be skeptical. I can only speak for myself. I've decided to follow Jesus…and I invite you to go with me.

All are invited on this journey, so just tuck that New Testament into the top of the pack…and let's roll.

NOTES

The version of the Bible most widely-used nowadays is the New International Version (NIV). Scripture references used in *The Journey* are from the NIV and, where marked, *The Message*, which is a well-respected, contemporary-language translation by the late Eugene Peterson.

I recommend that you read the scripture in your Bible first, then the entry. The Gospels (Matthew, Mark, Luke, and John) have parallel narratives since four different men were reporting on the same story. I've chosen to cover the entire book of Matthew in depth. I'll only cover material in Mark, Luke, and John that wasn't in Matthew, generally-speaking. Like a good journey, it'll make sense when you get there.

If I've used a biblical quote from the passage being studied, for example, John 3:16 in the entry covering John chapter 3, I have not cited its "address" in the entry. However, when I've pulled in related scriptures from elsewhere in the Bible, you'll find those addresses listed.

Sometimes the entries are just a few verses long; other times they cover several chapters. It depends on the complexity of the text. In the book of Revelation, I deferred to the experts since it's quite cryptic. I condensed the entire twenty-two chapters into a few entries, but I encourage you to study every word of the Revelation narrative nonetheless. (Talk about a fascinating read!)

If you read an entry a day, you'll get through the New Testament in about three hundred days, but you can also read it straight through or use it as a companion with other types of Bible study.

Each entry ends with an "Item in the Backpack." Hopefully it captures the essence of the entry, like hope or compassion or forgiveness. I invite you to meditate on that word or phrase throughout the day. May it bless you.

I've been immersed in scripture since childhood, but I haven't been to seminary. I'm not a theological expert, but I've been a Christian since I was six and now I'm…well, never mind. Let's just say I've been at it for a while. But since, it's very important to me to be accurate. I wish to thank Dr. William Klein, professor of New Testament at Denver Seminary, who read through the entire manuscript and made suggestions and corrections. I'm deeply grateful for this.

Please know, however, that this isn't a theological tome. You might want to pick up *How to Read the Bible for All Its Worth* by Gordon D. Fee and Douglas Stuart, fourth edition Grand Rapids: Zondervan, 2014 or Eugene Peterson's *The Navigator Bible Studies Handbook* or attend classes through Bible Study Fellowship, Community Bible Study, or a local church for in-depth training. I've written from my own viewpoint, expressing my opinions, musing on the Word of God as a fellow pilgrim on this journey.

I've been told my writing is "contemplative with a fun voice." (I *think* that's a compliment.) I should tell you that I write like I talk. I'm honest. I'm sometimes "angsty." I ask questions. I'm a little self-deprecating because I'm well aware of my shortcomings. And frankly, I don't always find the Christian journey to be a walk in the park.

I do, however, find it to be incomparable. Priceless.

I think you'll find a fresh way to view the Bible on this journey, whether you're a skeptic or a long-time Christ follower.

And by the way, our destination is love…to love and be loved.

After all, God *is* love.

Why I Believe

1. We're all on the journey called life, so whether we've chosen the path or it has chosen us, we're on it nonetheless. I believe most of us (all of us?) want our lives to count, maybe even to transcend. Some people opt for the simple "Be a good person. Do well in school. Rise to the top. The End" path. Some draw inspiration from the hero's journey (adventure/crisis/victory/return) or *The Pilgrim's Progress* or *Hinds' Feet on High Places* (good people's pilgrimages through life) or *Life of Pi* (we choose the story we want to believe) or even *Star Wars*, which, according to George Lucas, is based on a synthesis of all religions.

   There are commonalities. There is a quest. There will be ordeals along the way. Evil clashes with good. Humanity searches for meaning. And hopefully, all will turn out okay in the end.

   But there are also questions. What if "The End" of the secular path isn't the end? What is truth? And where does love enter in?

   For me, the Christ journey is the only one that gets me where I want to go.

2. So on that note, we need to be clear as to our destination. For some, that might be happiness or health or wealth or acclaim or a life well-lived or the leaving of a legacy.

   For me, it's love plus the sense of "mission accomplished" in my life's work. Don't get me wrong, I would love to have all of those other things too, but in my core, what I want most is to love and be loved and to make a positive dent in my world.

"If I speak in the tongues of men or of angels, but do not have love…I am nothing" (1 Cor. 13:1–2).

"For we are God's handiwork, created in Christ Jesus to do good works" (Eph. 2:10).

3. As far as I know, there are no other paths that lead to the very essence of love itself, so why bother with a lesser when you can have the greater?

> Dear friends, let us love one another, for love comes from God. Everyone who loves has been born of God and knows God. Whoever does not love does not know God, because *God is love.* This is how God showed his love among us: He sent his one and only Son into the world that we might live through him. This is love: not that we loved God, but that he loved us and sent his Son as an atoning sacrifice for our sins. (1 John 4:7–10)

Here's a graphic depiction of most of the world's top religions.

Hinduism... infinite manifestations of God
Buddhism... believes no god or gods exist
New Age... believes we ourselves are God
Islam... devoted to one transcendent God
Christianity... an infinite & personal God

As you might guess, I like the Christianity one.

> Christians believe in one eternal God who is creator of all that is. He is viewed as a loving God who offers everyone a personal relationship with himself now in this life. In his life on earth, Jesus Christ did not identify himself as a prophet

pointing to God or as a teacher of enlightenment. Rather, Jesus claimed to be God in human form. He performed miracles, forgave people of their sin, and said that anyone who believed in him would have eternal life.

(The graphics and summary above are from www.everystudent.com. "Connecting with the Divine" by Marilyn Adamson)

4. Following Jesus has other perks too. It has transformative power because God the Father, Son, and Spirit are alive and active in the here and now, offering forgiveness, a future, and a hope.
5. On a practical level, the Bible is full of prophecies, many of which have already come to pass in history. This can't be accidental.
6. I *like* Jesus. He ate dinner with friends one minute, threw moneychangers out of the temple the next, healed someone blind or tormented by their inner demons the next, and then, you know, died for *me*.
7. So to sum up why I believe, let me put it this way. I want it *all*-the most life has to offer. To me, other religions, practices, and ideologies fall short. Humanism in its highest form is about being the best person you can be, which is admirable, but limited. Christianity isn't about trying harder; it's about surrendering. It's about letting God himself come in. It's not for the fainthearted though. One doesn't get a pass on the hard parts of the journey; it's just that you're never alone. You get to go with God—limitless, loving God.

Matthew 1
<u>Great Expectations</u>

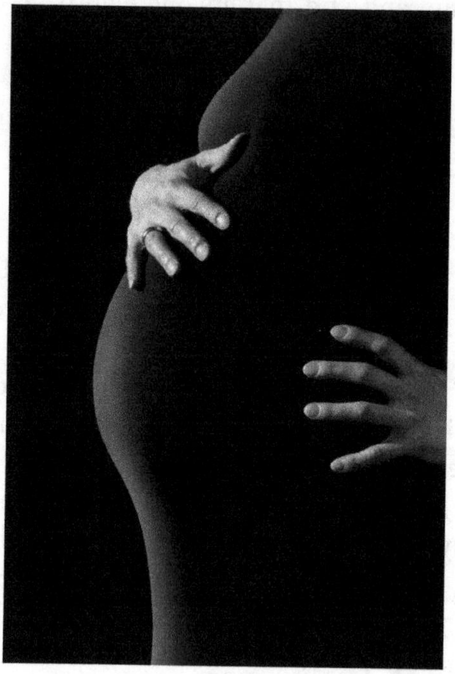

A young teenage girl was pregnant before she and her fiancé got together. An angel appeared to the fiancé and told him this baby was going to *save people from their sins.* (Can you imagine?) People had been anticipating this little boy for forty-two generations.

I just love books that hook you from page 1.

When I was younger, a pregnant woman was referred to as "expecting." "Pregnant" sounds scientific. "Expecting" sounds exciting and hopeful!

So they were expecting a *baby*! A child to cuddle and kiss and teach to ride a bike. (Okay, maybe not that last part.) They were awestruck by the miracle of it all, but they might not have anticipated what having this particular baby entailed. Scraped knees, yes. Gut-wrenching pain, hard to know.

Baby Jesus arrived as the promised Messiah, the King. His name meant "God with us." What a remarkable name. What great hope. He died, however, as a young adult without establishing an earthly kingdom. No doubt many were thinking, *What's up with that?*

We now understand he never intended to set up a kingdom based on people's expectations. He is birthed into our hearts, to change us from within, to love us far beyond what we could ever… expect.

But I'm getting ahead of myself. Suffice it to say that the journey began with great anticipation and the joy that only a baby can bring.

Item in the Backpack: Excitement

Matthew 2
New Realities

Baby Jesus was born in the little town of Bethlehem. You've sung the carols, given the gifts, decorated the Christmas trees—although there are no evergreens in Bethlehem, alas—but anyway, all to celebrate the newborn's arrival. It's quite festive and full of hope.

But the baby ushered in a couple of other newborn realities as well. The *New* Testament, for example. (Don't go away, we'll come back to the baby.)

What makes the New Testament new? It's chronologically newer than the Old Testament by four hundred-ish years. It's a new set of stories with a new cast of characters. The Old was only the beginning and one of its main purposes was to point to the New.

Matthew 2:6 is a throwback to an Old Testament verse, Micah 5:2: "But you, Bethlehem Ephrathah, though you are small among the clans of Judah, out of you will come for me one who will be ruler over Israel, whose origins are from of old, from ancient times."

The Old Testament laid down the Law, but God's people failed to keep it, over and over again. Something new was needed.

A baby. A baby so powerful that a few men (possibly three) travelled two years from their comfort zones to see him in person. A baby so threatening to King Herod that he had all young male children in the Bethlehem area slaughtered, to try to destroy this particular baby. A baby who grew up to serve as a sacrifice, not just for Israelites, but for everyone. The Old Testament prescribed all kinds of sacrifices, but this one was *way* new.

The result? It's in 2 Corinthians 5:17: "Therefore, if anyone is in Christ, the new creation has come: The old has gone, the new is here!"

Item in the Backpack: Hope

Matthew 3
Wild Things

Fast-forward about three decades. John the Baptist, somewhat of a wild man, appeared on the scene before the young man Jesus showed up (Jesus aka God with Us). John wore an outfit made of camel hair. He preached and baptized people, not in churches or other cleaned-up places but in the wilderness. He ate honey and grasshoppers. He dubbed the so-called religious giants a brood of snakes. And he basically said, "After me comes one who will seriously clean house and baptize you with fire. Unquenchable fire. You might want to get ready."

Then the scene dramatically changed. Jesus indeed arrived and asked John, who as it turns out was his cousin, to baptize him in the Jordan River. John hesitated. He didn't feel worthy to even touch Jesus's sandals, much less baptize him, but Jesus said to permit it, so John permitted it.

And lo and behold, when Jesus came up from the water, the Spirit of God settled on him as a dove. Not only that, but a voice rang out of the heavens, saying, "This is my Son, whom I love; with him I am well pleased."

(I'm not making this up. I told you it was going to be a fascinating story.)

Sometimes I wonder why there were so many wild souls in the Bible, not to mention the misfits and outright sinners. A lot of them were royal screwups. The First Couple thought they were being sneaky in their disobedience, but they were exposed. Firstborn Son killed Second-born Son. King David had an affair. It goes on and on and on, but God's love conquered all.

Maybe we're all wild souls. Jesus chose wild-thing John to baptize him. He seems to really care about all of us—whether we're royal screwups or just grasshopper eaters.

Item in the Backpack: Acceptance of Ourselves

Matthew 4
Journey Partners

After the glory of the baptism, Jesus went to the wilderness by himself, fasted forty days, and was tempted by the devil. Tempted by food, easy acclaim, and ownership of the world.

It would have been so easy.

But Jesus rebuffed the devil by *quoting scripture* and the devil left him. (What a lesson on how to resist temptation.)

After that, Jesus started preaching and healing people. He immediately came across two sets of brothers and said, "Follow me," and they did. Eventually there were twelve friends—a band of spiritual brothers. He was no longer by himself. He got to experience shared strength, the strength of friends.

My best friends and I remind each other that we're never alone, even though some of us live hundreds of miles apart. And for all of us who believe God is real and in a relationship with us, we're never apart from him either. Our beautiful challenge is to understand that fact more and more, *experientially*.

Life takes an enormous amount of personal strength. Jesus spent a lot of time in conversation with God to gain strength. (I'm guessing that's how he survived forty days in the wilderness.) And if Jesus needed that, how much more do we need it! But we can also draw strength, counsel, wisdom, and emotional safety from each other.

Companionship with God and companionship with others. I think Jesus loved alone time with his Father *and* his time with friends and family. I think he needed both. I think we do too.

Item in the Backpack: Companionship

Matthew 5:1–26
Soul Training

Most of Jesus's disciples were fishermen, respectable, but skilled at mending nets, not attending seminary. One was a tax collector, but not just your run-of-the-mill IRS employee. He was from a class of publicans called *mokhsa* who extorted money from travelers. (This was Matthew, who most likely wrote this Gospel.) And one had the moniker of zealot. We don't know the vocations of the rest, but one or two were likely tradesmen.

Let's just say they needed some training.

So Jesus sat them down on a mountainside and started teaching them with newfangled messages involving the perks of being poor in spirit, mournful, hungry, and persecuted. He told them they were the salt of the earth and the light of the world.

I visualize twelve guys sitting around on rocks just kind of staring at him, slack-jawed. This is not what these Jewish fellas had been taught, but Jesus was on it. He said, "Do not think that I have come to abolish the Law or the Prophets, I have not come to abolish them but to fulfill them."

And the brilliant, fascinating, counterintuitive Sermon of the Mount began. There's much to mull over. Each point could take a lifetime to master, but here's a hint. We don't have to master each one alone. We have a helper. (More on that later.)

Sometimes Jesus just laid things out, clear as can be, like this sermon. We can contemplate it, feed our souls with it, and build our lives on it.

Item in the Backpack: Contemplation

Matthew 5:27–48
High Bar

The Sermon on the Mount continues.

If you lust, you've already committed adultery in your heart. If your eye or hand causes you to sin, cut if off. If you divorce (except for unfaithfulness), it's back to the adultery thing. Don't resist an evil person; give him/her more than they demand. Love your enemies. Be perfect.

Okay, we're all in trouble.

Why can't the scriptures go something like this? If you lust, no big deal. Just don't act on it. If your eye or hand causes you to sin, join an accountability group. If you divorce, well, a lot of people divorce. If someone acts in an evil way, call 'em out on it and expose them to the public. About your enemies, try fight-or-flight. Be a good person.

But the scriptures don't go like that. In fact, Jesus sets the bar really high, actually at "perfect," not to torture us but so we can thrive. He settles for nothing less than the best for us.

Thankfully, later in Matthew, Jesus said, "Come to me, all you who are weary and burdened, and I will give you rest. Take my yoke upon you, and learn from me, for I am gentle and humble in heart" (Matt. 11:28–29). So there's hope.

And here's the kicker. "For all have sinned and fall short of the glory of God" (Rom. 3:23). And to bring things full circle: "If you declare with your mouth, 'Jesus is Lord,' and believe in your heart that God raised him from the dead, you will be saved" (Rom. 10:9). Saved, because on our own, we fall short of that high bar of perfection. Saved, because God settles for nothing less than the best for us.

Item in the Backpack: Salvation

Matthew 6:1–18
Spiritual Conversation

Jesus was *not* into people's self-righteousness, whether in giving or praying. What *is* prayer anyway? Let's first think about what it's not. It's not an opportunity to show off in public. It's not a wish, nice thought, or positive vibe.

It *is* a private conversation with God. It gets results. Your Father who sees in secret will repay you. It has components, like forgiveness. It has to be preceded by belief in God or at least by the possibility that God is real. Or this:

> A dad brought his son to be healed by Jesus and said, "If you can do anything, take pity on us and help us."
>
> "'If you can'?" asked Jesus. "Everything is possible for one who believes."
>
> Immediately the boy's father exclaimed, "I do believe; help me overcome my unbelief!" (Mark 9:22–24)

I love that verse. I've used it a lot in my own prayers. If we're really honest, believing in God, praying to God, living like God is real and not just a myth…those things are pretty bizarre to people who don't believe.

And sometimes, if we're really honest, we may have moments of doubt ourselves. "I *do* believe, but help me in my unbelief."

Prayer is a pretty bizarre thing. Jesus's friends and the crowds around him could see him and even touch him. We can't. We *can* choose to pray and believe, by faith. Then we can watch God work. It's all beyond natural.

Item in the Backpack: Prayer

Matthew 6:19–34
True Treasure

Here Jesus goes again—not mincing words! "You cannot serve both God and money." He didn't say you can't be materially wealthy. He just said you can't serve two masters, so you have to choose which one wins your heart.

Now, to invest our money, seek wise counsel about our money, be responsible with our money, give away a portion of our money… these are all good things that are taught in the Bible. I've never seen a passage that says, "Thou shalt not make money." It's all about what we love the most.

Jesus knows us. He was human. He knows we need food, clothes, education for our kids, reliable transportation, savings accounts. And he also knows we can easily get sidetracked with (A) the cares of the world or (B) greed. True treasure doesn't come easily.

About point A, Jesus gave a tangible solution: "But seek first his kingdom and his righteousness, and all these things will be given to you as well." "Can any one of you by worrying add a single hour to your life?" It takes trust. You can't worry and trust at the same time.

In my past, sometimes I had to work two or three jobs at a time, execute some serious money management, and, yes, massively trust when we were close to the financial edge; but guess what? We didn't miss any meals. God provided us with enough-ness.

And about point B. There are people who are selfish with their money. Jesus gave a tangible response to that too, in Luke 12:15: "Watch out! Be on your guard against all kinds of greed; life does not consist in an abundance of possessions."

Jesus loves us a lot. I think he wants us to get past stuff-seeking, worry and greed, and get on with Life with a capital *L*.

Item in the Backpack: Introspection about Money

Matthew 7
Golden Rules

The Golden Rule is found in Matthew 7: "So in everything, do to others what you would have them do to you." But there are lots of golden rules in this passage:

Do not judge lest you be judged.
Be proactive.
Ask. Seek. Knock.
Beware of false prophets.
Build your house upon the rock.

Here again, Jesus is spurring us on to greatness. (Notice that trend?) And he's so *practical.* Think about it.

Do not judge lest you be judged. (If we look inward to deal with our own sin before criticizing, we won't have the inclination, much less the time, to criticize others.)

Be proactive. Ask. Seek. Knock. (If we think like a parent, we'll realize God wants to give us good gifts.)

Beware of false prophets. (If we look at the fruit of a person's life, we can figure out who the posers are.)

Build your house upon the rock. (If we build our lives on solid principles, we'll most likely be more stable.)

Some people are rule followers; some hate rules. But God knows we need clarity. Take judging others, for example. Admittedly, it feels good to judge sometimes. (I can't believe I just wrote that!) But that's my point. God needed to make things crystal clear so there's no wiggle room for rationalizing.

In Matthew 22:36–40, Jesus was asked what the greatest commandment (rule) was. He replied that it's to love God with all your heart, soul, and mind. Then he added this: "And the second is like it: Love your neighbor as yourself."

I suppose if we had no other rules, this guidance could stand alone. And if we seriously and consistently obeyed it, the world would be changed.

Item in the Backpack: Guidance

Matthew 8:1–17
<u>Physical Healing</u>

The sermon ended, and Jesus came down the mountain and healed three people right off the bat. One had leprosy, one was paralyzed, and one had a fever. Even now the treatment for leprosy is at least six months of medication. Paralysis is, as we know, complicated. And fevers rarely go away so quickly that one could jump up and fix dinner.

Do you think miracles are possible? Once, a friend of mine prayed for a woman's compound-fractured arm, and the bone slipped back into place. (I'm telling you the truth.) Once, doctors treated my dad for stage IV lung cancer, and his scans came back clean until his death of natural causes six years later. There's possibility beyond the natural realm.

I believe Jesus healed the sick when he was God in the flesh. I believe he still does, sometimes miraculously. And . . . I believe he also uses the medical profession.

Both miracle workers *and* medical workers heal.

In some cases, Jesus touched people to heal them. In other cases, he spoke. This man was powerful. And in the deepest places of our souls, isn't that what we want? Why settle for the words of a fellow human like the Buddha or the myths of Hinduism when we have access to the God powerful enough to heal?

Item in the Backpack: Possibility

Matthew 8:18–34
Spiritual Healing

As Jesus continued on his journey, two violent, demon-possessed men stepped out from among the tombs. They started screaming at him about tormenting them. Jesus was tormenting *them*?

Bizarre. Demon possession might have looked a lot like mental illness or epilepsy. You know, something *explainable*. But to believe in God means believing in the unexplainable. It also means believing in a dimension beyond flesh and blood. *Spiritual* reality.

From what I understand, quantum physics describes the wacky behavior of particles that make up the universe, which baffles scientists. Scientists are baffled by a whole slew of things, just as we're *all* baffled by a whole slew of things, like demons being cast out.

Being baffled is not the same as those things being untrue.

Can you imagine being able to get up and walk after being paralyzed…or being free from some sort of inner demon? Baffling. But to that person, who cares? They are just happy and forever grateful.

These Matthew 8 demons were "beings" that inhabited certain people. Intruders from the outside. Evil spirits. I'm not an expert on those things, but we still speak about demons today. They're tormentors like traumatic memories, catastrophic choices, remnants of abuse, something more "minor" like low self-esteem (if there's such a thing as a minor demon), or something more major like witchcraft. We talk about people fighting their demons.

Jesus cast these particular demons into a herd of pigs. I know people who have asked him to cast out their inner demons, and he has. Sometimes instantaneously; sometimes over a period of time through prayer, counseling, and faith.

True to form, we again see Jesus loving people intensely by healing their bodies *and* their souls.

Item in the Backpack: Faith

Matthew 9:1–17
Forgiven Sinners

Okay, let's review. Jesus taught with unprecedented authority. He healed people. He cast out demons. And he forgave sins.

Let's set up a modern-day story. Say there was a tragic accident and a teenager broke her neck and became a quadriplegic, and this guy (we'll call him Josh) steps into her hospital room, forgives her sins, touches her on the arm, and she stands up. Then he goes outside and the latest politician (or entertainer) caught in some despicable act walks by and Josh forgives that person and says, "Go and sin no more. Case closed."

Healing people both physically and spiritually is one thing, but forgiving sin takes it to a whole new level.

Let's continue the story. Say that after this excitement-filled day, Josh and his friends are having dinner. Then the despicable politician (or entertainer) walks by, and Josh invites him and his friends to join them. Some holier-than-thou people watching Josh's every move freak out, to which Josh replies, "Hey, I'm here, not for the healthy people, but for those who are ill. And by the way, I desire compassion, not sacrifice. I came to call not the righteous but the sinners. *Compassion, people!*"

We're appalled by the moral failures of our politicians and entertainers. And we're disgusted at the "Pharisees" in our midst. But I believe that even the worst of the bunch can ask for forgiveness and turn from their ways and Jesus forgives.

Item in the Backpack: Forgiveness

Matthew 9:18–38
Emotional Reactions

People had such a variety of reactions to Jesus. After the pigs incident, the city dwellers asked him to leave. After he healed the paralytic, the crowds were filled with awe. After he went to the home of the dead girl, the mourners laughed at him. After the blind men were healed, they blatantly went against what he had asked of them. After he healed the man who couldn't speak, the Pharisees made a stupid indictment. "He casts out demons by the ruler of the demons." (What would be the purpose of that?)

Jesus knew the people didn't really get him and sometimes had dumb reactions; but he kept going around to their cities, teaching in their synagogues, proclaiming the Gospel, and healing every kind of disease.

He just didn't give up.

Seeing the multitudes, he felt compassion for them even after their rejection, mockery, disobedience, and stupid statements. He saw them as distressed and lost. He told the disciples there were lots of hurting people out there but not enough workers. More help was needed. He knew they would carry on the work after he was gone. Despite everything to the contrary, the rejecting, mocking, disobedient, distressed, and lost people were worth saving.

The people *are* worth saving. That includes you and me.

We can choose our reaction to Jesus—rejecting and disobedient…or grateful and filled with awe.

Item in the Backpack: Choice

Matthew 10:1–23
Hard Roads

This is not a fun passage. Jesus gave his twelve friends authority to do the most powerful and loving things in the world, like heal the sick, cast out demons, even *raise the dead.* He also instructed them to not be a pain to anyone by asking for payment.

You might think people would be rather fond of them.

Jesus knew some people would receive and take care of these friends but some would not. In fact, some would hate them, take them to court, and scourge them in their synagogues. A scourge is a whip used for punishment or torture. In church! For doing things like healing the sick and raising the dead. You know, good things.

But are you starting to see a pattern here? Jesus always seems to come through. In this case, he said for them not to be anxious about what they would say because *in that hour*, what to say would be given to them. There would be a presence, instructing them.

In other words, they would never be alone. The Spirit would be with them.

So I'm guessing the twelve exchanged furtive glances (I love that phrase) but decided to step into it anyway. Kind of like the eighteen-year-old who signs up for the military…or the couple who chooses the high road when their disabled child is born…or the whistle-blower.

Sometimes the way ahead is hard. We have to decide which hills we're willing to die on.

Item in the Backpack: Decisiveness

Matthew 10: 24–42
<u>Paradigm Shift</u>

Jesus didn't come to earth to coddle us. "Do not suppose that I have come to bring peace to the earth. I did not come to bring peace, but a sword."

"And anyone who does not take his cross and follow me is not worthy of me. Whoever finds his life will lose it, and whoever loses his life for my sake will find it."

There's just no way around Jesus's words. We can't pick and choose which passages we want to hear. It's all or nothing, but we can't fully understand Jesus unless we study the whole man.

Sometimes he's depicted with little children at his feet and chubby cherubim floating around his head. And sometimes he's raging mad, throwing money changers out of the temple. (That one's coming up soon.) I think he's both. And that's a good thing.

Notice the "buts" in this passage:

Life will be hard, *but* Jesus and his Father are more capable. Don't fear those who kill the body *but* are unable to kill the soul. Birds have value, *but* you have exponentially more value. Whoever confesses Me before men, I will also confess him before My Father, *but* whoever denies me…

He ends the passage with these words. "And whoever in the name of a disciple gives to one of these little ones even a cup of cold water to drink, truly I say to you he shall not lose his reward."

Just when we think he's asking too much, he makes a way. He's asking for our whole hearts, our everything, but he's already provided the means.

I think the moral of the story is that life may be profoundly difficult. We're called to surrender to that fact. We need to let go in order to find. It's a paradigm shift, and we get to decide whether or not to step into the ballgame, because it's a whole new ball game. We get to decide if having God in our lives is what we want.

Item in the Backpack: Surrender

Matthew 11
<u>Plain Sight</u>

Have you ever looked for something and it was right under your nose the whole time? Or gone hiking and tripped over a rock that was in plain sight? Or heard something with your ears but it didn't register with your brain?

I think that's Jesus's message in this passage. He seemed to be saying, "Here I am, in plain sight, but some will stumble over me."

Old Testament prophecies were being fulfilled. People were being healed and raised from the dead, but miracles weren't registering with the people. Or the people were flat-out rejecting them. Or maybe they were too busy or too cool. Or life was going just fine, thank-you-very-much.

How are people rejecting him these days? I can think of several ways:

"I'll ignore him and maybe he'll go away."

"I don't like those evangelicals."

"I'm a good person, so I don't need God."

"The clergy are worse than I am."

"The churches just want my money."

"I'm a humanist and don't believe in spiritual things or eternity. When we die, we die."

(Now, I've talked to several nonbelievers over the years who are really impressed with Jesus himself. They just don't like religion. Can't say I blame them sometimes. I just keep pointing them to the person, Jesus.) So we come to the end of the passage, and you guessed it. Just when we thought Jesus's words were a little too harsh, he finished the section with, "Come to me for rest."

He makes a way for even the most strident nonbeliever to become aware, to have the eyes to see and the ears to hear, and to stop stumbling.

Item in the Backpack: Awareness

Matthew 12:1–29
Those Pharisees

When I was a youngster, my family took Sundays pretty seriously. We went to church, and then Dad watched football in the afternoons, Mom made fudge with thousands of calories (I miss those days), the neighborhood kids played kickball or the boys chased the girls with snakes…you know, fun stuff. But we didn't get hung up on legalistic "Sunday" rules.

The Pharisees did.

Jesus healed a guy's withered hand on the Sabbath, and the disciples didn't get hung up on it.

But the Pharisees did.

Have you noticed how Jesus hung out with the less-than-perfect people but rebuked the holier-than-thou people?

Another thing I've noticed is the mention of the nations in this passage, twice actually: "And he will proclaim justice to the nations." "In his name the nations will put their hope." In the New American Standard version of the Bible, the word "Gentiles" was used for "nations."

I'm a Gentile.

So this is new. In the Old Testament, the Jews were God's chosen people. In the New Testament, all who believe in Jesus are chosen. That includes Jews and non-Jews (i.e., Gentiles).

I'm guessing the Pharisees weren't too happy about this Gentile outreach thing either.

Anyway, it's easy to criticize *those* people because nobody likes to be around people who think they're better than we are. They are sanctimonious, self-righteous, and hypocritical.

But sometimes I'm *that* person.

Just when we want to point a finger at *those* people, the Bible reminds us that we all need the Savior.

Item in the Backpack: Personal Inventory

Matthew 12:30–50
Hard Truths

Sometimes we come across hard-to-figure-out biblical passages. Take the unpardonable sin/blasphemy against the Spirit, for example (Matt. 12:31–32). Catholics believe there are six sins that blaspheme against the Holy Spirit: despair (believing that one's evil is beyond God's forgiveness), presumption (expectation of pardon without repentance), envying the goodness of another, obstinacy in sin, arguing against known points of faith, and final impenitence.

Here's another perspective on this concept of unpardonable sin (It seems to affirm the final impenitence sin above.): "For Christians today, we need not fear a specific moment of sin, but a kind of hardness of heart that would see Jesus as true and yet walk away—with a kind of hardness of heart incapable of repenting. Again, it's not that forgiveness isn't granted, but that it's not sought" (David Mathis, executive editor, www.desiringGod.org).

Here's another hard-to-figure-out thing. When an unclean spirit leaves a person, it can return to its now unoccupied house and bring along seven other spirits more wicked than itself. I've heard this explained that if we kick sin out of our lives, we need to fill the void with God or the sin can come back too easily. That makes sense to me. (Maybe it's not so hard to figure out after all.)

But some things in this passage are *easy* to figure out, like Matthew 12:37: "For out of the overflow of the heart the mouth speaks." Garbage in, garbage out.

Whether the scriptures present us with easy truths or hard ones, we won't even know what they are unless we do our homework.

Item in the Backpack: Study

Matthew 13:1–43
Seed Stories

Don't you just love a great story? The best ones have something to say *beyond* the story. Jesus could have *informed* his disciples that some people wouldn't understand their message…and that some would only listen temporarily…and that others would be distracted and so on, but he told them in story form. They could picture someone going out to sow seeds beside the road, on rocky places, among thorns, and on good soil.

With story, people remember.

The first story was about people's readiness to hear their "soil condition." The second was about evil people among the kingdom people and the fate of the former, which was not pretty. The third story was about a mustard seed. In Matthew 17, Jesus said that having faith as small as a mustard seed meant that nothing would be impossible for them. Pope Benedict XVI said, "I have a mustard seed, and I am not afraid to use it." (I love that.) Flip over to Mark 4:26–29 for another seed story that wasn't recorded in Matthew.

We too can use stories to communicate. A long time ago, my pastor asked me when God had become more than just a word to me. That opening line helped me fashion my testimony, my story. Maybe it can help you fashion yours as well.

Item in the Backpack: My Testimony

Matthew 13:44–58
Immeasurable Value

Have you ever seen a movie you didn't really understand? I have. Once I was discussing a movie with a friend and she went on and on about its deep symbolism. I sort of excused myself so I could slink away.

Although Jesus used deep symbolism often, he made things *very* clear about the kingdom of heaven. (Maybe for people like me, sigh.) The kingdom of heaven is worth selling everything we own in order to acquire it, like buying a pearl of great price.

And here's another quite clear thing. There are good fish and bad fish. The good are gathered up. The bad are tossed away. In other words, at the end of the age, wicked people will get tossed into the furnace of fire where there will be weeping and gnashing of teeth.

Any questions? (That's what he asked the disciples.)

The good news is that *every person* has the opportunity to be a good fish, meaning a righteous person, by becoming a follower of Jesus. The bad news is that not every person will say yes to him. And there are consequences. I know I'm walking on eggshells here because not everybody believes in an eternal furnace of fire, but my job isn't to soften the message.

I've been told I write with angst. It's true. I have huge angst over this passage. I wouldn't wish hell on my worst enemies, but Jesus doesn't either. In 2 Peter 3:9 it says, "The Lord is not slow in keeping his promise, as some understand slowness. Instead he is patient with you, not wanting anyone to perish, but everyone to come to repentance."

So back to the movies. Think *The Lord of the Rings*. The ring was worth the ultimate sacrifice. It had immeasurable value. And that particular story is an allegory about the kingdom of heaven.

Item in the Backpack: The Kingdom of Heaven

Matthew 14:1–21
Refilled Cups

Jesus once said that among those born of women, there had not arisen anyone greater than John the Baptist. This meant that John was the greatest person who had ever lived!

And he was murdered for someone's pleasure. Herodias was mad because John had told her husband an inconvenient truth. (Do we ever get mad when confronted with our inconvenient truths?)

But back to Jesus. When he heard the news, he went to a lonely place to grieve but perhaps also to get his emotional cup refilled.

It's impossible to drink from an empty cup. Jesus spent a lot of time with his Father getting replenishment. He knew he couldn't run on empty. And if Jesus needed that filling of the tank, how much more do *we* need it.

And right away we see why he needed it. The multitudes. Five thousand-plus people followed him, and true to form, he felt compassion and started healing them. By evening they were getting hungry, so Jesus fed them with five loaves and two fish.

From famine to feast, so to speak.

We can take a lesson here. We need to get filled up with God's love and instruction. We're going to need it. Then we can help others out of our abundance, not out of our lack.

Item in the Backpack: Replenishment

Matthew 14:22–36
Scary Storms

After feeding the five thousand, Jesus sent his disciples ahead in a boat and sent the multitudes on their way. Then he went up the mountain by himself to pray. (Have you noticed how much Jesus prayed?) Afterward, the boat was hundreds of yards away. It was sometime between 3:00 and 6:00 a.m., and the wind and waves were crazy bad.

But undeterred, Jesus walked out to the boat. The disciples were afraid. Jesus, however, said something like, "Hey, guys, take courage. It's me." So brash Peter wanted to walk on water too. Jesus invited him out, and Peter did indeed walk on the water, then panicked and began to sink.

And this is where it gets interesting. Jesus stretched out his hand and took hold of Peter, and they got into the boat. Then the wind stopped.

No surprises there. Jesus had already proven himself, and this was just another example.

I think what's interesting is what Jesus said to him and the way he might have said it: "O you of little faith, why did you doubt?" I always thought of this as a rebuke, but Jesus was saying it *as* he stretched out his hand and took hold of Peter, like a parent comforting a terrified child during a storm.

We don't rebuke the frightened. We hold them.

Do you ever need to be held by someone powerful enough to walk on water?

Item in the Backpack: Trust

Matthew 15:1–20
Pure Hearts

So far, I've seen several recurring themes in Jesus's life:

- His need to pray.
- His fulfillment of Old Testament law with New Testament grace.
- His balance of firmness and compassion.
- His provision. The bar is set at perfect and nobody is perfect, so he makes the way.

And, oh man, his disdain for the Pharisees!

He had serious issues with their *legalism*. "Why do you break the command of God for the sake of your tradition?"

He had serious issues with their *man-made rules*. "They worship me in vain; their teachings are merely human rules."

And he had serious issues with their *mouths*. "These people honor me with their lips, but their hearts are far from me."

I don't know about you, but sometimes I have less-than-charitable thoughts toward someone. I'm tempted to gossip. I feel judgmental. And the worst part is that sometimes I *act* on these things. I hate that! Things slip into my heart and come out of my mouth. Maybe this is why as people get older and wiser, they keep their mouths shut more often.

Psalm 51:10 says, "Create in me a pure heart, O God, and renew a steadfast spirit within me." Jesus knows we need discipline to guard ourselves and see the world from pure, clean hearts. Our words will follow suit.

Item in the Backpack: Discipline

Matthew 15:21–39
Dogged Persistence

A Canaanite woman cried out to Jesus, wanting healing for her demon-possessed daughter. (Demon possession was pervasive. I wonder if it still is, but we just don't call it that. Something to ponder.)

Interestingly, Jesus didn't respond. I think the disciples thought the woman was annoying, but Jesus simply said, "I was sent only to the lost sheep of Israel." Did he not answer because she was *Canaanite*? Well, she persisted with some honesty, which turned things around. He healed her daughter because of her faith.

I'm guessing he would have healed her daughter regardless, but he wanted to add a fine point to it—that of persistence. I've been praying for some things for years. Along the way, God has changed me or has answered on a different timeline or in an unexpected way.

Jesus persisted in doing compassionate things for the multitudes, so maybe he was giving us an object lesson. Maybe he wants us to persist in prayer. And maybe he's persistent in blessing us.

Maybe we don't always see his answers or even his blessings.

Maybe a devoted life can open our eyes if we are persistent and refuse to give up.

Item in the Backpack: Persistence

Matthew 16
Peter's Destiny

Simon Peter's a fascinating study. He walked on water *but* got scared and started to sink. He called Jesus the Son of the Living God *but* later denied him. He became outraged over Jesus's impending death *but* as it turns out, missed the bigger point. He was given the keys of the kingdom of heaven...and there are no "buts."

Jesus changed Simon's name to Peter, from the Greek word *petra*, which means "large rock or bedrock." Jesus said, "And I tell you that you are Peter, and on this rock I will build my church, and the gates of Hades will not overcome it."

Jesus founded the church on Peter and his confession. The church is the billions of people who have followed Jesus over thousands of years. Was Peter perfect? Not at *all*! But he hung in there with Jesus and kept learning, growing, stumbling, then getting back up to go follow him again.

Kind of like us.

Jesus said, "Whoever wants to be my disciple must deny themselves and take up their cross and follow me. For whoever wants to save their life will lose it, but whoever loses their life for me will find it. What good will it be for someone to gain the whole world, yet forfeit their soul?"

Deny self. Not an easy message. The most "worth it" message but not easy. It's one reason we need the church, so we can lean on and learn from each other.

Item in the Backpack: Church

Matthew 17
Mountaintop Experiences

Jesus took Peter, James, and John up to a high mountain where he was transfigured, meaning changed to an exalted state. Two Old Testament greats showed up, and a voice boomed out of a cloud, which was, obviously, God himself.

I think we sometimes forget that the disciples were regular men. We think of them as characters in a novel. Fiction. But they had real experiences, one of them being witnessing the transfiguration. This isn't science fiction. It's historical nonfiction.

It was a vision, but they *really* went up the mountain and it was a *real* vision to instruct them, and they got it. They understood. And no doubt their hearts were beating out of their chests.

Then they came down the mountain to a lunatic the disciples couldn't heal (meaning they needed more instruction). They also came down to something else.

Taxes.

How deflating.

We long to live on mountaintops with daily inspiration and outrageous joy, but that ain't real life. Real life is highs *and* lows *and* boring times in between. A song by Jason Crabb says, "You don't have to walk on water. It's how you walk on land." Sometimes we get mountaintop experiences, even miraculous experiences, but most of the time we walk on the flatlands.

Maybe our task is to keep the mountain vision alive in our daily walks through the flats and valleys.

Item in the Backpack: Vision

Matthew 18:1–14
Little Ones

Can you imagine going to your boss and asking him/her, "Who's the greatest in this company?" And your boss sees a child walking by and replies, "That kid. You have to be humble and teachable like a child to be great around here."

Jesus had little patience with puffed-up people or those who disregard children or those who cause little kids to stumble (probably by being a bad influence). In fact, he got quite graphic about it. He talked about elevating the little ones in our lives and taking special care with them. After all, their angels in heaven are continually in the presence of God the Father.

Wow, that's a picture.

And there is more to the "little ones" narrative. It has to do with a stray sheep. What person, if he has a hundred sheep and one strays, won't leave the ninety-nine and search for the stray? And when he finds it, rejoices over it more than over the ninety-nine who have not strayed.

Now the prudent thing would be to think of the stray as collateral damage, the cost of doing business...*unless you're that lamb.* Then you would want someone to care enough to save you.

Jesus stated that the Father isn't willing for even *one* little one to perish. God cares for the littles. And he wants the bigs to get some humility.

Item in the Backpack: Humility

Matthew 18:15–35
Two Models

Everybody sins.

Jesus dealt with it in a couple of ways.

First, by providing a conflict resolution model. If someone sins, go to the person privately. If that doesn't work, take others. If that doesn't work, take it to the church. Second, by providing a forgiveness model: "Lord, how many times shall I forgive my brother or sister who sins against me? Up to seven times?" Jesus answered, "I tell you, not seven times, but seventy-seven times." *Seven* might be figurative here, meaning, "Just keep forgiving."

I think it's interesting that these two passages are back-to-back. Are we supposed to reprove people or forgive them?

I think both. Matthew 10:16 says we're to be both shrewd and innocent. It's a sheep-among-wolves world out there.

Shrewd	= healthy conflict resolution
Innocent	= healthy forgiveness

Forgiveness doesn't necessarily mean the person is off the hook. They should be off the hook in our hearts (no lingering bitterness or retribution), but they likely need to take responsibility for their sin (i.e., repent). Forgiveness doesn't give a person carte blanche to keep on sinning.

Notice that when the king forgave slave A but slave A didn't forgive slave B, the king handed slave A over to the torturers. No second chances for him! Yikes.

I think we get what Jesus is saying. Sometimes, especially if we're in a leadership position, we need to deal with problems in the ranks and there's a process for that. To let things go would be disastrous. But in our *own* hearts, we are to forgive. That keeps our hearts innocent and free and loving. If someone takes advantage of forgiveness, it's back to being shrewd.

Reprove. Forgive. Both. And.

Item in the Backpack: Tools in the Relational Toolbox

Matthew 19
<u>God Possibilities</u>

Jesus always seemed to be surrounded by multitudes and Pharisees. The multitudes needed him. The Pharisees needled him.

In this case, the Pharisees asked him about divorce, which is a timely topic in our culture too. Jesus answered, "I tell you that anyone who divorces his wife, except for sexual immorality, and marries another woman commits adultery." Yeah, that means a giant percentage of Americans are adulterers, but we already knew that.

Then a wealthy young man came to Jesus and asked him what good thing he could do to obtain eternal life. He had already kept the Ten Commandments. Jesus told him that if he wished to be complete, meaning perfect, he needed to sell his possessions and give to the poor.

There's that word "perfect" again.

So the young man went away grieved, because he was rich. And Jesus turned to the disciples and said that it's easier for a camel to go through the eye of a needle than for a rich man to enter the kingdom of God.

Which is impossible. So the disciples asked, "Who then can be saved?"

And looking at them, Jesus said, "With man this is impossible, but with God all things are possible."

We fall far short of perfection. How many of us would sell *all* our possessions and give to the poor? Some would, although even they would fall short some other way.

God would love to see less divorce and more reconciliation, less greed and more generosity. Less violence and more peace, less bullying and more affection, less racial strife and more mending. The world would be a better place, but it seems to be getting worse. However, with God, all things are possible. *With* God.

Item in the Backpack: Unity with God

Matthew 20:1–16
Reversed Priorities

Jesus told a story about a generous landowner. This guy paid people who worked for him an hour the same as what he paid others who worked an entire day. That just doesn't seem fair.

Later, as Jesus was crucified, a robber who was crucified beside him asked him (Jesus) to remember him. Jesus told him he would be with him in paradise that very day. That just doesn't seem fair either. Some people faithfully follow the Lord for decades, and this robber slid in at the last minute.

A lot of things aren't fair. Some people are born with birth defects. Some have abusive parents. Some are born in wherever today's failed state happens to be. Some work their fingers to the bone for minimum wage and never get ahead. Others get a sports car for their sixteenth birthday.

What are we supposed to do about life's unfairness?

"So the last will be first, and the first will be last." "In humility consider others better than yourselves" (Phil. 2:3).

We can aspire to coming in last. This is the world's wisdom turned upside down.

Again, I think we get what Jesus is saying. He's not saying to deliberately lose races. He's not saying women should be paid less than men for the same job, but he *is* saying to guard against envy, because sometimes life isn't fair. And if we have high regard for others, we'll be happy if their lives go well.

It takes a lot of guts to live that well.

Item in the Backpack: Unselfishness

Matthew 20:17–34
Servant Greatness

Can't you just picture that Mama Bear asking Jesus to give her sons preferential treatment? It makes me smile and roll my eyes at the same time. I wonder if Jesus did the same. He turned to her two sons with a question: "Can you drink the cup I am going to drink?" (He had just told them what he was about to go through—mocking, scourging, crucifixion.) Whoever wishes to become great shall be your *servant.* Whoever wishes to be first shall be your *slave.*

We can't romanticize slavery. No rights. No respect. No one to stand up for you. No future for your children. Man's inhumanity to man.

In today's world, greatness doesn't look like the receiving end of man's inhumanity to man. Maybe the meting out end, but not the receiving end. Yet Jesus washed people's feet and ended up giving his life as a ransom. His murder wasn't just man's inhumanity to man. It was man's inhumanity to God.

We're to serve people: Wash their feet. Take care of their child when they're sick, even if that child is a brat. Get up in the night if they need us. Make time for them, even if it's inconvenient.

One of the spiritual gifts found in Romans 12 is service. It's a privilege, a form of worship, a lifestyle, a blessing to others. And interestingly, most of the servants I know are some of the happiest people I know.

Item in the Backpack: Service

Matthew 21:1–22
<u>Bad Days</u>

Jesus had a couple of bad days at this point. He came into Jerusalem riding a donkey. The multitudes made the path smooth with palm branches and their own clothes. Sort of like a Super Bowl winner parade, Jerusalem-style. Exciting, right? Jesus knew, however, that shortly the same people would turn on him. Crowd mentality would take over. They would shout for him to be killed. *Killed.*

He went to the temple, which had turned into a market. People were selling doves and such for the churchgoers to buy for sacrifices, apparently making a stiff profit. And he was *not* okay with that. He flipped over their tables and chairs, calling the temple a robbers' den. He was flat-out angry. Ephesians 4:26 says, "In your anger do not sin." In other words, *be* angry. Just don't sin. It's *good* to get mad over the right things.

The next morning, he went back to the city and along the way got hungry. A fig tree was by the road, figless. He spoke to it, and it withered.

Do you ever wonder how Jesus *felt* on his life journey? He was God in the flesh; so he had the full range of feelings, temptations, hunger, good and bad days, just like us. He shared humanity with us but *offers to take us far beyond our human limits.* "Truly I tell you, if you have faith and do not doubt, not only can you do what was done to the fig tree, but also you can say to this mountain, 'Go, throw yourself into the sea,' and it will be done. If you believe, you will receive whatever you ask for in prayer."

I want that kind of faith. I haven't even scratched the surface yet, but I want it. And the full range of emotions along the way, including anger handled well, is A-okay.

Item in the Backpack: Anger without Sin

Matthew 21:23–46
Useful Riddles

Jesus had authority. He also had spunk.

He had detractors even though he never did a single thing wrong. They just didn't like him, probably because he challenged their flimsy platforms. They really had no grounds for their arguments, but they had a form of power.

Jesus didn't try to convince them with evidence, like in a courtroom. They already had the evidence. He didn't use the finger-pointing approach by exposing their shortcomings.

He didn't even use a soft, reasoning method.

Now I could argue for each of these approaches, and we have the whole toolbox at our disposal. "There's a time for everything" (Eccles. 3).

But in this case, Jesus used riddles.

He knew their hearts and let them walk into their own traps. He was clever. He maintained his dignity. He didn't apologize for who he was, like "I'm sorry you guys don't like me, but..." He just let the chips fall where they would fall.

I can take a lesson from this. When I'm faced with detractors and those who scorn Christianity, I can hold my head high. I know whom I'm following. I trust his heart. He's the very definition of love. He's the rejected stone who, as it turned out, became the chief cornerstone. Some don't like him, but on what grounds? I can understand why they don't like some Christians, because we can get it wrong and screw things up. But him? When I point to him, their arguments fall flat.

Another thing about Jesus is that he was prepared. He had a working knowledge of the Old Testament, so he could quote it. That also speaks to me. I need those tools in my toolbox.

Item in the Backpack: Spunk

Matthew 22:1–22
Proper Attire

Why do you suppose Jesus used the term "kingdom of heaven" so much? It shows up thirty-one times in the book of Matthew alone.

What *is* the kingdom of heaven? Commentaries get really complex about the term, from *Second Temple Judaism* to *end-time millennialism*. Goodness! Maybe that's why Jesus had to explain it so much.

Many people of that time were looking for an earthly kingdom, but the kingdom of heaven is the *spiritual* rule of God for those who put their trust in Christ.

Easy…but not so easy. So Jesus told the parable about the marriage feast. The invitees were unwilling to come. Maybe they were looking for another kind of party. Since they declined, everyone else was invited, both evil and good people, and they came. But there was one guy who wasn't properly dressed. When confronted, even by the king, who addressed him as friend, the guy was speechless. He didn't make excuses or beg for mercy; he was just caught. Maybe he was trying to cheat his way in, hoping nobody would notice.

Perhaps being properly dressed means being humble. Aware of our shortcomings. Confessing them. Willing to become a member of the spiritual kingdom, in all that that means. Apparently, we're all invited, but only a few choose to dress properly.

Item in the Backpack: The Right Clothes

Matthew 22:23–46
Resurrected Souls

The Sadducees were religious; but they didn't believe in spirits, angels, or the resurrection, whereas the Pharisees did. Sounds like they didn't adhere to the *spirit* part of humanity, so of course, they wouldn't believe in an afterlife or eternity. They focused on the written Law alone.

I see some parallels between Sadducees and secular humanists, who focus on *human* activities and possibilities, downplaying or denying God and life after death.

In this passage, a little exchange ensued about a woman married to seven brothers. Jesus told the Sadducees they were missing the point. The question about marriage was a moot point since marriage isn't a thing in the resurrection. And why were they asking about the resurrection anyway, since they didn't even believe in it? Well, then he continued about God being the God of the living, meaning those who had previously died are…living. According to Jesus, the spirit lives on after death, obviously in resurrected bodies.

I have plenty of friends who are secular humanists. They are very good people, as a rule. When asked about the afterlife/eternity, they seem to answer one of two ways, either "I don't believe in that" or "I just don't think about that since it's all speculation."

But what if it's true?

I can't prove it. You can't prove it. A few people have gotten close to dying and report similar things, like seeing a bright light and experiencing profound peace, but there's no empirical evidence. It's a matter of faith, which is defined this way in Hebrews 11:1: "Faith is confidence in what we hope for and assurance about what we do not see."

Item in the Backpack: Eternity

Matthew 23:1–28
Despised Hypocrisy

Have you ever known someone who looks glamorous but is snotty and unkind? Or the candidate who makes lavish promises but neglects his people after the election? Or maybe the person who is "penny-wise but dollar foolish," keeping the minutia of the ledger but missing the investment opportunity?

The latter reminds me of the scribes and Pharisees in verse 23, who tithed nice spices (pennies) but neglected the big deals of justice, mercy, and faithfulness. Jesus called them hypocrites and whitewashed tombs, beautiful on the outside but full of dead men's bones and uncleanness. They were the blind leading the blind. And a big blind spot seemed to be money.

How can we keep ourselves *honorable*—the same on the outside as the inside?

It's just so easy to slip into those whitewashed tombs.

But the New Testament is full of ways to counter hypocrisy. I guess the Pharisees didn't pay attention, but we can. Hypocrisy and Micah 6:8 just don't mix. "He has shown you, O mortal, what is good. And what does the Lord require of you? To act justly and to love mercy and to walk humbly with your God."

Item in the Backpack: Honor

Matthew 23:29–39
Broken Heart

Jesus again called out hypocrisy in the scribes and Pharisees by quoting *them*: "If *we* had lived in the days of our fathers, *we* wouldn't have killed the prophets." Then he told them *they* would be the ones who would kill the prophets and righteous to come. In fact, he told them that the guilt of all the righteous blood shed on earth would fall on them, from A to Z (Abel to Zechariah).

This is intense. Truly.

Then the tide turned. He turned from anger to having a broken heart. He called out to Jerusalem: "How often I have longed to gather your children together, as a hen gathers her chicks under her wings, and you were not willing."

If I had been there, I would have cried at that point. Jesus seemed heartbroken. The picture of the hen gathering her chicks is too precious not to bring tears. And as I sit here, I'm aware that that's how Jesus wants *me* and *you*.

But Jerusalem was unwilling.

Remember, however, the parable of the marriage feast. All are invited. We can choose how to RSVP, whether we're good or evil, Jew or Gentile. We can choose whether or not to run under his wing.

Item in the Backpack: Jesus's Longing for Us

Matthew 24:1–28
Perilous Times

As Jesus stepped out of the temple, the disciples pointed out the temple buildings to him. Interestingly, he told them it would all be torn down, so they asked him when. A reasonable question. Then they asked what the signs would be. Somehow they understood he was talking about himself—his return and the perilous times ahead.

Not your run-of-the-mill conversation.

If this is your first time to read the New Testament, here's both the backstory and a preview. In the Old Testament (Daniel and other books), there's a lot of prophecy about the arrival of the Messiah and about times still ahead of us. In the New Testament book of Revelation and other passages like this one, much more detail is given. In Revelation, much is cryptic, but here, things are pretty straightforward. Jesus will return to earth at some point in the future; but leading up to that, there will be wars, famines, earthquakes, and a great tribulation.

The details of these things are still wildly open to debate. All will come clear when it happens.

That being said, one concept pops out to me in this passage. Jesus said that those who stand firm to the end will be saved.

"Perseverance must finish its work so that you may be mature and complete, not lacking anything" (James 1:4). Why is perseverance the key to such good things? Why can't the word be "victory" or "success"? Those words sound like a lot more fun than perseverance, but nonetheless, we're to stand firm.

Item in the Backpack: Endurance

Matthew 24:29–51
Constant Readiness

A definition of "integrity" is doing the right thing even when no one is looking. That's what strikes me in studying this passage. We're to have integrity *all* the time. Sometimes we get lax because we assume that the moon going dark won't happen for a long time. And maybe we assume nobody's really looking anyway.

We're to be like the faithful and sensible slave who feeds the family even when the master's away. You know, that person who does the right thing even when no one is looking.

So what does this mean for us? Let's imagine a scenario. Let's say we're going about our business and weird astronomy things happen and a sign appears in the sky. Could be figurative, could be literal, but let's say every person on the planet figures out that something supernatural is happening. And let's say that Jesus has come back to earth. (I mean, if we believe that he was here the first time, why would it be a stretch to believe he would come again?) And let's say the world is a mess. That is definitely not a stretch.

How many of us would be ready? Would we be embarrassed that we had let things slide? Would we be scrambling to cover up things done in secret? Would we be terrified?

Or would we be over the moon, so to speak? He might just say to us, "Well done, good and faithful slave." That phrase appears in the next chapter in a parable about a slave who made a wise investment. I can see similarities.

The point is to live with integrity…to live like Jesus could show up any minute. To live like Jesus is *already* here, spiritually speaking. So I ask myself, am I living out that truth or do I sometimes forget?

Item in the Backpack: Integrity

Matthew 25:1–30
Foolishness Exposed

The foolish virgins failed to take oil for their lamps, which is like taking a cookstove on your camping trip without any fuel. I believe Jesus told this parable because he wants people to think ahead. The downside for the foolish virgins was that they lost out on the bridegroom. That's a pretty serious consequence for being careless.

Jesus was straightforward about other negative traits too. Think about these folks: the improperly dressed dinner guest (Matt. 22:13), the evil slave who beat people and got drunk (Matt. 24:51), and the lazy slave who failed to invest the master's talent (Matt. 25:30).

All were presumptive and prideful. They felt they knew better than the king/master. The dinner guest just didn't try and didn't seem to care. He was disrespectful and took advantage of the lavish invitation. The Matthew 24 slave thought he could coast while the master was away. He indulged himself rather than exercising integrity. The Matthew 25 slave tried to deflect blame for his laziness.

The downside for them? Being thrown into outer darkness, where there's weeping and gnashing of teeth. Jesus *seriously* wants us to think ahead about our lives.

The virgins who were ready when the bridegroom arrived went to the wedding feast. The good guys in the slave stories were blessed and put in charge. These people had high regard for the king/master/bridegroom, and it paid off.

Item in the Backpack: High Regard for God

Matthew 25:31–46
Regarding Jesus

At some point in time, Jesus will sit in judgment and separate the people. To the right, he'll call the blessed ones to inherit the kingdom. To the left, he'll banish the cursed ones to eternal fire.

Why?

Again, because of their regard (or disregard) for him.

Interestingly, his measuring stick isn't how we fawn over him or make sacrifices. It's how we treat others. "Truly I tell you, whatever you did for one of the least of these brothers and sisters of mine, you did for me."

If we take care of our fellow humans, we're doing it for Jesus. This isn't a simile. The verse doesn't say that if we take care of our fellow humans, it's *like* we're doing it for Jesus. It says we're doing it for Jesus.

Mother Teresa once said, "It's not how much we give, but how much love we put into giving." We can do small things with great love.

Like giving a cup of cold water to someone who needs it or a flower to someone who's having a bad day. Or mentoring a kid who struggles. Or babysitting for a young mom who needs a break. Or visiting someone in prison. In doing so, it helps that person; but ultimately, in an enormous miraculous sense, it's all about loving Jesus himself. It's a way to live out our relationship with him.

Item in the Backpack: Relationship with Jesus

Matthew 26:1–25
Worthy Extravagance

I can barely write about Jesus's upcoming crucifixion. This is such holy ground, I'm almost afraid, but I *can* think about Jesus in human terms. That is my offering, such as it is. Mentally, he had to decide to do the right thing in the face of his impending murder. Can you imagine the agony? Physically, he was soon to sweat drops of blood in the garden of Gethsemane. (Sweating blood, called hematidrosis, although rare, is caused by acute fear or great stress.) Emotionally, he must have suffered from deep soul disappointment, intense dread, horror. Socially, some of his friends abandoned him. We'll soon see how they fell asleep, denied him, or betrayed him. Psychologically, I can't even imagine. Spiritually, he felt that even his father, God, had forsaken him, as we'll soon read.

And that precious woman with the vial of perfume knew what he needed. Not necessarily something practical that could be converted to funds for the poor, but comfort.

He needed comfort. Beautiful affection. Her heartfelt gift. Maybe this is why we speak in terms of giving him our hearts. Our centers. Our love. Like she did.

He wants a relationship with us. Not religiosity, but relationship. Love.

He was so appreciative of the love this woman showed him that he said this: "Truly I tell you, wherever this gospel is preached throughout the world, what she has done will also be told, in memory of her."

It boils down to love: "For God so loved the world that he gave his one and only Son, that whoever believes in him shall not perish but have eternal life" (John 3:16).

Item in the Backpack: Love

Matthew 26:26–50
Necessary Endings

Jesus went about doing his final things on earth. A symbolic supper. Instructions for Communion. Some last words to his guys. Agonizing prayer in the garden. Emotional preparation for his betrayal and arrest.

He also had to set some things in motion for his followers, which includes us. The first was his institution of the Lord's Supper. He gave instructions about the bread symbolizing his broken body and the cup symbolizing his blood. This memorial was set up for us to do continually, to remember him and his work on our behalf.

To remember. We can do this.

The second was his example in prayer. He laid his heart out before God in the garden—no holding back, no martyr complex. Just raw truth...but ending with surrender. "My Father, if it is possible, may this cup be taken from me. *Yet not as I will, but as you will.*" This is how we're to pray—honestly, but in the end, yielding to God's higher call.

To surrender. I wish I could easily write, "We can do this," but we know it's gut-wrenching at times. It was gut-wrenching for Jesus, but he *did* surrender to his destiny.

And this is how it turned out:

> He had equal status with God but didn't think so much of himself that he had to cling to the advantages of that status no matter what. Not at all. When the time came, he set aside the privileges of deity and took on the status of a slave, became *human*! Having become human, he stayed human. It was an incredibly humbling process. He didn't claim special privileges. Instead, he lived a selfless, obedient life and then died a selfless, obedient death—and the worst kind of death at that—a crucifixion. Because of that obedience, God lifted him high and honored him far beyond anyone or anything, ever, so that all created beings in heaven and on earth—even those long ago dead and buried—will bow in worship before this Jesus Christ, and call out in praise that he is the Master of all, to the glorious honor of God the Father. (Phil. 2:6–11, *The Message*).

It all worked out...for our benefit...and we will never forget.

Item in the Backpack: Remembrance

Matthew 26:51–75
Peer Pressure

Why did the crowd turn on Jesus? Within hours of his triumphal entry into Jerusalem, the people did a 180. And one of his best friends denied him three times, with cursing and swearing at that.

Peter feared for his life, but the crowd? I'm guessing some voices started infiltrating the ranks, making little disparaging comments here and there, casting doubt, and one by one people changed their minds about Jesus. Peer pressure created a raging wildfire.

Jesus, on the other hand, stood his ground. He stayed on top of the fact that everything happening was for a reason. He kept silent when someone skewed his words. He spoke up later even though it caused his death sentence. He endured being spit on, beaten, slapped, and mocked.

And the fire raged on within the crowd.

I'm finding an obscure but terrifying character in this story—the infiltrating voice. The voice that gained momentum and acceptance because it was loud and popular, obscuring the fact that it was dead wrong.

If we were to interview people in the crowd, asking why they were against him, they might scratch their heads, because a few days ago they had loved him. Crowd mentality. Peer pressure.

I ask myself, who would I have been in that crowd? A joiner? A coward? A lone ranger? A firefighter?

Next time we see crowd mentality taking over, we can remember this and pray for strength.

Item in the Backpack: Strength

Matthew 27:1–26
Individual Responsibility

The Apostles' Creed starts like this: "I believe in Jesus Christ, God's only Son, our Lord, who was conceived by the Holy Spirit, born of the Virgin Mary, *suffered under Pontius Pilate*, was crucified, died, and was buried."

Wouldn't you hate to go down in history like Pilate, the one who caused God to suffer?

Pilate was in a tough spot about Jesus. He was amazed by the man. Couldn't find anything wrong with him. His wife warned him to have nothing to do with "that righteous man." But as the governor, he had to govern and he chose his path. Fearing a riot, he had Jesus scourged and handed over for crucifixion.

It makes me aware of our leaders' responsibilities. Sometimes they have to make decisions they don't even agree with. That being said, Pilate still sentenced Jesus to death. Could he have made another choice? Of course.

It also makes me aware of my own responsibilities. Do I sometimes cause God to suffer? Yes. Could I make better choices at those times? Of course. It's not just Pontius Pilate, or even Judas for that matter.

So what are we to do? Live a tortured life? Pilate has been depicted in art as perpetually washing his hands, never able to banish his guilt. Judas took his own life.

But shortly we'll see that Jesus, *while being crucified*, prayed this about his torturers: "Father, forgive them; for they do not know what they are doing." Even at the pinnacle of suffering, he offered them forgiveness. He offers us forgiveness. Our responsibility is to accept it, whether we've caused a little suffering or a lot. We can perpetually wash our hands…or kill ourselves in one form or another…or gratefully accept the gift of forgiveness, plain and simple.

Item in the Backpack: Gratitude

Matthew 27:27–50
Darkest Hours

Jesus died.

At that point, nobody knew for a fact that he would come back to life three days later. Nobody remembered the symbolism of destroying the temple and rebuilding it in three days. Nobody seemed to put two and two together about this fulfillment of an Old Testament prophecy.

All they knew was that it was dark. Literally. (From noon until midafternoon, darkness fell on all the land.) And figuratively. It was the darkness that only Good Friday could cause.

Look at these scriptures about darkness:

> But if your eyes are bad, your whole body will be full of darkness. If then the light within you is darkness, how great is that darkness! (Matt. 6:23)

> This is the verdict: Light has come into the world, but men loved darkness instead of light because their deeds were evil. (John 3:19)

> If we claim to have fellowship with him and yet walk in the darkness, we lie and do not live by the truth. (1 John 1:6)

> Anyone who claims to be in the light but hates his brother is still in the darkness. (1 John 2:9)

I remember seeing a TV show years ago about darkness in a town. The sun just never came up, because the racial hatred between the people was too strong. What a picture.

We know how the Good Friday story ends. Light *does* arrive, but for three days, darkness reigned. The only glimmer of hope was that some remembered Jesus saying that after three days he would rise again. In John 8:12, Jesus said, "I am the light of the world. Whoever follows me will never walk in darkness, but will have the light of life."

Item in the Backpack: A Light

Matthew 27:51–66
<u>Torn Veil</u>

The moment Jesus died, the veil of the temple was torn in two from top to bottom. Small sentence. Enormous significance.

The Jerusalem temple was the center of Jewish religious life. The first temple was built by King Solomon in 957 BC and destroyed by the Babylonians in 586 BC. The second was built in 516 BC and destroyed by the Romans in AD 70. Jewish tradition maintains that a third and final temple will be built on the Temple Mount, which now houses the Islamic Dome of the Rock and other structures.

And herein is the significance. Jesus's point was that *he* is the third and final temple.

The veil separated the Holy of Holies, where God's presence dwelt, from the rest of the temple where people could be. Only the high priest could pass beyond the veil once a year to make atonement for their sins. The tearing signified that now the way into the Holy of Holies was open for all people, for all time, both Jew and Gentile.

God moved out of that place never again to dwell in a temple made with hands. There is no longer separation. It's now a matter of believing in Jesus and his atonement. There are no more animal sacrifices either. He became the once-and-for-all sacrifice for our sins.

It's a whole new thing. The price has been paid. We are free from our sins.

> Therefore, brothers and sisters, since we have confidence to enter the Most Holy Place by the blood of Jesus, by a new and living way opened for us through the curtain, that is, his body, and since we have a great priest over the house of God, let us draw near to God with a sincere heart and with the full assurance that faith brings, having our hearts sprinkled to cleanse us from a guilty conscience and having our bodies washed with pure water. Let us hold unswervingly to the hope

> we profess, for he who promised is faithful. (Heb. 10:19–23)

Item in the Backpack: Freedom

Matthew 28
Startling Discovery

Two friends, both named Mary, went to Jesus's grave at dawn on Sunday morning. There had been earthquakes since he died, but right now, all they sensed was the pounding of their hearts. They got there and an angel that looked like lightning was at the open tomb. No wonder the guards looked dead.

After listening to the angel, they took off in fear and joy to tell the disciples. Then Jesus was just there…on the path. They grabbed his feet, probably sobbing one minute and laughing the next. I visualize Jesus throwing his head back in laughter too. After all, it was *finished.*

Can you imagine the joy of someone you love so much being alive again, this time forever?

They raced on to tell their friends, likely tripping now and then in that running-too-fast kind of way. They reached the disciples and blubbered out his message. "Meet me in Galilee. Stat."

They did…and Jesus commissioned them. Because the disciples obeyed, I'm a believer today. A handful of followers, both men and women, spread the word and the world has never been the same.

Of course, the biggest reason the world has never been the same is that he's not in the tomb. Like the orthodox greeting says, "He is risen. He is risen indeed." I believe it's true. Do you? If so, let's throw a party. If not, you can just tell him you believe him and trust him, plain and simple, *this very moment.*

And welcome to the party!

Item in the Backpack: A Victory Celebration

Mark 1–3
Mark's Viewpoint

The author of the book of Mark was probably John Mark, who transcribed the teachings of Peter and later joined Paul and Barnabas on their missionary journeys. We get to see things from his seat on the bus. The book is fast-paced and highlights Jesus's emotions.

Here are some points to ponder in chapters 1–3. Remember, for the most part, we'll cover narratives in Mark, Luke, and John that were not covered in Matthew. It's interesting to note what each of them thought to be most important. Jesus chose the twelve from a group "he himself wanted." Best friends, in a way. He gave nicknames to James and John (i.e., Sons of Thunder). (I wonder what their personalities were like!) He changed Simon's name to Peter, which means "rock." (I wonder if he called him Rocky.)

Jesus healed many more people and cast out many more demons. The demons would cry out, "You are the Son of God!" Seems that almost every time, Jesus would tell the healed or freed person not to tell anyone. Maybe it was just a practical matter because of the crowds.

He healed the paralytic whose friends hoisted him up to the roof, dug an opening, and lowered him down into the room. I love that picture of friendship.

Jesus healed on the Sabbath, which was a big no-no to the Pharisees. Jesus saw through their legalism. He didn't want them to get hung up on the details and miss the point. Two points actually. One was that he's bigger than Sabbath rules. Two, the idea of the Sabbath is to rest, and legalism is far from restful. Healing someone, on the other hand…

Resting at least one-seventh of the time was God's idea for our benefit. Jesus seemed to have done a fair amount of hanging out with friends and family, resting.

Do you know anyone who is frenetic? Trying to be God Jr.? I think if we're really following God, we'll take time to stay balanced and rest.

Item in the Backpack: A Sleeping Bag (Rest)

Mark 4–6
Happy People

Here again we see "seed" stories and as you might know, seeds make me happy! I love that a whole life is contained in a tiny seed... and that seeds can be planted to spread life. We can ask ourselves if we spread life or death. A funny question maybe, but think about it. Have you made the world a better place today? Made someone happy? Jesus used a lot of seed symbolism. Maybe seeds made him happy too.

And I love the picture of the woman who had been bleeding for twelve years touching Jesus's cloak. Crowds were pressing against him, but he knew! She was healed but thought at first that she was in trouble. Can't you just visualize him turning and smiling at her and saying, "Go in peace"? Yep, that was one happy lady.

And what about the man from the tombs with the unclean spirits. Their name was Legion (many). The man had been chained, cried out constantly, and gashed himself with stones. Some mentally ill people hear voices, harm themselves, harm others, end up in prison ("chained"), or commit suicide. Are there parallels?

Don't you love Mark 5:15? The man is sitting down, clothed, and in his right mind. Healed. Happy. We can pray for physical, mental, and spiritual health for ourselves and others. Something miraculous could happen. Something unbelievably happy.

Item in the Backpack: Health

Mark 7–9
<u>Salty Disciples</u>

The disciples spent a lot of time being confused. Take Mark 8:17 for example. Jesus had *just* fed four thousand people with seven loaves and a few fish, with lots of leftovers, yet the disciples were fretting because they only had one loaf in the boat with them. Hello! Why couldn't they understand that Jesus could easily provide? And why did they question the meaning of his parables so much?

(We have the benefit of understanding *after* reading his explanations.)

Anyway, I get their confusion. Often I wish I could ask Jesus questions face-to-face: "What do you mean by so-and-so?" "Why isn't everyone healed when we pray?" "Can you elaborate on hell?"

But Jesus loved the disciples in spite of their confusion, so I guess he loves me too. And with some things, maybe we're not meant to understand yet. The older I get, the more comfortable I am living with questions. There *are* answers; I just don't have them yet.

Lastly, in this passage, we read about salt. "Have salt in yourselves!" What is salt used for? It's a nutrient that seasons and preserves. It also creates thirst. I've read that it has over fourteen thousand uses.

So we, like the disciples, press on—gaining understanding to mitigate our confusion and refilling our salt shakers to bless those around us. We don't have to have our acts totally together before we're able to live out our saltiness.

Item in the Backpack: Salt

Mark 10–12
Childlike Trust

I took education classes in college; so I studied about lesson plans, opening hooks, practical applications, useful homework as opposed to busy work, etc. I've been musing on all that as I observe Jesus as a teacher. He was a master. He was direct at times and illustrative at times. He used object lessons. When little kids were around, you know, *being little kids*, the disciples tried to shoo them away, but Jesus said, "Anyone who will not receive the kingdom of God like a little child will never enter it."

So what does "like a little child" mean? Children *believe* those they trust. They have innocent faith. What a beautiful picture for those of us who have lost sight of our childlikeness. Maybe we need to reclaim it a bit.

Jesus elaborated on what the kingdom of God means. Having faith without doubting means granted requests. Leaving everything and following Jesus means eternal life. Serving is key to true greatness. Forgiving others is parallel to God's forgiveness of us. Ascertaining things intelligently rather than "following the party line" means the kingdom is near.

I like the idea of trusting God in a childlike way. It's so easy to get cynical and focused on why things *won't* work, when sometimes we just need to receive like a child…with delight.

Item in the Backpack: A Sense of Innocence

Mark 12:38–44
Last Cent

For me, the idea of poor widows doesn't make me think of hunched-over old women wrapped in dark shawls. I think of sari-clad Dalit ladies in India, impoverished, many "widowed" due to absent, alcoholic husbands, but with ironic joy on their faces, because the ladies I'm thinking of have become Christians. They're no longer outcasts. God loves them, and they totally get it.

The widow in this story put her last cent into the treasury at the church. She wasn't giving because someone was holding a gun to her head; she was doing it out of love. Because she got it. If she had given grudgingly, Jesus wouldn't have singled her out.

No doubt she knew the risk she was taking. She gave all she had to live on. She was either willing to starve or knew that somehow she would be taken care of. To her, it was a win-win. She certainly earned the respect of Jesus himself.

Luke 6:38 says this, "Give, and it will be given to you. A good measure, pressed down, shaken together and running over, will be poured into your lap. For with the measure you use, it will be measured to you."

"Last-cent sacrifice" is ultimate abandon, complete surrender without restraint or moderation. "Martyr sacrifice" is self-serving. I think we need to examine our motives when we sacrifice. Jesus noticed the poor widow's abandon.

Item in the Backpack: Abandon

Mark 13
Second Coming

Wars. Earthquakes. Famines. Persecution. Arrests. Family discord. The abomination of desolation. Tribulation. False Christs. Astronomical changes. Heaven and earth passing away.

Bad stuff. Really. Bad.

Even the most brilliant biblical scholars disagree on the return of Christ. When? How? Have some of these signs already been fulfilled? We certainly coexist with several items on the list.

And what is the abomination of desolation?

And why is the world such a hellish place for so many even now?

And why can't we all just get along?

And why can't we just ignore all that stuff and live in the moment, happy, happy, happy?

For two reasons. One, Jesus said to be on the alert, not ignoring what's going on. Two, life *is* hellish for so many, and who are we to ignore that? We aren't in paradise yet, folks.

Murders. Rapes. Civilians in the crossfire. Child abuse. School shootings. Mental illness. Suicides. Kidnappings. Caste discrimination. Terrorism. On and on.

Why will Jesus return? Because we can't get it right without him. He is...

Redeemer. Prince of Peace. Bread of Life. Alpha and Omega. Chief Cornerstone. Light of the World. Deliverer. Good Shepherd. Great High Priest. King of Kings. Mediator. Mighty One. The Door. Savior. Resurrection and the Life.

Item in the Backpack: The Answer

Mark 14–16
Easter Power

Easter Sunday celebrates Jesus's resurrection, but it wasn't called Easter that day. Everyone thought it was an ordinary Sabbath at first. The actual celebration of Easter (Pascha) didn't even begin until the mid-second century.

But on Resurrection Day "death was swallowed up in victory" (Isa. 25:8 and 1 Cor. 15:54). It took a while for everyone to figure out what had happened, but eventually the disciples *got it*. Mark 16:19–20 says this in *The Message*: "Then the Master Jesus, after briefing them, was taken up to heaven, and he sat down beside God in the place of honor. And the disciples went everywhere preaching, the Master working right with them, validating the Message with indisputable evidence."

The Lord *worked with them.* That's gotta be one of my favorite passages in the Bible. True to form, even after his death and resurrection, Jesus knew his people needed "working with." They needed a new dose of power to move into their next chapter. The baton had been passed to them.

Now, centuries later, we celebrate Easter. We dye the eggs and decorate the church with lilies, both symbols of the resurrection, but do we live in Easter power all year long?

I know my answer. Not enough.

It's like sitting in my car by the gas pump without filling up. That doesn't get me very far.

But with the Lord *working with me*? Reminding me? Empowering me? "I can do all this through him who gives me strength" (Phil. 4:13).

I just need to fill up the tank.

Item in the Backpack: Fuel

Luke 1:1–25
<u>God's Timing</u>

Have you ever thrown a surprise party for someone? *You* knew what was coming, but that person didn't? He/she assumed everyone forgot or worse, didn't care. You had the details worked out to a tee and could hardly hide that smile. You knew they would be so happy!

Sometimes I think our view of God is like that. We pray and pray and assume he forgot or, worse, doesn't care, when all along he has the details worked out to a tee and is probably a bit giddy during the wait.

Maybe that happened to Zacharias and Elizabeth. God knew they would have this baby even though they were old. Zacharias was a little doubtful, so there was a consequence for that. Elizabeth was just happy. They had wanted a baby for such a long time. God wants to give us good gifts, but in his timing.

The Dalits have been waiting for justice and wholeness for three thousand years, but I get impatient when my laptop won't boot up fast enough. Ugh. Why do we have to wait? Why can't God just give us a little hint of good things to come? It would make patience so much easier.

But that's not the way things work in God Reality.

I've heard there are three potential answers to prayer—yes, no, or wait. I rarely get an instant sense of yes or no. Often my prayers launch a course in Debbie Preparation 101, which can take years. The scriptures tell us to ask and we'll receive. We'll receive what we asked for or a greater gift, which might take a lot of loving preparation behind the scenes, kind of like a surprise party.

Item in the Backpack: Patience

Luke 1:26–45
<u>Girl Time</u>

Mary and Elizabeth were relatives. Mary was young. Elizabeth was old. They got to spend a few months together while each was pregnant with a son. It was sacred time and likely a lot of fun. (Those two concepts don't have to be mutually exclusive.)

The words "favored," "blessed," and "holy" are used a lot in this passage. Elizabeth knew her baby was special, but she knew Mary was carrying *God*. "How has it happened to me, that the mother of my Lord should come to me?" Can you imagine? The baby Elizabeth was carrying leaped in her womb for joy.

I think women need each other. Honestly, I don't know what I would do without my girlfriends. There are invisible threads among women—threads of understanding, support, connection, empathy—often wordless threads (although we're generally more than happy to use words). I love visualizing Mary and Elizabeth chatting over a cup of tea. It makes me feel as if I'm right there with them.

And I believe men need each other too. Don't you think Jesus and his guy friends kicked a soccer ball around every once in a while? And that they had each other's backs? Even when they denied him, all but Judas came back, and they set the world on fire.

"Though one may be overpowered, two can defend themselves. A cord of three strands is not quickly broken" (Eccles. 4:12).

The community of friends is so important. Mary made the elderly Elizabeth happy. Elizabeth encouraged young Mary in her faith. "*Blessed is she* who has believed that what the Lord has said to her will be accomplished!"

Item in the Backpack: Friend Time

Luke 1:46–56
The Magnificat

Confession: Sometimes when I pray, it's sort of like this: "Let's see, where were we? Oh yeah, that's right. Okay, so, thank you for this, I'm still concerned about that, etc."

I don't mean to make light of it or be *too* self-deprecating, but I think you understand. I cut to the chase too often. I don't spend nearly enough time in praise or remembrance of the greatness of God. I can take a lesson from the young Mary. Here's what she said (per *The Message*):

> I'm bursting with God-news; I'm dancing the song of my Savior God. God took one good look at me and look what happened—I'm the most fortunate woman on earth! What God has done for me will never be forgotten, the God whose very name is holy, set apart from all others. His mercy flows in wave after wave on those who are in awe before him. He bared his arm and showed his strength, scattered the bluffing braggarts. He knocked tyrants off their high horses, pulled victims out of the mud. The starving poor sat down

> to a banquet; the callous rich were left out in the cold. He embraced his chosen child, Israel; he remembered and piled on the mercies, piled them high. It's exactly what he promised, beginning with Abraham and right up to now.

Item in the Backpack: Praise

Luke 1:57–80
Prophetic Words

Zacharias prophesied this about John: "And you, my child, 'Prophet of the Highest,' will go ahead of the Master to prepare his ways, present the offer of salvation to his people, the forgiveness of their sins. Through the heartfelt mercies of our God, God's Sunrise will break in upon us" (Luke 1:76–78, *The Message*).

What an amazing thing for a dad to proclaim about his child! And, of course, the prophecy came to pass.

According to J. Barton Payne's *Encyclopedia of Biblical Prophecy*, 1,239 prophecies are found in the Old Testament and 578 in the New for a total of 1,817, Zacharias's being one of them. Prophecies are a *big deal* in the Bible. We'll touch on many more throughout our journey. They've been given to prepare us, bless us, and give us signs to point the way. To me, they're "evidence that demands a verdict" in the words of Josh McDowell, Christian apologist. Tracking their progress (past, present, and future) is one of the most compelling reasons to believe.

Item in the Backpack: Attention to the Prophecies

Luke 2:1–38
Temple Happenings

I never get tired of reading about Jesus's birth, just like I never get tired of looking at the Rocky Mountains or sitting on a beach. There's always something new to see. I love the part about the shepherds in this passage. Shepherds were lowly, but they were handpicked by God to be the first to visit the Christ. That is *so* like God. And I love the part about a multitude of the heavenly host praising God. Oh my!

I love thinking about Jesus's first few days from the perspective of happy-but-sleep-deprived Mary and Joseph, getting prepared for their baby's circumcision, picking out a pair of birds for the temple sacrifice, meeting Simeon and Anna. The passage says they were amazed at the things Simeon said about Jesus. Maybe they didn't fully understand that their baby was going to be a light of revelation to Gentiles or the glory of God's people Israel or the fall and rise of many or a sign or a sword. They knew Jesus was God's Son, and that they were chosen to raise him, but I'm guessing they didn't know that even time would be measured by his birth.

Can you imagine the wonder of it all?

Item in the Backpack: Musings on the Miracle

Luke 2:39–52
Young Jesus

We don't know much about Jesus as a youngster, but this story gets me every time! If you've ever lost track of a child in a store, even for a couple of minutes, frantic doesn't even begin to describe it. But three days? No wonder Mary let him have it!

If they had understood, they would have smacked their foreheads, realizing they had left him at church (i.e., his Father's house).

I use verse 52 when I pray for all the children and grandkids in my life, including those of extended family and friends. I have a running list of several, called my League of Extraordinaries. Frankly, they're mostly boys that are having a hard time in life. (Seems that's epidemic these days.) I have a strong sense that these guys have extraordinary potential and that society has failed them in some way.

I pray that they'll increase in wisdom, stature, and favor with God and people. I pray for their brains and their educations. I pray that their physical bodies will develop, strong and healthy. I pray that they'll become believers. And I pray that they'll find favor with people and not be rebellious and difficult, unless that behavior is some kind of sign that we, the adults, need to pay attention to. Sometimes young ones have struggles we can help with. That's our job.

An interesting thing about Jesus is that he listened to the temple teachers and asked them questions. He already had the understanding and answers, but he listened. There is a passage in Hebrews 5 that says this: "Son though he was, he learned obedience from what he suffered." Apparently, Jesus had to learn, just like us. Maybe his listening and question-asking helped him gain what he needed. Note that he listened to the temple teachers, not to the voices of the world. What a lesson for us…and our kiddos.

Item in the Backpack: Listening Skills

Luke 3–4
Holy Spirit

"He (Jesus) will *baptize* you in the Holy Spirit."
"And the Holy Spirit *descended upon* him like a dove."
"And Jesus, *full of* the Holy Spirit…"
"And Jesus returned to Galilee *in the power of* the Spirit…"
"The Spirit of the Lord is *upon* Me…"

Who or what *is* the Holy Spirit?

The Holy Spirit is the third person of the Father/Son/Spirit trio (the Trinity). Orthodox theology asserts that the Trinity consists of three distinct persons who can interact with each other, yet all existing in one essence.

What does the Holy Spirit *do*?

He enables us to do what needs to be done. Isaiah 61:1–2, which Jesus quoted in Luke 4, says this (per *The Message)*: "*God's Spirit is on me*; he's chosen me to preach the Message of good news to the poor, sent me to announce pardon to prisoners and recovery of sight to the blind, to set the burdened and battered free, to announce, 'This is God's year to act!'"

Our power source is the Holy Spirit. He indwells us.

The Spirit is somewhat of a mystery, but a welcome mystery.

Watch how many times you'll see words about the Spirit in the Bible. They often precede a supernatural act of power. Power that heals, casts out evil, sets people free.

Need power? Call on the Spirit.

Item in the Backpack: Holy Spirit

Luke 5:1–11
Full Nets

A few years ago, I was puzzling over a peculiar mental health trait in a friend. I was praying about it and sensed this: "Go to the Internet and research it one more time," to which I replied, "I've already done that to no avail, but okay."

I padded over to my laptop, plunked around a bit, and there it was. *Abundant* information that described the trait. Researching it has made an enormous difference in our relationship.

I immediately thought of Simon, casting that net one more time. We need to obey even when we think we know better. *Especially* when we think we know better.

God has the big picture. We don't. It's like that tapestry illustration. We see the tapestry of life from the underside, and it looks like a clot of random threads, but God sees it from the topside, orderly and beautiful.

Sometimes I need obedience training, like my dog. When she doesn't want to obey, she won't make eye contact with me. Sometimes I do that with God. I avoid eye contact. I rationalize. I compare myself to others who are "worse" than I am. And sometimes I disobey, hoping God won't notice or will let me off the hook. And you know what? There are always consequences. He forgives and restores, but I've found that there's a process. Restoration may be painful, but blessing seems to follow obedience.

What if Simon had said no? Disobeyed Jesus? It might have changed history, because as it turns out, this catch plus the fact that

Jesus told him he would become a fisher of men, caused him to leave everything and follow Jesus.

Item in the Backpack: Obedience

Luke 5:12–6:49
Solid Foundation

Luke 6 is full of rock-solid teaching about building life on a firm foundation.

Our home is built on a rocky ridge with boulders and caves and ponderosa pines. It overlooks the front range of the Rocky Mountains. It's solid. When I need solitude and God time, I scramble up through our hillside orchard and perch on a bench at our overlook. Jesus's words come to mind. "As for everyone who comes to me and hears my words and puts them into practice, I will show you what they are like. They are like a man building a house, who dug down deep and laid the foundation on rock. When a flood came, the torrent struck that house but could not shake it, because it was well built."

Building a rock-solid life isn't about hearing his words and then going about our business. It's about *acting* on those words. Not *intending* to act on them, but literally acting on them. The words are powerful and life-altering, but not easy.

Here are verses 22–26 from *The Message*:

> It's trouble ahead if you think you have it made. What you have is all you'll ever get. And it's trouble ahead if you're satisfied with yourself. Your *self* will not satisfy you for long. And it's trouble ahead if you think life's all fun and games. There's suffering to be met, and you're going to meet it. There's trouble ahead when you live only for the approval of others, saying what flatters them, doing what indulges them. Popularity contests are not truth contests—look how many scoundrel preachers were approved by your ancestors! Your task is to be true, not popular.

Nobody ever said building a life on a solid foundation would be easy, just worth it.

Item in the Backpack: Foundation

Luke 7–8
Fear Not

Jairus's daughter died. When Jesus heard of it, he said, "Don't be *afraid*," and went to their house. He took her by the hand and she rose up.

Earlier, the woman who had had a hemorrhage was *afraid*. She thought she was in trouble, so she fell down before him, trembling. (She needn't have been afraid. He healed her, happily so.)

It's been said that some form of "fear not" or "don't be afraid" appears in the Bible 365 times. That exact number is a bit disputed, but it's safe to say it appears a lot.

People back then had a lot of fear. People today have a lot of fear.

Here's the definition of fear: "a distressing emotion aroused by impending danger, evil, pain, etc., whether the threat is real or imagined." Real or imagined.

I know what it's like to live fearfully, and I know what it's like to live contented and safe. I prefer the latter, but trusting God means doing so whether we're doing fine or suffering. Trusting God means seeing life as a win-win. We have good times and bad times. We will hurt, grieve, and suffer, sometimes horribly, but we can look for silver linings, lessons, and beauty out of the ashes. If we know God is *for* us, we can trust his heart. God never tricks us. We might go through terrible things, but he is with us.

Remember Matthew 28:20: "And surely I am with you always, to the very end of the age."

Item in the Backpack: Win-Win Attitude

Luke 9:1–10:24
Happy Results

Jesus made it clear what following him meant. Denying self. Taking up one's cross every day. Setting one's face forward without turning back.

Think of times when you've chosen to deny yourself. Like biting your tongue when somebody was wrong about you. Or taking a stand for something that went against popular culture. Or choosing not to align with somebody enticing but harmful, even though part of you really wanted to. Or saying, "I'm a Christian." In some countries, saying that could cost you your job or even your life.

This stuff is not for the fainthearted.

However, there are happy results! When the seventy Jesus had sent out returned, they had success stories and Jesus rejoiced greatly. They had operated on a whole new level.

We can operate on a whole new level as well. We just need to follow Jesus.

In Colorado, some of us climb 14ers (fourteen-thousand-plus-foot peaks) for fun, believe it or not. Those hikes are like climbing stairs for seven hours, exhausting and sometimes terrifying. To me, mountain climbing is a picture of following Christ. Once you get to the serious climbing part, you have to deny what you want to do, which is to sit down or turn around. You're exhausted. You wonder why you took this on in the first place! You have to set your face forward with resolve. You must choose to follow the leader, one step at a time. Then, finally, finally, *finally*, you make it to the top.

And you rejoice greatly!

Item in the Backpack: Resolve

Luke 10:25–42
Correct Priorities

There's the story about the seminary professor who had a strict deadline for his students' Good Samaritan essay. Unbeknownst to them, he staged an accident in front of the building. As the students bounded up the stairs to turn in their papers, each one sidestepped the accident…and failed the essay.

And there's the story that goes on in households across the world even today—the conflict between the Marthas and the Marys, the type A "get 'er done" person and the laid-back social butterfly.

Both stories in this passage have to do with priorities.

Why did the priest and Levite not stop to help the man who was beaten? Maybe they were late for an appointment. Maybe they thought somebody else would stop. They had other priorities. But a Samaritan stopped even though there were strong tensions between the Jews and Samaritans. He had his priorities straight. He knew about the tensions, and he didn't care. It was more important to help the guy.

And Martha and Mary had different priorities. Martha was concerned about logistics. Mary wanted to curl up and listen to Jesus. I'm one of those people focused on deadlines, a clean house, a nice dinner on the table. I'm more of a Martha than a Mary. It's the way I'm wired, and that's okay, but sometimes wiring gets in the way.

As Jesus said, only a few things are necessary. Really, only one. To be like Jesus. And to do that, we need to stop for the hurting person or slow down enough to listen. The former means we need to pay attention to interruptions. The latter means we might not be able to put a check mark on our to-do list. However, like Mary, we will have chosen the good part.

Item in the Backpack: Priorities

Luke 11
No Darkness

"Your eye is the lamp of your body. When your eyes are healthy, your whole body also is full of light."

Well, that's pretty direct. Watch what we watch, right? I'm one of those people impacted by sight. I avoid horror movies, for example. (And to my young friends, I don't care if it's fake!) I come undone over war movies, but sometimes I force myself to watch them. I need to see reality if it helps my formation.

That being said, however, I believe Jesus was talking about the eye leading us astray, as any of the senses can do. Wrong music to the ears. Wrong touch. Wrong tastes.

Think about how the world would be if everyone guarded their eyes. It would seriously set back the porn industry. It might lessen violent acts after people play violent video games. I know I sound *old* right now, but could it be true? And what about our addictions to our smartphones? Sometimes I hate them.

What would it be like to have a Darkness-Free Day? To choose Philippians 4:8? "Whatever is…true, noble, right, pure, lovely, admirable, excellent or praiseworthy…think about such things."

Jesus said if we're full of light, we'll be wholly illumined. Darkness free.

Item in the Backpack: Living in the Light

Luke 12
Given Much

"Be on your guard against all kinds of greed."

"From everyone who has been given much, much will be demanded."

In America, we've been given much. Actually, we're at the top, pretty inarguably, largely because of blood, sweat, tears, hard work, and living our ideals. And I'm on-my-knees thankful, but to hear "America First" touted all around bothers me badly because of the verses above.

(Let the hate mail begin!)

As enticing as "Me First" sounds, Jesus wants us to be ready, caught in the act of laying up treasures in heaven, not in bigger barns. Caught in the act of doing good, not in indulging ourselves with disregard for others. Caught in the act of "you first."

And you know what? "For the pagan world runs after all such things, and your Father knows that you need them. But seek his kingdom, and these things will be given to you as well."

And remember Luke 6:38? "Give, and it will be given to you. A good measure, pressed down, shaken together and running over, will be poured into your lap. For with the measure you use, it will be measured to you."

I think God wants us to be our very best, meaning having a spirit of generosity, not selfishness.

Item in the Backpack: Generosity

Luke 13:1–17
No Kidding

Jesus didn't mess around with small talk. *I tell you*, unless you repent, you will perish. "Strive to enter through the narrow door; for many, *I tell you*, will seek to enter and will not be able."

Jesus made things crystal clear. He doesn't toy with us. There aren't many paths to God, just one. He wants us with him. He said this in John 10:9–10, using a sheep pen analogy: "I am the gate; whoever enters through me will be saved. They will come in and go out, and find pasture. The thief comes only to steal and kill and destroy; I have come that they may have life, and have it to the full."

We humans can try our best to earn our way into heaven, consult charts or crystals, or choose a different religious path; but Jesus stands his ground. He's not kidding. He is our true north, so to speak. He died for us to prove his point.

Item in the Backpack: Compass

Luke 13:31–14:35
Counting Cost

This morning, I reread an article about five missionaries who had been killed in a drive-by shooting in northern Iraq. Good Baptist folk from the Southern United States. Had they counted the cost beforehand? I'm quite sure they had. They had decided to hoist the cross…and they paid the ultimate price for it.

Jesus wants us to count the cost, just like we would before starting a building project or going on a journey. He wants us to prethink and make plans accordingly. Being a Christian means making distinctive decisions. It's wise to let our loved ones know of them in advance too, because being a Christian affects how we spend money, how we give money, how we make career decisions, how we parent, how we treat people, what we live for…and what we are willing to die for.

Remember the story of the pearl of great price? God wants us to decide if that's what we want, then to plan the way to acquire it.

Item in the Backpack: Planning

Luke 15
Second Chances

In writing this book, I feel like I've been born again, *again.* I want each entry to be fresh and personal (even the hard parts), and to that end, God has lavished a whole new awareness on me. It took a while to write this one though. I wanted a fresh take on the Prodigal Son story, and I got it. Unfortunately.

See, I feel like the big brother in the story. Sometimes I feel like the prodigal son and sometimes I feel like the father, *always* welcoming his children no matter what, but today I feel like the older brother. Jealous. (Ugly.)

Suffice it to say I've been subconsciously comparing myself to an acquaintance and coming up short. If you knew the details, you'd say I'm justified because the situation isn't exactly fair. However, the situation wasn't exactly "fair" for the older brother either. Younger Brother (aka brat) was getting all the attention. Their father had to set Older Brother straight. He was jealous for no good reason.

BTW, an antonym to jealousy is "satisfied." Older Brother was having trouble being satisfied. Jealousy is so *human.* God, however, wants us to rise above. Older Brother could have chosen a satisfied heart and joined his dad in welcoming his brother home.

The good news is that when we're aware of our less than savory features, we're always welcome to come home. And there's no place like home.

Item in the Backpack: Ticket Home

Luke 16:1–18
Savvy Steward

This passage could be confusing until you dig into it. Jesus praised an unrighteous steward! Odd, but reading verses 8–9 in *The Message* clarifies things: "Now here's a surprise: The master praised the crooked manager! And why? Because he knew how to look after himself. Streetwise people are smarter in this regard than law-abiding citizens. They are on constant alert, looking for angles, surviving by their wits. I want you to be smart in the same way—but for what is *right*—using every adversity to stimulate you to creative survival, to concentrate your attention on the bare essentials, so you'll live, really live, and not complacently just get by on good behavior."

To get a complete picture of Jesus, we need these adjectives: *savvy, gutsy, shrewd.* He praised the steward's shrewdness, and he most definitely wants *us* to be savvy, gutsy, and shrewd too.

"To the pure you show yourself pure, but to the devious you show yourself *shrewd*" (Ps. 18:26).

"I am sending you out like sheep among wolves. Therefore be as *shrewd* as snakes and as innocent as doves" (Matt. 10:16).

Another important word in this passage is "manager" (or "steward" in the New American Standard version). A steward is one who manages or is in charge of another's household or affairs. "Let a man regard us in this manner, as servants of Christ, and *stewards of the mysteries of God.* In this case, moreover, it is required of stewards that one be found trustworthy" (1 Cor. 4:1–2). Stewards of the mysteries of God. Can you think of anything more demanding than that? We're to be faithful stewards on behalf of God, which includes shrewdness and lots and lots of practice.

Item in the Backpack: Shrewdness

Luke 16:19–31
Lazarus's Destiny

Years ago, Paul Harvey told a story on the radio. It was about a man who decided against going to church with his wife on Christmas Eve because he couldn't buy that Jesus story, about God coming to earth as a man. That night snow started falling, and birds started crashing into his window, lost in the blizzard. He tried to shoo the birds into the barn in every way he could think of, but to no avail. He was upset and thought, *If only I could be a bird and mingle with them and speak their language. Then I could tell them not to be afraid. Then I could show them the way to safety. But I would have to be one of them.*

At that moment the church bells began to ring...and he sank to his knees in the snow.

"He [Jesus] said to him, 'If they do not listen to Moses and the Prophets, they will not be convinced even if someone rises from the dead'" (Luke 16:31). Jesus became a person and mingled with us and spoke our language so we could see, hear, understand. Then he died and three days later rose from the dead. Yet many are still unpersuaded.

Why risk it? Why not run into the arms of the one who loves you, where you'll be safe? God is love. In this passage, the poor man Lazarus somehow understood the message and is spending eternity in paradise. The rich man missed the point.

God sent Jesus to be our "bird" to show us the way.

Item in the Backpack: Promise of Paradise

Luke 17

Road Signs

This passage is full of road signs. The Samaritan leper did a "U-turn" to thank Jesus.

And here's a "straight arrow" sign. When Jesus returns, we're to follow full steam ahead and not turn back. The same holds true for the here and now. We're to be focused and forward moving.

So the key is to always know where he is. If he's behind us, we do a U-turn to get to him. If he's ahead of us, we follow him.

Sometimes it helps to literally, physically do a U-turn, like doing a 180 to walk away from that tempting second doughnut.

And sometimes it helps to envision following him. Stepping in his footprints, just a handhold away when times get rough. "Never will I leave you; never will I forsake you." So we say with confidence, "The Lord is my helper; I will not be afraid. What can mere mortals do to me?"(Heb. 13:5–6).

What road sign reminders do you need today? U-turn? Danger Ahead? Caution? Rest Area Ahead? Stop? Do Not Enter? One Way?

Figure out your direction and proceed.

Item in the Backpack: Reminders

Luke 18
Merciful Justice

God is just.

In this passage, Jesus talked about bringing swift justice to his elect. He also talked about bringing justice to both the Pharisee and the tax gatherer. The self-righteous one would be humbled. The repentant sinner would be exalted.

We love that God provides justice for the bad guys.

But what about us? We're not always good guys. We stumble. We flat-out sin. Do we cry out to God to have justice on us? Um, no.

We cry out for mercy.

Fortunately, God is merciful. "Mercy triumphs over judgment" (James 2:13).

In our dealings with others, I believe God calls us to be just (fair) *and* merciful. "But the wisdom that comes from heaven is first of all pure; then peace-loving, considerate, submissive, full of mercy and good fruit, impartial and sincere" (James 3:17).

Item in the Backpack: Mercy

Luke 19
Smart Dealings

Jesus used money illustrations a lot, probably because money is a big deal to us, so we pay attention.

Zacchaeus told Jesus he would give half of his possessions to the poor and that he'd repay those he had defrauded fourfold.

That's a lot of money!

The nobleman in this passage gave his slaves some cash and said, "Put this money to work until I come back." The ones who invested well were told, "Well done!" Because they were faithful with a little, he put them in authority over much.

That's good investing!

This passage is likely literal, meaning we're to use money well. We can hoard, or we can invest. In the parallel parable in Matthew, the currency is called not a mina but a talent. A mina was worth about one hundred days' wages, and a talent was worth about $1,000 in silver.

We can invest whether we have a little or a lot. Investing $50 in a microloan to a woman in a developing country produces (a) means for her to start a small business, (b) payback of the loan, (c) reinvestment of the loan, (d) means for another woman to start a small business, (e) payback of the loan, (f) reinvestment. You get the picture. That $50 investment could go on forever.

Same with our nonmonetary talents, like our business savvy, musicianship, teaching ability, cooking skills, etc. They're for investing.

Item in the Backpack: Good Investments

Luke 20–23
Seven Sentences

While Jesus was dying on the cross, he was mostly silent. He spoke just seven times, often called the Seven Last Words of Christ. We have to look at all four Gospel accounts to get all seven sentences.

"Father, forgive them, for they do not know what they are doing" (Luke 23:34).

"Truly I tell you, today you will be with me in paradise" (Luke 23:43).

"'Woman, here is your son,' and to the disciple, 'Here is your mother'" (John 19:26–27).

"My God, my God, why have you forsaken me?" (Mark 15:34, Matthew 27:46).

"I am thirsty" (John 19:28).

"It is finished" (John 19:30).

"Father, into your hands I commit my spirit" (Luke 23:46).

Jesus was forgiving, loving, protective, honest, human, complete, and victorious. Seven words, in a sense. Then this part of his journey ended.

If you knew you were about to die, what would your last words be? Jesus didn't use his last hours to summarize his mission or preach one last time. He didn't lash out at the crowd or his killers. He didn't defend himself. He *did* make sure his mom was taken care of. It seems he had lived his life and had already said what needed to be said. And then his time came to die.

Maybe that's a lesson for us—to do the life we want while we're living. To not wait until we're older or dying to make corrections. What life do you want? Who do you want to be? It might be interesting to write it in seven adjectives while you're fully alive.

Item in the Backpack: Self-Assessment

Luke 24
<u>Love Won</u>

Jesus did it. He defeated death. Killed it.

"When the perishable has been clothed with the imperishable, and the mortal with immortality, then the saying that is written will come true: '*Death has been swallowed up in victory.*' 'Where, O death, is your victory? Where, O death, is your sting?'" (1 Cor.15:54–55).

"For God so loved the world that he gave his one and only Son, that whoever believes in him shall not perish but have eternal life" (John 3:16).

We'll die physically, but not spiritually.

Jesus died but came back fully alive and almost giddy, it seems. He was practically teasing the two on the road to Emmaus, getting them to tell the story. He appeared to others, and as soon as they recognized him, he vanished. He seemed to relish rehashing the fulfilled prophecies from the *victory* side of the grave so they would finally put two and two together. He ate. He blessed. He disappeared in the middle of his Bethany blessing. It's like he was saying, "To be continued."

He knew that they were going to have to suffer for his sake, but it didn't dampen his spirits. Suffering is temporary. He knew they would ultimately be okay. He had their backs.

David said it like this: "I will exalt you, LORD, for you lifted me out of the depths and did not let my enemies gloat over me. LORD my God, I called to you for help, and you healed me. You, LORD, brought me up from the realm of the dead; you spared me from going down to the pit. Sing the praises of the LORD, you his faithful people; praise his holy name. For his anger lasts only a moment, but his favor lasts a lifetime; weeping may stay for the night, but rejoicing comes in the morning" (Ps. 30:1–5).

We can count on that for all eternity.

Item in the Backpack: Assurance

John 1
God Clothes

This Gospel was likely written by John, son of Zebedee, one of Jesus's disciples. He also wrote 1, 2, and 3 John and the book of Revelation. He's got to be one of the most interesting writers in history. The revelation he was given in exile is quite something. Stay tuned!

He packed a lot about Jesus into this one chapter. He called Jesus "the Word." Jesus was in the beginning, was with God, *was* God, and became flesh and lived among us. All things came into being by him. In him was life and light, which enlightens everyone. The world was made through him. God was explained by him. Glory, grace, and truth were realized through him. He takes away the sin of the world. He's called the Lamb of God, Son of God, Son of Man, King of Israel, and the Messiah.

Wow.

God squished into a body. God clothed in flesh and blood. God, who was there when it all began. God, who knows how the earth story will play out. God, who knows what you'll experience five minutes from now. God, who has the key to abundant life. And eternal life. And love we can only begin to understand.

All within this one man, a man who wants a relationship with us.

Sometimes I wonder why. Some of us are pretty cool, and some of us are pretty limited, but compared to God, we're just tiny slivers. I wonder if he can see something in us we can't see.

Item in the Backpack: Wonder

John 2
Everyday Miracles

There are two kinds of people in the world—those who believe in miracles and those who don't. There are people who look for "God sightings" in everyday life. They are open to something beyond the physical world.

Others just don't. To them, life is what it is. The concept of praying to God is ridiculous. There's no afterlife. And miracles? Explainable somehow.

I happen to believe in miracles. Jesus performed miracles out of compassion or to show people his power, but turning the water to wine at Cana was a necessity, is the mother-of-invention kind of miracle. Embarrassingly, the host was running out of wine, and Jesus helped him out.

And Jesus commissioned his followers to keep miracles going. Just how far into the future was that to extend? I'm really not sure… except in a way, I *am* sure. God's done some miracles in my life. He changes my heart if it needs a tune-up or an overhaul. And when I'm at the top of my game (walking in the Spirit as the Bible calls it), I spend my time watching him work. So far I've not seen any water turned into wine, but I wouldn't be terribly shocked if it happened.

Reading about this miracle just reaffirms my desire to watch him do everyday miracles in my world. It's about intent and awareness. They're likely all around me. I just need better focus.

Item in the Backpack: Binoculars

John 3
<u>Birth Certificates</u>

"Very truly I tell you, no one can see the kingdom of God unless they are *born again*."

"Therefore, if anyone is in Christ, the *new creation* has come: The old has gone, the new is here!" (2 Cor. 5:17)

"To the one who is victorious, I will give some of the hidden manna. I will also give that person a white stone with a *new name* written on it, known only to the one who receives it" (Rev. 2:17).

Seems that spiritually speaking, we need two birth certificates—one for our physical birth and a second when we're born again. After all, we're new creations. The old has passed away; the new has arrived. We even get a new name on a white stone.

I'm not the tattoo type, but if I were to get one, it would be a small fish on my wrist. Just after Jesus's time on earth when there was a lot of persecution, fish symbols were code for being a Christ-follower. I have a doctor friend who works with gang kids. She has that tattoo, and it opens a lot of conversational doors for her. It's documentation of her faith. Words without words.

Jews at Auschwitz had to have their ID numbers tattooed on their arms. They were marked. Some tattoos are by choice; some are not.

Christians don't get second birth certificates or tattoos or any outward signs of being born again. *Our documentation is the lives we lead.* We are born of the Spirit. As we progress through the Bible, we'll get a lot of info on how to walk in the Spirit so we won't carry out the desires of the flesh. Our goal? To document our faith, with and without words.

Item in the Backpack: Documentation

John 4:1–30
No Bias

Notice that the woman at the well was Samaritan. She was shocked that Jesus talked to her, because Jews had no dealings with Samaritans. He used something completely ordinary, water, to segue to living water and to introduce himself as the Messiah.

I love this on so many levels. One, we too can use ordinary stuff (like water or parenthood or the weather) to segue to spiritual conversations. Two, we can see Jesus's power because he knew about her life. Three, we can see where he stood regarding gender and racial prejudice.

He had none.

Furthermore, part of what makes his death and resurrection so spectacular is that it was for all people.

The major issue between Jews and Samaritans was the chosen place to worship God: Mount Zion in Jerusalem according to the Jewish faith or Mount Gerizim according to the Samaritan faith. Samaria is located on the West Bank, the disputed West Bank.

Yet Samaritans are mentioned over and over in the New Testament, quite favorably, I might add. Jesus told the woman that "a time is coming when you will worship the Father neither on this mountain nor in Jerusalem." In other words, it's not about place or skin color or gender. It's about *anyone* being welcomed to worship the Father in spirit and truth.

Our churches should be the most diverse places on the planet. All are welcome to come together under the banner of the Jesus message. We could be the worst person on earth, yet if we desire to worship the Father in spirit and truth, the well is open for business.

Item in the Backpack: Impartiality

John 4:31–54
Journey Food

I love camping food. Sausage sizzling on the camp stove, hot coffee, s'mores! Today's item in the backpack is food. Jesus said, "My food is to do the will of him who sent me and to finish his work."

Food is another big biblical theme. Loaves and fish. Figs. Burnt offerings. Fruit of the vine. The bread of life (John 6). We would die without food. Bad food makes us sick. Scarce food makes us weak. Too much food makes us obese.

But Jesus said his food was to do God's will. That's what sustained him. There was something more vital to him than the pleasures of food. Don't get me wrong—he seemed to really enjoy a good meal with friends. In fact, he got in trouble for eating with tax gatherers and such, but he knew better than to get too carried away with food…or any good thing that can be misused.

The other part of this passage I love is about the Samaritans (again). Jesus wasn't honored in his own region, but the Samaritans welcomed him. Many started believing. No wonder he felt the urgency to get on with things. People must have been so hungry for the food he had to share.

Are today's people hungry for the food he has to share? In America, not so much. Too many are self-made and look to politics or the stock market for answers. Good things, in a way, but misused if that's all there is. Wealth, even relative wealth compared to the rest of the world, can be so numbing.

Even so, he offers his body as bread and his blood as wine—food that will take us far beyond politics and the stock market. Food that will open us to a more abundant life.

Item in the Backpack: Food

John 5
Expert Witnesses

Lawyers call expert witnesses to testify in court. Jesus made his case using expert witnesses too—the witness of John, of works, of God the Father, and of scripture.

The people liked John the Baptist, who, of course, was just pointing them to Jesus. The people noticed the miracles Jesus was doing. The people were mostly Jews who had a long history with God. The people knew the Old Testament scriptures but seemed blind to the fact that the scriptures were pointing them to Jesus.

I rely on expert witnesses too. If I hear an odd statement or a criticism, I test the waters. "Dear friends, do not believe every spirit, but test the spirits to see whether they are from God, because many false prophets have gone out into the world" (1 John 4:1).

Jesus was omniscient (all-knowing). He knew the facts. He knew he and the Father were one. It's the people who needed evidence and proof. And people still do.

I personally believe in Jesus for several reasons, as I've already shared. Of all the religious and philosophical stories (Islam, Hinduism, Buddhism, ancestor worship, human effort, and the rest), the Jesus story makes the most sense to me. I believe because of the already-fulfilled prophecies. I believe because of God's work in my life. I believe love will ultimately prevail. These witnesses coalesced for me when I was younger, and I took the leap of faith. Now, in turn, I can witness to the reality of God in my life.

Item in the Backpack: Witnessing

John 6
Individual Attention

"This, in a nutshell, is [God's] will: that everything handed over to me by the Father be completed—not a single detail missed—and at the wrap-up of time I have everything and everyone put together, upright and whole. This is what my Father wants: that anyone who sees the Son and trusts who he is and what he does and then aligns with him will enter *real* life, *eternal* life. My part is to put them on their feet alive and whole at the completion of time" (John 6:39–40, *The Message*).

In other words, there are no little people. It's Jesus's will to *not lose anything or anybody.*

We read a lot about the twelve disciples, the healed people, various Pharisees, etc.; but there are so many nameless but equally significant folks too: the little boy who gave Jesus his sack lunch, the headwaiter at Cana, the man who provided his guest room for the Passover meal, each individual in the multitude.

Jesus paid attention to individuals. He paid attention to *one* guy at the Bethesda pool. Nobody had helped this man into the healing waters for thirty-eight years, but Jesus stopped and healed him.

Salvation is individualized. Jesus didn't make saving pronouncements over swaths of people. Each of us must decide. Each of us is worth dying for, and each of us must decide how to respond to him, to this: "I am the living bread that came down from heaven. Whoever eats this bread will live forever."

If you feel insignificant, you are wanted. If you think you're pretty hot stuff on your own, Jesus said the first shall be last and the last, first. If you are just an individual in the morass of humanity, Jesus knows you.

His body was broken for *you*. His blood was shed for *you*.

Item in the Backpack: Significance

John 7:1–39
True Grit

Jesus spoke his mind. He let the chips fall wherever they would fall. He had grit. Courage. "The world cannot hate you, but it hates me because I testify that its works are evil."

These were strong, no-nonsense words. The people were confused and mad. On one hand they marveled and wondered how he had become educated. On the other hand, they felt he was claiming to be God (which he was), and they didn't believe it. They were looking for the Messiah, but this guy didn't fit their expectations.

Plus, he flat-out confronted and challenged them all the time.

Jesus knew his mission. He had nothing to lose. When facing the world, he essentially said, "Bring it. Hit me with your best shot." It was important for him to be clear. There could be no ambiguity. Still, he was human and such courage had its fallout. Maybe it shook him, maybe not.

Am I that gutsy? No. But I want to be.

Today I met with an old friend who's full of courage. He's constantly stepping out of his comfort zone to sit with a homeless person on the sidewalk or to speak boldly for God in a world that tries to tamp down the message. I think our paths crossed again after many years to fill up my courage tank. We need courage to do the right things when the world nudges us to do otherwise…or when we're fearful…or when it's time to speak up.

Item in the Backpack: Courage

John 7:40–8:11
Grace Zone

Here Jesus goes again! Showing grace to someone caught in the very act and exposing the hypocrisy of her accusers.

What person among us can withstand the statement, "Let any one of you who is without sin be the first to throw a stone…"?

Do you read the order in which the accusers turned around and left? Beginning with the older ones.

And what do you suppose Jesus was writing on the ground while all this was happening? I wonder if he was just drawing in the dirt to keep his cool. Or maybe he was writing something profound. Anyway, he didn't condemn her. He just told her to go and sin no more. And he gives us the same message. He doesn't condemn us when we sin. He just says to go and sin no more.

Romans 6:14–15 says this: "For sin shall no longer be your master, because you are not under the law, but under grace. What then? Shall we sin because we are not under the law but under grace? By no means!"

Do we get a thousand second chances? Yes, in a sense, although God expects us to move from sin to righteousness. The woman caught in adultery stepped into the grace zone. We, as believers, *live* in the grace zone; but is that license to keep on sinning?

May it never be.

We have the tools to move away from our sins to righteousness. And likewise, we have the tools to show grace to others. No rocks allowed.

Item in the Backpack: Grace

John 8:12–59
True Freedom

The truth will make you free.

The people had a hard time believing what Jesus was saying. He called himself God. "Very truly I tell you," Jesus answered, "before Abraham was born, I am!"

In Exodus 3:14, "God said to Moses, "I AM WHO I AM. This is what you are to say to the Israelites: 'I AM has sent me to you.'" Jesus was trying to explain the truest truth, but the people couldn't grasp it. Why couldn't they discern that he fulfilled the prophecies?

He blew up their sense of order, their world view. If they acquiesced, he would usurp their positions of power. He would be at the top of the heap without their permission. This was not their idea.

Do you know of anyone who only acts on things that are *their* idea?

True freedom is making room for Jesus, being open to his ideas over our own. We probably wouldn't have thought of these people as bad guys. They were sticking with what they thought was true, but somehow they couldn't see that he fulfilled the messianic prophecies. Why were they blind and deaf to that? I don't know.

Are we blind and deaf sometimes? For example, when we rationalize a sin rather than falling on our knees and confessing it, telling ourselves the truth? We can keep that up for long periods. Some keep it up their whole lives. And miss out on freedom.

May we have eyes to see and ears to hear the truth. May we have the courage to say yes to it.

Item in the Backpack: Truth

John 9
<u>Silver Linings</u>

Does God allow bad things to happen? Yes…but for a reason. About the man born blind, Jesus said, "Neither this man nor his parents sinned, but this happened so that the works of God might be displayed in him." Sometimes we suffer because of our own choices. Sometimes through no fault of our own. Sometimes for some other reason.

Are there silver linings of meaning and hope in our suffering?

I just got back from the funeral of a forty-nine-year-old friend. She died *completely* unexpectedly, so looking for answers eludes us for now, but I want to share with you the scripture presented at her service. "I consider that our present sufferings are not worth comparing with the glory that will be revealed in us" (Rom. 8:18).

For those of us in Christ, glory awaits. There's hope that surpasses the suffering.

In the book of Acts, we're told about Stephen, one of the first deacons of the church. He was full of faith, grace, power, and the Holy Spirit; but because of false accusers, he ended up being stoned to death. A bad thing happened to a very good person. But hear this. As he was about to be killed, he looked to heaven and said, "Look, I see heaven open and the Son of Man standing at the right hand of God." Standing. To welcome him.

At the funeral today, we gave my deceased friend a standing ovation, because to be absent from the body is to be present with God. She's there. That's a silver lining.

Item in the Backpack: A Future and a Hope

John 10:1–11:44
His Voice

"He calls his own sheep by name and leads them out. When he has brought out all his own, he goes on ahead of them, and his sheep follow him because they know his *voice*." "Jesus called in a loud *voice*, 'Lazarus, come out!' The dead man came out."

Do you recognize the voices of your loved ones? Of course. (Well, maybe except in a busy place where a hundred little kids are calling "Mom!" and all the moms turn around. Oh well, *again*, I digress.)

My point is that generally speaking, we recognize voices, but do we recognize the voice of Jesus? I now hear him better than I did in the past. His voice brings me peace. The words may be hard, but the internal sense I get is one of peace, not fear.

I'm skeptical of the voices of some people in our world—the narcissists, those who have personality disorders, the angry-disguised-as-strong, the hypercritical. Their voices can mimic healthy ones. We must be aware.

The voice flows out of what's in the heart.

One of my favorite verses is John 10:10: "I have come that they may have life, and have it to the full."

In that verse, I can hear his voice...and his heart.

Item in the Backpack: Ears to Hear

John 11:44–57
Caiaphas Calculations

The high priest, Caiaphas, had some calculated dealings with Jesus. In this passage, the priests and Pharisees were concerned about the Romans. "If we let him go on like this, everyone will believe in him, and then the Romans will come and take away both our temple and our nation."

In Matthew, Caiaphas tore his robes, saying Jesus was a blasphemer. In Acts, he tried to silence Peter and John from spreading the Jesus message, but they refused.

Caiaphas was not a fan.

He had a high position and a platform. He was religious but also had an eye on the Romans. He had a voice people listened to. So what did Jesus, and later Peter and John, do when standing before Caiaphas? Jesus either was silent in order to make a point or reiterated truth. Peter and John replied, "Which is right in God's eyes: to listen to you, or to him? You be the judges! As for us, we cannot help speaking about what we have seen and heard" (Acts 4:19–20). In other words, in an act of civil disobedience, they chose to obey God rather than man.

I'm not generally a rabble rouser, but there are times when we must take a stand.

Calculated attacks have gone on for a long time. They got Jesus killed, and they'll continue because someone will always try to subvert God. We can take lessons from Jesus, Peter, and John (i.e., to stand our ground). Jesus had to stand alone. Peter and John got to stand together.

Item in the Backpack: Bravery

John 12:1–26
Ego Death

A counselor friend once told me about an illustration she uses with clients who need to make a hard choice. She has them walk across the room and grab the doorknob. Then she tells them to return to their chair which is, say, ten feet away, *without letting go of the doorknob*. To move from a negative to a positive, the person needs to let go.

That reminds me of this passage about the grain of wheat. The kernel has to die in order to live. It has to let go in order to bear fruit. To pursue salvation, a person must "first allow their current convictions and ideas about the world to die and be shed, before they can be reborn with a purer, more virtuous self that is stronger than the original" ("A Grain of Wheat," *America Magazine*, March 27, 2009).

It seems that this dying-to-self happens two ways. It begins with a decision to follow Jesus, no matter what.

Second, it happens in a million small ways—ego death daily. I'm not talking about one's self*hood,* just one's self-*importance.* And I'm not advocating any kind of weird spiritual masochism. I just believe Jesus can draw us to a place that's better than where our limited selves can take us. If we know that God is God and we're not, it makes abundant sense.

Easy? Rarely, but it's how we step into the kingdom of God. We let go of sin and self in order to believe and follow.

Item in the Backpack: Relinquishment

John 12:27–50
The Verdict

This passage is largely about judgment, which is an interesting topic in today's world, where right and wrong/good and evil can be moving targets, less defined by absolutes than by culture. That being said, most of the time we know the difference. We recognize evil, and we need to fight it, not let it nestle in our lives in a cooperative kind of way.

Good vs. Evil is a real thing, and we are accountable for our choices, but herein lies the interesting part. We would all be doomed, guilty, except for this: Jesus said, "For I did not come to judge the world, but to save the world."

And here's the *key*.

"If anyone acknowledges that Jesus is the Son of God, God lives in them and they in God. And so we know and rely on the love God has for us. God is love. Whoever lives in love lives in God, and God in them. This is how love is made complete among us so that we will have confidence on the day of judgment: In this world we are like Jesus. There is no fear in love. But perfect love drives out fear, because fear has to do with punishment. The one who fears is not made perfect in love. We love because he first loved us" (1 John 4:15–19).

Item in the Backpack: The Key

John 13–14
Comfort Words

Jesus had been talking about going away. The disciples were probably getting a little nervous and insecure, so he comforted them. He told them about their new homes! (John 14:1–3)

When we were backpacking across Europe, our tent was our refuge—our home away from home. But by the end of the trip, "there's no place like home" took on a different meaning. We couldn't wait to get back to our house in the good ol' USA. A real bathroom! Sheets! Stability. Comfort.

No doubt the image of an eternal dwelling place comforted the disciples. Well…somewhat. It seems they couldn't quite understand. Have you noticed how much reiterating Jesus had to do? In a variety of ways, he kept teaching them about the Father and his love. It's almost like they were a bit dense, until you realize that the Helper hadn't yet arrived. The Spirit of truth would later be sent to abide in them in order to explain and assist.

And comfort.

Twice in chapter 14 we read, "Do not let your hearts be troubled." Jesus spoke of two sources of comfort to come—heaven and the Spirit. The Spirit would help them, abide with them forever, teach them, bring Jesus's words to their remembrance, and indwell them so they wouldn't feel orphaned.

They were beginning to understand that their friend Jesus was God. "Anyone who loves me will obey my teaching. My Father will love them, and *we* will come to them and make our home with them."

We.

Item in the Backpack: God's Presence

John 15
Vine Life

Jesus said, "Remain in me, as I also remain in you." Other versions of the Bible use the word "abide" for "remain." The words mean to take up inner residence, like branches connected to the vine, so the life force can flow.

Abiding in Christ results in

- good fruit/good works,
- positive answers to prayers,
- love,
- obedience,
- joy,
- friendship with God.

If we don't abide in Christ, we're useless except for kindling. What does that mean to you? To me, it has to do with that "life force" analogy. If a branch is cut off, it dies. It just needs to be raked up and thrown into the slash pile. To live, it needs the juicy sap from the vine.

I hate it when I feel separated from God, which is only due to *me* choosing not to do things his way. He didn't move; I did. But I love it when I feel connected to God. And I love the sense that his life force is flowing through me. I don't have to strain to generate it. All I have to do is stay hooked up. I don't have to strain to bear fruit, just stay attached.

The vinedresser does the work. Our job is to keep that inner spigot open so the juice can flow.

Item in the Backpack: Spigot

John 16
<u>True Math</u>

"The Father himself loves you because you have loved me and have believed that I came from God." "Unless I go away, the Advocate will not come to you; but if I go, I will send him to you."

A mathematical formula could sum this up, but suffice it to say that the Father, Son, and Spirit work together as God, and they love you and me.

The problem is that we can't graph, quantify, or measure love (or prayer either, for that matter). Prayer seems like simple math. If (A), you ask the Father for anything, then (B) he will give it to you in Jesus's name. But it's not that cut-and-dried. We must ask according to God's will. And not all of our requests get answered the way *we* think is best. They get answered the way *he* thinks is best.

This is where the math gets fuzzy, not because it's not true, but because we can't fully grasp how it works. Faith is required (which is another thing we can't graph, quantify, or measure).

At the end of chapter 16, Jesus told the disciples, "I have told you these things, so that in me you may have peace. In this world you will have trouble. But take heart! I have overcome the world."

Life is hard, but God is in charge. We just can't see the whole picture yet. "For now we see only a reflection as in a mirror; then we shall see face to face. Now I know in part; then I shall know fully, even as I am fully known" (1 Cor. 13:12).

It's hard to operate with un-graphable, unmeasurable faith while we're in the thick of a trouble-filled world, but there's serenity in knowing how the story ends. Jesus has overcome the world.

Item in the Backpack: Serenity

John 17
Big Picture

Jesus prayed for *you and me*. I say this because of John 17:20. He had been praying for his disciples, then inserted this: "My prayer is not for them alone. I pray also for those who will believe in me through their message."

He asked his Father God for these things for us:

1. That our joy may be full
2. That God would keep us from the evil one
3. That God would *sanctify* us in truth
4. That we would be one with other believers and with God the Father and Jesus the Son
5. That we would be with them forever

To be sanctified means to be *set apart as holy*. Consecrated. I think we miss the hugeness of what Jesus was asking on our behalf. Sometimes it seems that becoming a Christian is a choice and a lifestyle change. You know, going to church, living biblically, etc.; but in God Reality, we have entered another dimension.

God sees the big picture. We are set apart as holy, but can we see that? We take photos of earthly things, but wouldn't it be amazing to see through the thin places of God Reality? Like taking a selfie with Jesus beside you?

As the song goes, "I can only imagine."

Item in the Backpack: Set Apart as Holy

John 18–19
Crossing Over

As I write this, my father is dying. He's about to cross the bridge into eternity. I'm literally waiting on a meeting between family and doctors for decision-making. Why am I writing at a time such as this? Because it comforts me. I'm experiencing a kinship with Jesus, his friends and relatives, and my own. A cloud of witnesses.

"Therefore, since we are surrounded by such a great cloud of witnesses, let us throw off everything that hinders and the sin that so easily entangles. And let us run with perseverance the race marked out for us, fixing our eyes on Jesus, the pioneer and perfecter of faith. For the joy set before him he endured the cross, scorning its shame, and sat down at the right hand of the throne of God" (Heb. 12:1–2).

At death, we come face-to-face with God Reality. With eternity. With what matters the most.

Jesus could see to the other side. He was ready to be reunited with his Father. He knew there would be excruciating pain in the short run, but he chose the greater thing.

I pray that my father has eyes to see to the other side. As he approaches his "it is finished," I pray he's getting excited to cross over to the place of no more pain, just the fullness of love itself.

We can only imagine, but Dad is close to seeing Jesus face-to-face.

And somehow, through my tears, that makes me smile.

Item in the Backpack: Comfort

John 20
Homeward Bound

My dad died.

His funeral was a few days ago. I did the eulogy and concluded with these words written by F. B. Myer to his friend George Truett in 1928:

> Our lives on earth may not meet as often as we'd like but this thought expresses my hope. "The only thing to do is for us to make a tryst to meet, as soon as possible, if not before our arriving in heaven, at the Middle Gate on the East Side of the New Jerusalem. Then we will go off together, for a ramble by the River of Water of Life, and will doubtless find a nook, where we can have a quiet talk...and perhaps the Prince Himself will join us. There will be much to talk about."

I love that visual. For Christ followers, death isn't just an end but a launch to our next location—Heaven.

But lest you think I'm in denial about the gravity of death, let me just say that I identify with the disciples and the women in John 20. They were starting their grief process. So am I. It's been a mixture of sadness, tiredness, a few laughs over shared memories, a bit of anger, and triggered emotions of all sorts. There's a lot of work to do. There are plans to change for the future.

It's no wonder Jesus's friends didn't understand or, like Thomas, doubted when he reappeared, alive and quite well. They were in the throes of grief and misunderstanding. Their worlds had turned upside down a few days back, then turned upside down *again.*

Jesus probably just smiled. Then he got down to business, like imparting the Holy Spirit to them, because he was headed to heaven and they needed help until it was their time to join him there.

Item in the Backpack: Heaven

John 21
End Notes

John wrapped up his version of the Jesus-on-earth story. I love his telling of Jesus's appearance on a beach where he fixed breakfast for the disciples over a charcoal fire. What an ordinary thing! It would be like me walking into the kitchen a few mornings after my dad's funeral to see Dad frying up bacon and eggs. Yeah, not really ordinary at all.

Well, anyway, after breakfast, Jesus asked Simon if he loved him, meaning *agape* love. Simon said, "You know I love you!" meaning *phileo* love. *Agape* means "love" or "affection" and is usually seen as the highest Christian virtue. *Phileo* means "affectionate regard between friends."

He posed the *agape* question a second time and got the *phileo* response. The third time, he posed the question as *phileo* and got the *phileo* response.

What's up with that? It seems like agape is a higher form of love and Simon was falling short. But maybe not. Maybe Jesus was asking Simon if he was his "forever friend." He knew Simon would soon die for him and for the cause. Maybe he just needed his pal.

I really, really love that. Jesus was fully divine but fully human.

In summary, I don't view Jesus as a myth or an icon or a gilded piece of art with a sad face. I'm getting to know him. I really *like* him in addition to loving him. What he did for you and me is the greatest thing in the world. He offers us abundant, eternal life. We don't have to fear death or to be blunt, hell. Jesus did the needful.

John summarized it all with these words spoken by Jesus: "I am the gate; whoever enters through me will be saved" (John 10:9). Remember that only one item is essential for the backpack. It's not hard work or being good or even sacrifice. It's obedient belief. It's choosing to walk through the gate.

Item in the Backpack: Belief

Acts 1

Super Power

Luke, who was a physician, wrote both Luke and Acts. He used power words when discussing Jesus in Acts 1.

Jesus had given the apostles orders to stay put. It was time to get on with business. No messing around. No more staring up into the sky.

Real power must have a source. Jesus is God; but his followers are, you know, people. These men and women in Acts needed help, and Jesus knew it. He told them to wait in Jerusalem for what the Father had promised, which would be their power source. I'm guessing they had no idea what he meant by the Holy Spirit.

I think we're a little fuzzy on the Holy Spirit too.

The Spirit indwells believers. He actually lives inside us. That sets us apart from nonbelievers. Some of the Spirit's roles are to empower us, convict us when we fall short, teach us, comfort us, bear fruit through us (Fruit of the Spirit), and equip us (Gifts of the Spirit). Walking in the Spirit helps us not carry out the desires of the flesh.

So back to the narrative. Jesus's followers returned to the Upper Room. About 120 people gathered, prayed, chose a replacement for Judas...and waited.

But waited for what?

Their superpower?

Yes. As believers, we have a giant power source inside us, but so many of us fail to access it—

I mean *him*. Let's make a commitment, you and I, to be more open to the Spirit's power in our lives as we read through the book of Acts.

If we don't access power, we're like an unscrewed-in light bulb. Useless. But *with* power, we can light up the world.

Item in the Backpack: Power

Acts 2:1–36
Wind Energy

The day arrived. Pentecost. The followers were all together, and things started happening. Think: sitting in church when a sound like violent wind rushes through and little flames appear over people's heads and everyone starts speaking in foreign languages, real bona fide languages that they didn't technically know.

No wonder some people thought they were drunk.

But Peter stood up and explained. He was empowered. No more denying Christ for him! He explained that this had all been predicted in the Old Testament book of Joel. Then he really started preaching. He summarized the Jesus story in three verses (22–24) followed by a rendering of David's words from Psalm 16:8–11: "I have set the Lord continually before me. He is at my right hand. He won't abandon me. He'll make known to me the path of life. In his presence is fulness of joy."

In short, Peter said *Jesus is the guy David was talking about.* Godless men killed him, but God raised him up again.

Peter was talking to people who knew that passage in Psalms. Some believed that Jesus was the guy David was talking about and some did not, but the spread of Christianity started that day—first to the Jews, then to the Gentiles, then to the remotest parts of the earth.

Wind energy began at Pentecost. The Spirit is still empowering believers to do miraculous things every day, like stewarding the mysteries of God in languages others can understand.

Item in the Backpack: Miracles

Acts 2:37–47
Revival Time

In this short passage, we get a glimpse of the original revival service. Think Billy Graham style. Three thousand walked the aisle on one day, which is in itself a remarkable thing. What's even more remarkable though is what happened afterward.

The church. That's what happened.

The early converts had a radical lifestyle change. They devoted themselves to the apostles' teaching, hanging out together (fellowship), eating together (breaking of bread), and prayer. They had all things in common and shared with each other as needs presented themselves.

If it weren't for the abuses of the word, I would call this a commune, but not the drinking-the-Kool-Aid kind. Think about the intense love it would take to sell your property to help your fellow Christians. Think about the joy. Think about the trajectory.

Even today, although we rarely live communally, our churches are full of fellowship, shared meals, helping our fellow believers around the world, teaching, prayer, praise.

St. Catherine of Siena said, "We are of such value to God that He came to live among us…and to guide us home. He will go to any length to seek us, even to being lifted high upon the cross to draw us back to Himself. We can only respond by loving God for His love."

She also said, "Be who you were meant to be and you will set the world on fire."

And that's exactly what the early church did.

Item in the Backpack: Zeal

Acts 3
Free Pass

After Peter's first two sermons, some of the people were mortified. They had the insight and self-awareness to realize *they* had turned on Jesus. After his first sermon (chapter 2), they were pierced to the heart and asked, "What shall we do?" So Peter gave them the "repent/be baptized/receive the Holy Spirit" answer. He elaborated on his answer in his second sermon (chap. 3:17–19, 26). Here's a paraphrase: "Look. I know you acted in ignorance, just as your rulers did. Repent and return to him. You'll be refreshed. You're the first to be given this opportunity. Jesus came to bless you by turning every single one of you from your wicked ways."

He gave them a free pass! They had just been collectively guilty of Jesus's murder and they got a pass.

And this, friends, is the whole point. We *all* get a pass. He paid the bill.

Item in the Backpack: Pass Marked "Paid in Full"

Acts 4:1–22
Civil Disobedience

I know, I know, we're supposed to obey the laws of the land. Romans 13:1–4 says this:

> Let everyone be subject to the governing authorities, for there is no authority except that which God has established. The authorities that exist have been established by God. Consequently, whoever rebels against the authority is rebelling against what God has instituted, and those who do so will bring judgment on themselves. For rulers hold no terror for those who do right, but for those who do wrong. Do you want to be free from fear of the one in authority? Then do what is right and you will be commended. For the one in authority is God's servant for your good. But if you do wrong, be afraid, for rulers do not bear the sword for no reason. They are God's servants, agents of wrath to bring punishment on the wrongdoer.

But Peter and John chose not to obey the authorities. Jesus healed on the Sabbath and got in trouble for it. Peter and John healed a man in the name of Jesus and got in trouble for it. All three asked the authorities why they were in trouble for doing something good, which left the authorities pretty speechless.

So we're to obey the law…except when we're not supposed to obey the law. Following Jesus supersedes the law.

One more point about this passage. "Salvation is found in no one else, for there is no other name under heaven given to mankind by which we must be saved" (vs. 12). This means there aren't multiple paths to God, which puts Christ followers in the crosshairs of some people's sentiments. This is when we can cite verses 19–20: "Which is right in God's eyes: to listen to you, or to him? You be the judges! As for us, we cannot help speaking about what we have seen and heard."

In other words, the Jesus the world spurns is so remarkable, we just can't keep quiet about him.

Item in the Backpack: Voice

Acts 4:23–37
Predestined Outcome

We've read about predestination several times and here it is again in verses 27–28. Herod, Pontius Pilate, the Gentiles, and the people of Israel were *predestined* to oppose Jesus, which fulfilled God's purposes.

What? Predetermined to do something bad?

Romans 8:29 says this: "For those God foreknew he also *predestined* to be conformed to the image of his Son, that he might be the firstborn among many brothers and sisters."

What? Predetermined to do something good?

I've heard it explained that God has foreknowledge of our decisions but doesn't force those decisions. I really don't know the technicalities, but I believe in free will. I believe Herod and Pilate had a choice, as do you and I, but whole religious traditions are based on a brand of Reformed theology that affirms that God determines everything that happens.

Joshua 24:15 says, "But if serving the LORD seems undesirable to you, then choose for yourselves this day whom you will serve, whether the gods your ancestors served beyond the Euphrates, or the gods of the Amorites, in whose land you are living. But as for me and my household, we will serve the LORD."

Predestined to believe or choosing to believe? Tough theological question, but like Joshua, I can only speak for myself…and what I know is that I was once spiritually blind and now I see, so I've chosen to serve the Lord. And he's chosen me. And if you've chosen him, then he's chosen you. Therefore, you and I are entirely secure.

Item in the Backpack: Security

Acts 5
Investment Returns

Okay, this is a troubling passage if you look at it from a strictly monetary point of view. Nowadays, if someone were to sell a piece of property and give a chunk of the proceeds to the church, that would be a good thing. But Ananias and Sapphira did that and *died.*

In the previous verses, Joseph the Cyprian Levite sold some land and laid 100 percent of the proceeds at the apostles' feet. Ananias and Sapphira held back (or lied about the amount). Maybe the issue is a spiritual one. God wants us at 100 percent, which is risky. No fall-back measures in case he (God) fails. Ananias and Sapphira hedged their bets and went with a smaller percentage. They were hypocrites.

It *is* risky to go with God. The process is easy, but you have to calculate the cost/benefit ratio. *Or maybe not.* Maybe you just take the leap of faith, because here's what the believers got as a return on their 100 percent investment:

- an ongoing sense of awe
- signs and wonders in their midst
- the sharing of *all* things
- gladness and sincerity of heart
- favor with all the people
- abundant grace

That being said, when Ananias and Sapphira dropped dead, the people had great fear and none of the rest dared to associate with the apostles. No surprises there, but the people saw that God meant business.

Gamaliel summed it up something like this: "Hey, if this movement is of man it'll dissipate. But if it's of God, nothing can stop it."

Notice that it's still going on. One hundred percent investments have been worth it for a couple of millennia for Christ followers.

Item in the Backpack: Full Commitment

Acts 6
Conflict Resolution

Well, it seems some things will never change. There'll be head-butting, even within the church. After all, we're humans, but there's more to it than that. God used a head-butting situation to provide a practical solution. He doesn't want our humanity to limit us. He wants the church to thrive.

The Hellenistic Jews complained that the Palestinian Jews weren't being fair, so the solution was to choose seven reputable men to take care of church business. These were the first deacons. Servants. Problem solvers. Arbiters. The deacon system worked then and still works today.

The church needs spiritual leaders but also *practical* servants like Stephen. Both are to be full of the Holy Spirit, equipped with skills to address head-butting and problems. We all need those skills whether we're church leaders or not. God equips us with what we need to live productive, abundant lives in the here and now.

So why do churches (and relationships) still split sometimes? We can hone our own conflict resolution skills, but when we hit brick walls, we can look to the deacons in our lives for help. We need each other, especially when we get stuck.

Item in the Backpack: Problem-Solving Skills

Acts 7
Secret Sauce

Stephen summed up the whole Old Testament in fifty verses, then addressed the people who claimed the Old Testament as their foundation. He called them stiff-necked, uncircumcised in heart, resistant to the Holy Spirit, descendants of persecutors and killers, betrayers, murderers, lawbreakers. Yikes.

They couldn't see the prophecy-Jesus connection, so they killed Stephen. However, before they started stoning him, he gazed into heaven and saw Jesus *standing* at the right hand of God. (We usually think of Jesus as sitting at the right hand of God.) What a welcome party.

Stephen is intriguing. He was bold and full of faith, grace, and power. He served his fellow churchgoers. He forgave the people who were heaving rocks at him *while* they were doing it.

What made him able to supersede his humanity? Why aren't all Christians that way?

The only thing I can come up with is the Holy Spirit's work in his life. He wasn't an angel. He was just like you and me—fully human. For some reason, he got it. He yielded to the Spirit, so even a horrific death didn't faze him.

With all my heart, I want that beautiful ingredient, that not-so-secret sauce, which is available to all of us. The Holy Spirit. God calls us to Stephen-ness (i.e., a life yielded to the Spirit).

Item in the Backpack: Yielded-ness

Acts 8:1–24
Due Time

God has given us a great gift…the gift of time. Saul didn't get "kicked off the island" because he ravaged the church. *In due time,* God intervened in his life, as we'll see in chapter 9.

And Simon the Magician thought he could buy the ability to perform miracles. Peter let him have it for missing the point. We don't know the end of the story, whether *in due time* he ended up saying yes or no to truth over tricks.

I believe this is the tale of two timetables. Saul's enlightenment happened in a flash. He ended up getting it right when the time was right—instantaneously. Simon's process was slower. He became a believer, but he still had a lot of growing to do.

I think most of us have a lot of growing to do. Some, like Saul, change quickly and dramatically; but most of us grow incrementally. Two steps forward, one step back. Drop by drop. Tiny movements that create a canyon…or a mature life.

Sometimes we get off track. We hear a teaching, philosophy, or "big idea" and latch on to it. It might be 180 degrees or 1 degree from the truth. The latter is the hardest. We latch on to certain concepts about money, politics, parenting, dieting, moral hot topics, even religion, and sometimes that concept is wrong. Both Saul and Simon thought they were right, but God showed each the better way, in his time, by his means, through his people.

Once we realize we may have been misguided by some belief, we too can take time to study, question, agonize, and grow. God will show us the better way. The prayer God always answers is, "Help me to be more like you."

Sometimes that happens quickly. Sometimes, incrementally.

Item in the Backpack: Growth

Acts 8:25–40
Redeemed Time

Do you ever wake up wondering, "What in the world is going to happen today?"

Philip and friends started back to Jerusalem, but Philip was redirected to a desert road leading to Gaza. There he met an Ethiopian eunuch, a court official, who was returning from worship time in Jerusalem. What are the odds? A castrated African man worshipping the Hebrew God? And there's more. The man happened to be sitting in his chariot, reading the scroll of Isaiah, perplexed. So Philip ran up to the chariot and explained it all to him. The eunuch got it and immediately wanted to be baptized, which happened. Then Philip was snatched away.

Okay, that's pretty farfetched, don't you think?

But such is the spice of life for Christ followers. We don't know what each day will bring. Take today for example. I ended up having a conversation with a friend over theological issues she brought up, from a perspective I had never even heard of before. It pushed me. It pushed her. But I have no doubt that this "accidental" encounter was the whole point of the day for both of us. God redeemed an otherwise humdrum day.

I think God wants us to be aware of the "Ethiopian eunuchs" that cross our paths. He wants our time to count, no matter what or whom each day may bring.

Item in the Backpack: Readiness

Acts 9:1–20
Serious Pursuit

Saul was a scary man. He breathed threats and murder. He asked for permission to bind up the Christ followers and haul them back to Jerusalem. He reminds me of a bounty hunter from the movies. Can you imagine being hunted by a powerful man with a license to kill you?

Likely, a soft approach couldn't have gotten through his rage, so God pulled out all the stops with the bright light, bodiless voice, and blindness. God does stuff like that sometimes.

I have a friend who was rabbit hunting by himself along a country road; and God spoke to him, not verbally, but just as real as verbally. God told him to lay down his burdens and follow him, which my friend did. I have another friend who was standing on a cliff to commit suicide, when God spoke to him too. Again, not verbally, but just as real. He went home and began a long career in the Christian arts. Still another friend became a believer after a meth addiction.

Me? I was a little kid who wanted to follow Jesus, so my parents took me to meet with our pastor. And right there in his quiet, book-lined office, I prayed the prayer. No bright lights, no despair, no addictions.

After Saul's conversion, he was a man on fire. In 1 Corinthians 9:22 he wrote, "To the weak I became weak, to win the weak. I have become all things to all people so that by all possible means I might save some."

He would do whatever it took to save people. Seems God does that too. If it takes something wildly dramatic, check. If it takes a still, small voice, check.

Back to the subject of friends. I have another one who couldn't care less about God. He scoffs. Of all the information out there about Christians, he only gloms onto the stories about abusive priests or fallen evangelists. The transformative quiet, everyday Christian stories go unnoticed.

What will it take for God to get his attention? I don't know, but if he can get Saul's attention, he can do anything.

Item in the Backpack: Assurance of God's Attention

Acts 9:21–43
Miraculous Deeds

People rarely get raised from the dead at my church. Okay, "rarely" isn't the right word. To my knowledge, it's never happened. But impossible? No.

Back in the day, however, miracles abounded. People near and far heard about them. The church was in full swing.

So why don't we see more miracles today? Although the church is under attack, it's still in full swing. Here are a couple of thoughts on this miracle thing. One, that miracles were performed only back then. The radical confirmation of miracles was needed to validate the Jesus narrative—that Jesus rose from the dead, changed lives, and was setting a new order in place. Two, that miracles still occur.

What is a miracle anyway? It's "an event in the physical world that surpasses known powers and is ascribed to the supernatural." For example, known science can't create life out of nothingness. It can do amazing things with a living cell in a chemistry lab, but not a dead cell. The spark of life had to have begun at some point, supernaturally. Miraculously.

In the beginning, God created…

It's hard to believe in God without believing in the supernatural…and vice versa.

It would take a miracle for my aforementioned scoffing friend to believe in God. He would become spiritually resurrected, but Jesus (and Tabitha, in this passage) was physically resurrected, so why would I doubt spiritual resurrection for him?

I believe in option number 2, that miracles still occur.

Item in the Backpack: Belief in the Supernatural

Acts 10:1–11:18
Gentile Time

Peter essentially said in verses 34 and 35 that he understood that God doesn't show partiality. *Every person of any race who stands in awe of him and does what is right is welcome to God.*

It took some courage for Peter to say yes to Cornelius because of that Jewish law about not associating with a foreigner. But Jesus was a rule breaker, and one by one the laws of love had to be put into place to supersede the old laws. In this case, God chose Peter to bushwhack through the old to set up the new. What a job.

In the past, the Jews weren't supposed to associate with the Gentiles, but that was no longer true for Christ followers. That *is* no longer true. Nobody's unclean. All have equal access.

God's chosen people are now people from *all* nations who fear him and do what is right. Some people took issue with Peter when he told them the Gentiles had received the Spirit and been baptized, but when he explained everything to them, guess what happened? They quieted down and glorified God and said, "So then, even to Gentiles God has granted repentance that leads to life."

Maybe we would do well to quiet down and glorify God when people are treated equally.

Item in the Backpack: Justice

Acts 11:19–30
First Christians

The Christ followers started to scatter because of what had happened to Stephen. Some started preaching in Antioch, which was a Roman military and commercial center. It's where the followers of Jesus were first called Christians.

In a sense, this was a Christian diaspora. Today, Christians live all over the planet, but according to the Joshua Project, 29 percent of the world's people have had virtually zero exposure to the message of Christ. Thirty-nine percent have heard but have not responded.

The message of Christ is transforming people in India. The largest congregation in the world is in South Korea. In 2015, three-fourths of polled Americans identified themselves as Christian. And it all started in Bethlehem, about six miles south of Jerusalem, a long way from India or Korea or the United States.

All told, roughly 32 percent of the world's 7.3 billion people are Christian, 24 percent are Muslim, 15 percent are Hindu, 7 percent are Buddhist, and the rest are various other religions. Only 0.2 percent are Jewish (2017 statistics from the Pew Research Center).

There's a lot of power in a few committed souls banding together, living for the spread of a message. The first Christians began what we're to keep going. Our work is not yet done.

Item in the Backpack: Great Commission

Acts 12
Jail Break

Peter was thrown into prison, chained up, and guarded by four squads of soldiers. Then an angel set him free, and the soldiers were executed, and the king who had thrown him into prison was eaten by worms and died. The End.

Have you ever been in jail? Not a literal jail, but a place in life that held you captive? Did you wish death by worms on your captors?

Some things in life are so binding, awful, and soul-destroying that there seems to be no way out.

Addiction. Poverty mind-set. Abuse. Political oppression. Ingrained crippling thinking. Illness. Depression. A loved one with a personality disorder. Your own personality disorder.

What or who is your captor? And what can you do about it? Peter couldn't do anything about his captors. God had to intervene.

Years ago, I was stuck in depression prison. I couldn't do anything about it. I tried. I shook the metal bars every way I could. Turns out it was because of my body's reaction to the Pill—a simple chemical thing. When I quit taking it, my depression went away.

Was that divine intervention? Simple science? Both, probably.

Jesus said this about himself in Luke 4:18: "The Spirit of the Lord is on me, because he has anointed me to proclaim good news to the poor. He has sent me to proclaim freedom for the prisoners and recovery of sight for the blind, to set the oppressed free, to proclaim the year of the Lord's favor."

There are a number of tools in God's toolbox, divine intervention being one of them. He set Peter free. He can do it for you and me too. I might be stuck again, maybe in a literal prison if Christian persecution heats up. If so, I'm not going to rule out divine intervention.

Item in the Backpack: Divine Intervention

Acts 13:1–43
Missionary Journey No.1

A lot of scoffers. A few believers. That was the story of Paul's missionary journeys. People who heard the message were having a hard time believing, even though Paul said, "Through him everyone who believes is set free from every sin, a justification you were not able to obtain under the law of Moses." The old didn't work, so God made a New Deal.

And Paul went on to say this in verses 40–41: "Take care that what the prophets have said does not happen to you: 'Look, you scoffers, wonder and perish, for I am going to do something in your days that you would never believe, even if someone told you.'"

Many are called, but few are chosen. The way is wide that leads to destruction, but narrow is the path that leads to life.

If you're ever asked to talk about Jesus, Acts 13:16–43 is a great summary yet many won't believe. Some, like Elymas the magician, will try to make crooked the straight ways of the Lord.

So what are we twenty-first century believers to do? *Just keep going.*

Item in the Backpack: Perseverance

Acts 13:44–14:18
<u>Vain Things</u>

God has always made himself known. Every person who has ever been born has a sense of God. According to this passage, he allowed the nations to go their own ways but always gave them rain, fruitful seasons, food, and gladness. My personal feeling is that all who were searching for God pre-Jesus were able to find him, because he's always made himself known.

Then, at the right time, Jesus came on the scene. The great "I Am" became a regular guy with a common name. In Acts, the preaching of Jesus took off. Once people knew about Jesus, they had their God-Quest Answer yet so many didn't believe.

In this passage, the people couldn't quite grasp the idea of Jesus so they recategorized Barnabas and Paul as Zeus and Hermes. Barnabas and Paul smacked their foreheads and asked something like, "Why are you doing this? We're regular humans giving you info about turning from vain things to the living God."

People still skirt around him all the time, thinking vain things can lead to God. It's easier that way. I can't think of anyone who worships Zeus or Hermes, putting their trust in Greek mythology, but Hinduism is a collection of myths about its thirty-three million gods. A lot of people worship those gods. And people everywhere seek answers to the meaning of life through meditation or philosophy or vegan diets.

Please don't think I'm minimizing healthy thinking or healthy lifestyles. Of course I'm not. I *encourage* them, just not as the end-all. I think there's danger in *substituting* lesser things for the Jesus path, which calls for our heart and soul, not just our eating habits.

Item in the Backpack: Reality Check

Acts 14:19–28
<u>Short-term Pain</u>

Short-term pain, long-term gain.

Short-term pain = verse 19, "Then some Jews came from Antioch and Iconium and won the crowd over. They stoned Paul and dragged him outside the city, thinking he was dead."

Like Paul, we'll have times when the crowds seem to be against us. We'll feel that those who scoff at us or harm us are winning.

Long-term gain = verse 20, "But after the disciples had gathered around him, he got up and went back into the city. The next day he and Barnabas left for Derbe."

Like Paul, we'll have times when, despite all odds, we can get up and go.

Short-term pain = verse 22, "We must go through many hardships to enter the kingdom of God."

Like Paul, we'll have our share of suffering.

Long-term gain = verse 27, "On arriving there, they gathered the church together and reported all that God had done through them and how he had opened a door of faith to the Gentiles."

Like Paul, we'll have victories in spite of our suffering.

Maybe suffering is a key ingredient. We wish otherwise, but a message this unusual and transformative is bound to have opposition. Sometimes being a Christ follower means going against popular opinion or political correctness. Sometimes it means great sacrifice. We must be strong.

(The first Christian martyr at the Colosseum in Rome was believed to be Saint Ignatius who had been, interestingly, the bishop of Antioch.)

Our message is about love. I guess there will always be opposition to love.

Item in the Backpack: Fortitude

Acts 15:1–31
<u>New Ways</u>

A little clash arose regarding circumcision. Here's the back story. When Abraham was ninety-nine years old, God made a covenant with him.

> I will make you very fruitful; I will make nations of you, and kings will come from you. I will establish my covenant as an everlasting covenant between me and you and your descendants after you for the generations to come, to be your God and the God of your descendants after you.
>
> This is my covenant with you and your descendants after you, the covenant you are to keep: Every male among you shall be circumcised. You are to undergo circumcision, and it will be the sign of the covenant between me and you. (Gen. 17:6–7, 10–11)

Circumcision was a sign of the covenant between God and the Jews, but there was no covenant between God and the Gentiles. The apostles and elders needed to create new ways of operating for the Gentile Christ followers.

So, long story short, the apostles and elders decided that from that day forward, no physical sign was required when people became Christ followers.(Circumcision was now of the heart, so there was, in a sense, a spiritual sign—and the Holy Spirit.)

No physical circumcision. No tattoo. No paperwork. Just a reminder to "abstain from food polluted by idols, from sexual immorality, from the meat of strangled animals and from blood." Three of these had to do with Jewish customs and health advisories (confusing to us in modern times), but we know what sexual immorality means.

I believe the apostles and elders wanted the sign to be *a holy life*. 1 Corinthians 7:19 reiterates it this way: "Circumcision is nothing and uncircumcision is nothing. Keeping God's commands is what counts."

Some days it would be easier to just have that tattoo.

Item in the Backpack: Holiness

Acts 15:32–16:21
Missionary Journey No. 2

Paul and Barnabas had a little tiff, so Barnabas went one way with John-also-called-Mark. Paul went another way with Silas. Paul had a strong personality, to put it mildly.

This was Paul pre-conversion, when he was called Saul. "But Saul began to destroy the church. Going from house to house, he dragged off both men and women and put them in prison" (Acts 8:3). "Meanwhile, Saul was still breathing out murderous threats against the Lord's disciples" (Acts 9:1). But Paul, post-conversion, still had a fiery personality. Conversion didn't mean his whole disposition changed; it just meant that after meeting Jesus on the Damascus road, he started *yielding* to God. Throughout the whole New Testament, Paul was outspoken, direct, decisive, and unafraid of taking risks.

Maybe a moral of the story is that God doesn't use us in spite of our personalities, he uses us *through* our personalities. Remember those PBPGIFWMY buttons people used to wear? (Please be patient. God isn't finished with me yet.)

Do you feel that God uses you? Do you know your mission in life? Discovering your spiritual gifting helps. (Stay tuned for 1 Corinthians!) Writing out your personal mission statement helps.

God can and will use unique you.

Item in the Backpack: Sense of Mission

Acts 16:22–40
Impossible Circumstances

Once upon a time, I was facing an impossible circumstance. At least it seemed that way, so I prayed and released it to God.

God's response? "Watch me work."

Paul and Silas were facing an impossible circumstance too. They were beaten with rods and thrown into an inner prison with their feet in stocks. No way out.

I'm guessing they also decided to watch God work, so they spent their time singing hymns. (I need to remember that next time I'm facing an impossible situation.)

And God *did* work. Not only did he spring them out of prison, but he gave them the opportunity to invite the jailer and his family into the kingdom of God.

This impossible circumstance had a quick resolution and happy ending, but not all circumstances have a quick resolution or the ending we want. According to many sources, Paul died a martyr's death but that doesn't mean God abandoned him. I think Paul and Silas were getting into the groove of watching God work, so by the time Paul died, he likely understood that this was just the next step in watching God work.

God is *always* working. Trusting God means a win-win, no matter what. I think Paul and Silas sang hymns because if this was going to be the end, they would sing. If God was going to release them from jail, they would sing.

My impossible circumstance? God is working in ways that make me marvel every day. It took a while for things to turn around though. The earthquake has been slow and incremental, but it's an earthquake nonetheless.

This watching and singing can become a lifestyle, so if you're not sure what to do, might as well sing.

Item in the Backpack: Songs

Acts 17
<u>Bridge Building</u>

"Now the Berean Jews were of more noble character than those in Thessalonica, for they received the message with great eagerness and examined the Scriptures every day to see if what Paul said was true."

God honors examination of his words.

I love Paul's sermon to the people of Athens in the meeting of the Areopagus. He was clever and wise. He honored their religiosity without mocking them. He observed their altar built to an unknown god and used it as his figurative jumping-off point. He proclaimed that the unknown was now known!

He found two common denominators with his audience: (1) that particular altar and (2) the words of one of their own poets. He then explained that what they called new was really old-Old Testament fulfillment. He let them know that what they had worshipped in ignorance now had a flesh-and-blood answer, so God was going to overlook their times of ignorance.

Paul met them at the point of their unknowns, their questions, their reality, and their need.

He built bridges rather than walls.

Item in the Backpack: Wisdom

Acts 18
Missionary Journey No. 3

In this passage, we're introduced to some new faces, like a new tent-making buddy named Aquila and his wife, Priscilla; Titius Justus who lived next door to the church; Crispus, the leader of the synagogue; and Proconsul Gallio, who believed in the separation of church and state. We hear about Paul getting his hair cut. We hear about his eighteen-month stay in one place, then about more travels.

A word about a couple of these things before we move on. One is that Paul had a job apart from his missionary duties. Some people are career missionaries or full-time paid ministers, but most Christ followers make tents or art or microchips or whatever…and serve God on the job. Paul apparently did both simultaneously, often making enough from tent making to help support his travels. He did what he needed to do.

And about that haircut. He had been taking a vow, perhaps a temporary Nazarite vow to live a more austere life out of consecration or thanksgiving or discipline. *He did what he needed to do.*

Now, from what I understand, his third missionary journey began with verse 23 when he took off to the Galatian region. At this point, we meet Apollos, the new preacher in town. His theology of baptism seemed a bit sketchy, so Aquila and Priscilla schooled him in the ways of God more accurately. But he was eloquent, fervent, and bold.

God did what he needed to do. He raised up new preachers to spread the message around the world. So whether we preach (or teach) or make tents (or weavings) or take care of kids (or patients), God wants us to integrate our faith with our work. That's what Paul did.

Item in the Backpack: Integration

Acts 19:1–10
<u>Spirit Power</u>

Sooner or later, every Christ follower must face the reality of the Holy Spirit. Some Christian traditions barely acknowledge the Spirit. Others barely touch on anything *but.*

How did/do people "acquire" the Holy Spirit? Check out these scriptures from Acts. "You will be baptized with the Holy Spirit" (1:5, 11:16). "You will receive power when the Holy Spirit comes on you" (1:8). "All of them were filled with the Holy Spirit" (2:4, 4:8, 4:31, 7:54, 9:17, 13:9, and 52). "You will receive the gift of the Holy Spirit" (2:38, 10:47). "God anointed Jesus of Nazareth with the Holy Spirit" (10:38). "When Paul placed his hands on them, the Holy Spirit came on them" (19:6).

So do we acquire the Spirit by baptism, filling, receiving, being anointed with, or the laying on of hands? The answer is yes. Only believers in Jesus can receive the Holy Spirit, but do all Christians automatically get the whole Trinity (God the Father, God the Son, and God the Holy Spirit) at salvation, or does the Spirit arrive separately?

I believe the former, at salvation, because of John chapter 3; but I also believe many of us fall short of experiencing (and appropriating) the fullness of God through the Spirit. The Spirit provides us with power, comfort, and help. He seals us, intercedes for us, perfects us, gifts and equips us, convicts us of sin, and gives us wisdom so we can understand God. Oh, and he restrains the evil one.

In Acts, the people filled with the Spirit also spoke in languages unknown to them but understood by others. They prophesied, had visions, and performed miracles.

What about now? Tomes have been written about the Spirit's work beyond the early church, and I don't have room for tomes, but I can say this. No matter where you are on this particular spectrum, we as believers can ask God for the filling of the Spirit. Why stop short of the fullness of God, including miraculous works? This is *God* we're talking about.

Item in the Backpack: Infilling

Acts 19:11–41
<u>Money Matters</u>

A certain ministry in my city is located near a notorious street. By notorious I mean that certain industries flourish there—prostitution, the drug trade, even human trafficking. The ministry loves the street people in the neighborhood through housing, programs, and church. A while back, the liquor store nearby filed a complaint with the city because the ministry was negatively affecting their business. They were losing their market.

That story reminds me of the silversmith in this passage who stirred up his fellow tradesmen. They, too, were losing their market.

Seems things always come down to economics. Wallets.

Look at Acts 19:13–19. Because of the miraculous things happening through Paul, even exorcists and magicians started converting, confessing, and disclosing their tricks. And it came down to economics for them too, but in a beautiful way. The books they burned equaled fifty thousand Greek drachmas. A drachma was about a day's wage, so that meant a lot of wages on the parts of a lot of magicians.

People are affected when it comes to their wallets. The Artemis tradesmen may have tried to ignore the Christian message had it not affected their wallets. And on the flip side, when the magicians converted, they demonstrated it with their wallets—giving up income and renouncing their lucrative careers.

The Bible speaks a lot about money, but not in the way some people think. Sure, churches and ministries need money to run, but God just longs for our souls to be free of the insane entrapment of *more* when he provides *enough*. The magicians figured that out.

We need to be wise with our money, but we need to hold it loosely in our hands so it doesn't wrap around our hearts.

Item in the Backpack: Loose Hands

Acts 20:1–16
Actual Accomplishments

Here again we find an action passage. Paul went here and there, dodging uproars. A young man fell out of a window. Paul embraced him and announced that he was still living. Then more sailing. Logistical stuff.

I think the word "action" needs a little attention. These weren't the thoughts of the apostles or the intentions of the apostles. They were the acts. Someone once said, "I would rather play cards with someone who doesn't cheat at cards than with someone who *intends* not to cheat at cards."

Intentions are no good if they don't result in action.

This book of Acts is full of things the early church folks *did*. They wrote the book on it, literally. They didn't have any protocol; they just stepped out and performed miracles and shared their possessions with each other and did unprecedented things like that, all with the power of their recently deceased-and-resurrected friend Jesus.

James 1:25 says, "But whoever looks intently into the perfect law that gives freedom, and continues in it—not forgetting what they have heard, *but doing it*—they will be blessed in what they do." Studying the Bible is one thing; acting on it is quite another.

Paul was a changed man after his Damascus road experience. He couldn't contain himself. He had to act. He had to spread the message as widely as possible. Sitting around intending to do so wouldn't have changed the world.

Item in the Backpack: Action

Acts 20:17–38
Fond Farewell

Paul poured his heart out to the Ephesian believers. He was in turmoil on a monumental scale. My heart is beating fast just thinking about it. And herein is a lesson.

Be real. Be vulnerable.

He said good-bye to them, then turned from his own issues to theirs. "I know that after I leave, savage wolves will come in among you and will not spare the flock."

Then I love what he did in verse 32. He gave up control. He turned it over to God. "Now I commit you to God and to the word of his grace." He encouraged them to work hard and remember the sacred words of Jesus. And he dropped to his knees and prayed with them.

And herein is another lesson.

Surrender it.

I believe that once God gets ahold of us, we start the journey, but it's imperfect. We have epiphanies. Then we screw up. Then we're forgiven, and we "get back on that horse." Then we grow. Then we falter. Then we…you get the picture. God wants us to grow, but it's often by a serpentine path. Paul was holding the human condition and God's salvation simultaneously, and he gave it all over to God.

In the end, they accompanied him to the ship. I can't think of a fonder farewell.

Item in the Backpack: Vulnerability

Acts 21 and 22
Relentless Opposition

Persecution was fierce and relentless for the first-century Christians, and it's alive and well today. Historically, Christianity has experienced ebbs and flows. Here's a Wikipedia summary.

> A form of Christianity was legalized by the Edict of Milan and eventually became the state religion of the Roman Empire. The schisms of the Middle Ages and especially the Protestant Reformation sometimes provoked severe conflicts between Christian denominations to the point of persecuting each other.
>
> In the 20th century, Christians were persecuted by various groups, including the Islamic Ottoman Empire in the form of the Armenian Genocide, the Assyrian Genocide and the Greek Genocide, as well as atheistic states such as the Soviet Union and North Korea.
>
> In more recent times, the Christian missionary organization Open Doors (UK) estimates that over 200 million Christians face persecution, particularly in Middle Eastern countries such as Pakistan and Saudi Arabia.

Can you imagine being killed by a mob because of your religion? It's part of the calculated risk we take when we say yes to Christ. If Christianity messes with others' closely held views or lifestyles, persecution can happen. The Holocaust happened to Jews, and not very long ago. We need to be hyperaware of the mob mentality. Some German churches gave assent to Nazi ideology. Other churches were persecuted for resisting it. And we need to be hyperprepared if we're ever confronted by a mob, as Paul was. He was ready. He was solid.

Item in the Backpack: Calculated Risk

Acts 23 and 24
Imaginative Opportunities

Paul pushed the envelope big time in chapter 23. He called the high priest a whitewashed wall and told him God was going to strike him. A dissension arose between the Sadducees and the Pharisees. There was a plot to kill Paul.

But Paul took these potentially fatal situations and turned them into opportunities to share the message.

In chapter 24, after brownnosing Governor Felix, Tertullus the Attorney laid into Paul, calling him a real pest. Then he (Tertullus) lied and twisted the truth. Paul never desecrated the temple, for example. Taking advantage of the opportunity, Paul replied in a straightforward way about his blamelessness. He had strictly served God, believing the Law and the Prophets to a tee. In fact, that was his point! The Way of Jesus *fulfilled* the Law and the Prophets.

Okay, he did admit to one misdeed, that of shouting out about the resurrection of the dead, even though it was true.

Anyway, the end result was that Felix stalled, wanting a bribe, but gave Paul a lot of freedom. During the two-year stall, Paul was able to meet with him and talk about Jesus, righteousness, self-control, and judgment, which freaked Felix out but he nonetheless heard the whole message. Another creative opportunity.

In 1 Corinthians 9:22, Paul wrote this: "I have become all things to all people so that by all possible means I might save some."

By all means to save some. Paul counted every experience as an opportunity, whether that meant yelling at the high priest or creating a diversion or listening to his nephew or forming a relationship with the governor.

Do I see every experience of every day as an opportunity? Am I that imaginative and positive?

Item in the Backpack: Creativity

Acts 25 and 26
Mission Statement

The voice of Jesus said this to Paul, who then recounted it to King Agrippa: "I'm sending you off to open the eyes of the outsiders so they can see the difference between dark and light, and choose light, see the difference between Satan and God, and choose God. I'm sending you off to present my offer of sins forgiven, and a place in the family, inviting them into the company of those who begin real living by believing in me" (*The Message)*.

Frankly, I was beginning to think the "prison-and-defense" narrative was a bit of overkill. Paul before the Jews. Paul before the council. Paul before Felix. Paul before Festus. Paul before Agrippa. Same story over and over. But then I realized this. He was consistent. I'm less so. I get sidetracked and sometimes lose my focus.

Take today for example. I met with a friend, and she asked me why I was so into the Bible. And you know what happened? I started telling her but got sidetracked. I stopped short of turning my story into an invitation like Paul did. His message was so concise and effective that Agrippa said, "Keep this up much longer and you'll make a Christian out of me!"

After a while, I got back on track and next Sunday we're going to church together, but I'm freshly aware of my need to practice my story, which goes something like this:

"I realized, even as a little kid, that there was a God and I wasn't him. I'm from good ol' Southern Baptist stock, so I went to church all the time and even attended a Christian college, but that's no guarantee of salvation. But the Jesus message really took hold during my youth, and I chose to devote myself to it, to him. First John 4:8 says God is love and that following Jesus is the way to know God. So that's my spiritual journey. What's yours?"

Item in the Backpack: Message

Acts 27
Perfect Storm

This chapter is the stuff of movies, except movies don't always end so well. A big storm was coming up. Paul had figured out that the voyage would result in damage and loss, but the captain overrode him. After all, he was the master and commander; Paul was a prisoner. The ship was destroyed off the coast of Malta, but all 276 people on board survived.

Do you think Paul had some special revelation about the storm coming up, or did he just voice what everyone else was thinking? And what are we to make of this when we encounter storms?

This, I think.

1. Sometimes we're to use our brains and the commonsense God gave us.
2. Sometimes we're to use our "God ears."

Stay with me here. I've never gotten an audible from God, but there have been many times I would pretty much bet my life on the sense I was getting. Once in church, while we were singing "Jesus, Lover of My Soul," I was overcome with the sense of being profoundly loved. I'll never forget that. It changed my life. So yes, I believe God speaks if we have the ears to hear. We have to *want* to hear him. We need keen spiritual sensitivity.

I believe Paul heard from God, both time no. 1 (v. 10) as well as time no. 2 (vv. 23–25). I believe we can hear from God constantly, if we have the ears to hear.

Item in the Backpack: Sensitivity

Acts 28
Alive Hearts

Paul went from Malta to Rome and stayed there over two years, but predictably, a lot of people rejected his message, which had been prophesied in Isaiah. "Go to this people and tell them this: 'You're going to listen with your ears, but you won't hear a word; You're going to stare with your eyes, but you won't see a thing. These people are blockheads!'" (*The Message)* However, this was not true of the natives.

Why do some people have open hearts and others, dull hearts, even today? And the big question is, how can we have *alive* hearts? We can read the Old Testament scriptures predicting the Messiah. There are hundreds. We can ask God for understanding, not just with our heads, but with our hearts. We can believe Hebrews 4:12: "For the word of God is alive and active. Sharper than any double-edged sword." We can give our assent and choose to step into the God-filled life. An active relationship with God makes for quite a lively heart.

If we ask for an alive heart, we will receive an alive heart. "Seek and you will find" (Matt. 7:7).

Item in the Backpack: Assent

Romans 1:1–20
Without Excuse

Paul wanted to make sure the Romans got the facts straight. And he was proud of his calling. Not proud as in "prideful" but proud as in "honored." He wasn't ashamed of the message he was preaching; he knew its power.

I think one of the most intriguing passages in the Bible is in Romans 1. Here it is in *The Message*: "The basic reality of God is plain enough. Open your eyes and there it is! By taking a long and thoughtful look at what God has created, people have always been able to see what their eyes as such can't see: eternal power, for instance, and the mystery of his divine being. So nobody has a good excuse."

In other words, even if people don't know about Jesus, they're without excuse when it comes to having a sense of God. Since the beginning of time, God's invisible attributes, eternal power, and divine nature have been evident through what's been made. The people who lived before Jesus and people who have never heard about Jesus can still believe in God. God is obvious in creation and also within the human soul that recognizes its limitations and its desire for love…and God *is* love.

God gives us a jillion chances to accept him; but he's against straight-up unbelief, ungodliness, and unrighteousness. He planted a sense of himself in all of us. We have the sense of right and wrong. We can't say, "Sorry I beat that guy up. I didn't know it was wrong."

Only God can judge who is truly unbelieving. I don't have that measuring stick, but maybe if we truly understood the pure love of God, *nobody* would reject him.

Item in the Backpack: Awareness of Consequences

Romans 1:21–32
<u>Course Junctions</u>

Most reasonable people spurn things like depravity, unrighteousness, wickedness, greed, malice, envy, murder, strife, deceit, gossip, slander, God-hate, insolence, arrogance, boasting, evil-inventing, disobedience to parents, lack of understanding/love/mercy, and untrustworthiness.

But if we're honest, we've been guilty of some of those things and/or approved of them in others.

If we screw up but ask for forgiveness, God forgives. There's a difference between screwing up and asking for forgiveness and choosing to not acknowledge God any longer. Those who *did not see fit to acknowledge God any longer*, God gave over to a depraved mind, to do those things that aren't proper.

The Jesus Life means we hang in there even if we want to do otherwise. We don't give up or give in, or if we do temporarily, we can run back home into his always-open arms.

However, if we just don't see fit to acknowledge God any longer, making a deliberate choice to go a different direction, God lets us go. We're free to stay or make a trade, exchanging our relationship with God for something else. "Although they claimed to be wise, they became fools and exchanged the glory of the immortal God for images." They *exchanged* the truth of God for a lie.

The prodigal son made a bad trade, then changed his mind. And his father was waiting for him, with open arms.

We can't acknowledge God and *not* acknowledge God at the same time. We can be confused and kick and scream, but in the end, we must choose. To acknowledge or not acknowledge, that is the question. So maybe, as we look at our choices, the core question should be, "Am I acknowledging God?" That answer will determine our course.

Item in the Backpack: Acknowledgment

Romans 2:1–16
<u>No Checklists</u>

We aren't to condemn people, then turn around and practice the same things.

What if we had to fill out a checklist before entering church each Sunday and even one check mark disqualified us from entering? Here's a short list. (The real one would be much longer.)

Unrighteousness
Greed
Envy
Gossip
Boasting
Judging

Talk about empty pews.

Sometimes I wonder why some sins seem to be ranked more highly than others in our churches. Depravity (perversion) gets top billing, but arrogance gets a pass. And passing judgment on a particular perversion or on an arrogant person is just as bad as the perversion or arrogance itself. Seems we can't do anything wrong and get away with it. Which is exactly the point.

My belief is that all are welcome at church—the depraved, the greedy, the holier-than-thou folks, you, me—all sitting side by side, packing a pew. But I also believe that some churches dumb down the Gospel. They say that such and such on "the list" doesn't really count. I think our churches should preach the message as is and let God do the judging. God makes it very clear in this passage that judging is not our job; it's his.

Paul reiterated in chapter 2 what he had said in chapter 1. Whether or not we know "the law," the law of God is written on our hearts. Our consciences bear witness. Our thoughts accuse or defend us. Those who do right are justified.

The New Testament messages are consistent. We fall short; God saves us. I'm so thankful there are no checklists. Our hearts accuse or defend us. God knows our secrets. And his kindness leads us to repentance.

Item in the Backpack: Repentance

Romans 2:17–29
<u>Circumcised Hearts</u>

I often wear a little cross necklace, but it doesn't make me a Christian. The Jews were circumcised, but Paul said that didn't make them Jewish. Essentially, he said, "Don't brag about your outward appearances. God looks at your heart, at what has been done in your life by the Holy Spirit, not by the letter of the law. You'll get your applause from God, not from people."

Our walk needs to line up with our talk.

Circumcision of males was an outward sign of membership in the covenant people of God, set up in the Old Testament, but frankly, it's about cutting and pain. The metaphor of a circumcised heart is not to be taken lightly.

As we've considered before, there aren't many outward signs of becoming a Christian in America today. We don't have to shave our heads or wear long dresses. In other countries, however, becoming a Christian could mean death. In India, churches are burned, pastors are killed, and crowds of Christians are rounded up by Hindu extremists for reconversion ceremonies, with serious threats for noncompliance.

When I was six years old, I "gave my heart to Jesus." I was sitting with my mom in our pastor's office, and he led me in prayer. It made an impact on me. (I even remember the little red-and-blue corduroy skirt I was wearing.) I remember being aware of my sin, like being mean to my little sister. (So sorry, dear sister.) Anyway, I wanted Jesus in my heart. I knew I needed a circumcised heart, although not in those words. He's been in my heart ever since. Even though I've given him a run for his money at times, I'm committed to him, and he's committed to me.

A circumcised heart is a profound and sacred thing.

Item in the Backpack: Inward Commitment

Romans 3
<u>The Gift</u>

Romans 3:23–24 just might be the best gift in the whole wide world. "For all have sinned and fall short of the glory of God, and

all are justified freely by his grace through the redemption that came by Christ Jesus."

In other words, we can lay our burdens down—our guilt, regrets, little sins, big sins. The reason? The gift. The gift of grace, unmerited favor. Some people spend their whole lives striving for approval, trying to be good enough, when all along, God has said all we have to do is have faith. And BTW, what is good enough anyway?

"For we maintain that a person is *justified by faith apart from works of the law*."

I understand that some people don't want the gift. They feel they don't need it. Some may feel Christians are a little sin-obsessed and that they're pretty good people without the gift. (You have to recognize your sin in order to accept the gift.)

Some feel *they* are the gift to mankind. Um, they're not. Some just don't want to think about it. Some seek God or answers in other religions or philosophies.

But nobody else offers the gift. The gift is twofold, *forgiveness and wholeness*, because God himself comes in to dwell.

All we have to do is ask God for the gift. In Paul's theological terminology, it's called justification by faith. In lay terms, it's akin to being handed a million-dollar bill.

Every day.

Item in the Backpack: Justification by Faith

Romans 4
<u>Sola Fide</u>

When we work, we get paid. The boss isn't just doing us a favor; we earn that payment. That's like the Law of the Old Testament. Well, sort of. Back then, keeping the Law meant blessing; but the problem was that even Abraham, the father of the whole Jewish nation, couldn't *earn* righteousness.

Righteousness is a whole different animal. We can't earn it. God gives it to those who believe in him by faith.

Abraham believed God, not after he was circumcised, but before. He believed God was telling the truth about his promise. He didn't have to clean up his act and get the outward sign beforehand.

Sometimes people think they have to get their acts together, *then* come to God, which is the exact opposite of what God is saying. Abraham believed God, and *it was credited to him as righteousness.* He didn't get a follow-up memo that read, "And afterward there will be a six-week probation period for you to tidy up your life. Then we'll have a posttest." Nope—just believe.

Abraham believed that God would make him the father of many nations, even though he and his wife were way past the childbearing years. He didn't waver in his belief...and then the most amazing thing happened. He grew strong in faith. *Belief was a choice. Then strength followed.* I'm not sure it always happens that way, but it happened to Abraham in verse 20. As a result, he was assured that what God promised, he would be able to complete.

Which God indeed did.

Item in the Backpack: Righteousness

Romans 5
<u>The Sequence</u>

Paul loved multisyllable words like "justification," "tribulation," "reconciliation," and "transgression." (You get the picture.) And the picture he painted in this chapter is clear. Sin and death came through one man, Adam, and salvation came through one man, Jesus. While we were sinners, Christ died for us, and the rest is history, literally.

I've read Romans 5 a lot, but this time my brain landed on the word "exult." That little word shows up several times in this chapter. We're to *exult* in hope of the glory of God. We're to *exult* in our tribulations. We're to *exult* in God through Christ, through whom we've received reconciliation.

About that "exulting in our tribulations" sentence. This does not sound fun, yet here's the sequence. Tribulation brings perseverance. Perseverance brings proven character. Proven character brings hope. Hope does not disappoint.

(Everything works out.)

Say you're going through a tribulation. And say it lasts a long time. And you stay with it, praying, getting counsel from wise friends, taking brave steps along the way. That's perseverance. And let's say that this process keeps you from doing stupid things, because you and God are linked and you aren't about to let go of his hand. That builds character. And now here you are. And you two have been through such blood, sweat, and tears together that you're inextricably connected; and you know everything is going to be okay…and that with God, no matter how things turn out, you win. The process brings hope.

And hope does not disappoint.

Item in the Backpack: Exulting in Tribulation

Romans 6
<u>Sin Issues</u>

Believe me, I've heard lots of sermons on this passage, all very theological. "If you're a believer, you're sin free because you're positionally aligned with Jesus. Your old self was crucified with him and the dead self is freed from sin."

Which is awesome, except that I still sin. What am I supposed to do about my stupid sin?

I find comfort in verses 12–14. Here they are in *The Message*: "You must not give sin a vote in the way you conduct your lives. Don't give it the time of day. Don't even run little errands that are connected with that old way of life. Throw yourselves wholeheartedly and full-time—remember, you've been raised from the dead!—into God's way of doing things. Sin can't tell you how to live. After all, you're not living under that old tyranny any longer. You're living in the freedom of God."

A-ha! *Because* all the theological stuff is true, I can choose how to present myself.

I've heard this described like a cross. The vertical post is my alignment with God. The horizontal crosspiece is my relationship with people and my physical world. If the vertical is on track, the horizontal will follow suit.

This reminds me of a loved one. (I write this with his permission.) Until he accepted enough love to overcome his self-doubt, he stayed stuck. He looked for love in all the wrong places. He got into stuff. But as he started digging into the depths of his life and accepting real love, he chose against the negative stuff because he *wanted* to. Because he became positionally aligned with love, his whole life started changing.

Once we accept alignment with Love Incarnate, our lives start changing. We can choose enslavement to righteousness. We'll do righteousness imperfectly, but we're still spiritually, positionally, vertically aligned with Jesus. Period. And we have the rest of our lives to work on the horizontal part.

Item in the Backpack: Alignment

Romans 7
<u>Two Natures</u>

This is war. "I do not understand what I do. For what I want to do I do not do, but what I hate I do."

There's a battle between our sinful passions and living for God. This passage talks about the nature of the enemy (sin), and it goes into a lot of detail about how we're *attracted* to the enemy. Now I can understand not recognizing the enemy or wanting to kill the enemy, but being attracted to it?

I don't think this is a Stockholm syndrome situation. I think we've always kind of liked the enemy. It usually fulfills its promise of a temporary feel-good. It can be terribly attractive, almost irresistible. And if we can just keep it sort of hidden and harmless, maybe it's not that big a deal, right?

It's so easy to rationalize, or on the flip side, despair, because there are times when the battle seems impossible to win. "What a wretched man I am! Who will rescue me from this body that is subject to death?" Paul called it the conflict of our two natures. *Conflict.*

But we get a glimpse of the hope of victory in verse 25. "Thanks be to God, who delivers me through Jesus Christ our Lord!"

Hang on! Chapter 8 is coming! In my Bible, chapter 8 is subtitled "Deliverance from Bondage." Maybe chapter 7 was included so we wouldn't have that "everyone must find this easy but me" kind of feeling.

The whole point of the New Testament is that we humans, in our own power, can't win the war. In the end, God will win. In the meantime, we must contend with the conflict of our two natures. It all goes back to that alignment thing. The battles continue, but the war has already been won.

Item in the Backpack: Warfare

Romans 8:1–11
Spiritual Freedom

Warfare is terrifying and exhausting, but we were never intended to be defined by it, ultimately. There is deliverance. There is no condemnation for those who are in Christ Jesus. The mind set on the Spirit is life and peace. If Christ is in you, the spirit is alive. He who raised Jesus from the dead will also give life to your mortal bodies.

But what's the catch? Seems we should have to do *something* to deserve this.

I think the onus is mostly on God. "God went for the jugular when he sent his own Son. He didn't deal with the problem as something remote and unimportant. In his Son, Jesus, he personally took on the human condition, entered the disordered mess of struggling humanity in order to set it right once and for all. The law code, weakened as it always was by fractured human nature, could never have done that. The law always ended up being used as a Band-Aid on sin instead of a deep healing of it. And now what the law code asked for but we couldn't deliver is accomplished as we, instead of redoubling our own efforts, simply embrace what the Spirit is doing in us" (Rom. 8:3–4, *The Message*).

And here are the following two verses from the NIV. "Those who live according to the flesh have their minds set on what the flesh desires; but those who live in accordance with the Spirit have their minds set on what the Spirit desires. The mind governed by the flesh is death, but the mind governed by the Spirit is life and peace."

Our job is to set our minds on the things of the Spirit.

Miraculously, there's the equation. The mind set on the flesh is death, but the mind set on the Spirit is life and peace. The verse doesn't say that the person who has *mastered* the spiritual mind-set will have life and peace. It says to simply *set our minds* on what the Spirit wants.

When I get up in the mornings, sometimes I need to get my mind set for the day. (I might have gotten up on the wrong side of the bed, so to speak.) I might need to choose joy over melancholy. I might need to review what is good and right. I might need to pray. Sometimes I don't know what the Spirit wants, so I need to ask. My job is to set my mind on the things of the Spirit and keep it set there until it's, well, set. Then I can continue on with my day. And if I mess up along the way, I can hit the reset button. That's where the spiritual victory is. We do the setting, and God does the miracle.

Item in the Backpack: Mind-Set

Romans 8:12–25
Profound Truths

I thought about breaking this passage into single verses, because each one holds a *profundity*. There's so much here, from putting to death the deeds of the body to having the first fruits of the Spirit to groaning! But to take that much time would send our journey into overtime, so I've just decided to itemize the profundities, then comment on them as a whole.

If by the Spirit you are putting to death the deeds of the body, you will live. All who are led by the Spirit are children of God. You have not received a spirit of slavery leading to fear. You have received a spirit of adoption as sons and daughters. We are heirs of God and fellow heirs with Christ, if we suffer with him. The sufferings of this time are not worthy to be compared with the glory to come. The creation will be set free from corruption into the freedom of glory.

Commentary: It's all good!

No *Cliffs Notes* or *Dummies* books can capture the breadth of this passage. There are times when we need to meditate on small passages and let them sink deep into our souls. Meditation is a spiritual discipline along with practices such as prayer, fasting, study, simplicity, solitude, submission, service, confession, worship, guidance, and celebration. (For more, see Richard Foster's book *Celebration of Discipline.*)

The New Testament contains 184,600 words, give or take, depending on the translation. That's a lot of profundities. It's good to read the whole thing to get the whole picture. And I also recommend taking time to meditate on a phrase…or even a word.

Item in the Backpack: Meditation

Romans 8:26–39
More Profundities

The last passage was profound, but things get even better! This passage is worth even more meditation—or better yet, memorization. Imagine having this passage memorized, as handy as your back pocket, when life is tough. Here are some highlights. Notice the verbs.

He *helps* us when we're weak. He *intercedes* for us with power beyond words. He *causes* all things to work for good. He *justifies* us (makes us right) and *glorifies* us (makes us splendid). He *gives* us all things with Christ. He *makes* it impossible to be separated from him.

Have you ever been so weak (physically or will power-wise) that you could barely hang on? He helps us when we're weak. Have you ever not been able to pray? He intercedes for us. Have you ever thought things would never get better? He causes all things to work together for good…somehow, eventually, always. Have you ever felt wronged and belittled? He justifies. He glorifies. Have you ever felt poor in spirit? He gives us all things in Christ. Have you ever felt alone and powerless? He reminds us that we are never alone. Nothing, *nothing*, can separate us from his love.

In writing this, I'm shaking a bit. Seriously. I'm astounded by the realities. All these *profundities* are available. It's like there's a parallel universe, a spiritual world, that I can't always access. But the truth is (and this is worth memorizing)... "We know that in all things God works for the good of those who love him, who have been called according to his purpose" (Rom, 8:28). God has something victorious in mind.

Item in the Backpack: Memorization

Romans 9
Promise Children

The children of God are children of the *promise.*

"The Lord is not slow in keeping his *promise,* as some understand slowness. Instead he is patient with you, not wanting anyone to perish, but everyone to come to repentance" (2 Pet. 3:9).

To me, the promise discussed in Romans 9 and the one discussed in 2 Peter 3 are the same promise.

So what *is* the promise?

That if we believe and accept the gift of Jesus by faith, we'll be saved. And we won't be disappointed.

He gives us a lifetime of opportunity to believe. And since time hasn't ended yet, there's still opportunity.

And get this! Second Peter 3:13 says, "But in keeping with his *promise* we are looking forward to a new heaven and a new earth, where righteousness dwells."

Item in the Backpack: The Promise

Romans 10
God's Hands

Paul used body imagery and the senses in this chapter. We *hear* the message of Christ and decide in our *hearts* whether or not to believe. If we choose to believe, we confess that Jesus is Lord with our *mouth,* and when we do, we're saved.

Paul was never one to tone down his message just to be nice. He made it very clear that choosing the "righteousness" of the law over righteousness based on faith was a dead end. A dead end that grieves God, and the last verse in the chapter paints a graphic picture using, interestingly, another body part: *hands.* "All day long I have held out my hands to a disobedient and obstinate people."

What a visual. God stretching out his hands to people he wants. This makes me think of Michelangelo's depiction of the creation of Adam on the ceiling of the Sistine Chapel. God's hand touching Adam's hand. And then there are the hands of Jesus. Hands touching lepers and blind people and the demon-possessed and children and Peter when he was sinking and the high priest's slave's ear...and the wood of the cross.

It's interesting that people killed Jesus by disabling his hands and feet. In crucifixions, the inability to lift oneself up by the arms or feet to breathe meant asphyxiation. But Jesus got full use of his hands and feet back. Remember when he talked to Thomas after the resurrection? "'Put your finger here; see my hands. Reach out your hand and put it into my side. Stop doubting and believe.' Thomas said to him, 'My Lord and my God!'" (John 20:27–28)

Sometimes, if I'm going through something hard, I wake up with sore hands from "gripping God's hand" in my sleep, begging him not to let go.

But I don't need to beg. He never lets go. I'm safe.

Item in the Backpack: Safety

Romans 11
<u>God's Offer</u>

Because of the transgression of Israel, salvation came to the Gentiles, but by God's grace, a remnant of Israel will be saved. And after the fullness of the Gentiles has come in, all Israel will be saved. All is irrevocable. "For God has bound everyone over to disobedience so that he may have mercy on them all."

Now this is a conundrum. Will everyone be saved? Even all of Israel? After all, God is love, but so many scriptures speak about individual choice.

This is where I land on things. God does his part. We can be assured of that. God, in his mercy, will make himself known to every single person; yet he doesn't force his will on us. How unsearchable are his judgments and unfathomable his ways.

Maybe the last verse of the chapter holds the key: "For from him and through him and for him are all things." He's the Alpha and the Omega, the beginning and the end and everything in between. He's very clear about the path to himself. Sometimes people call it the Roman Road to Salvation (*Rom. 3:10, 3:23, 5:8, 5:12, 6:23, 10:9–10, and 10:13*).

God is God. I'm not. You're not. God has extended his love to you and me. We don't need to worry about who's in and who's not. We just need to consider his offer to us individually and respond… sort of like a proposal.

Item in the Backpack: Response

Romans 12:1–8
Dedicated Service

In case there was doubt, Paul reminded believers how we're supposed to act. We're to present our bodies a living and holy sacrifice. We're to not conform to the world. We're to be transformed by the renewing of our minds. We're to not think of ourselves more highly than we ought to think. We're to have sound judgment. We're to exercise our gifts appropriately.

So what do these line items look like in real life? The first few are about the body; the second few about the mind. God can personalize them for each of us.

We're to present our bodies as living and holy sacrifices. This impacts what we eat and drink. How we dress. Our morality.

We're to present our minds to God. We're not to conform to the world if the world is creeping away from God's values. This takes guts. I just read a news clip suggesting pedophilia be listed as a gender variance. That sounds bizarre, but how many other things have sounded bizarre at first but have crept into the "okay" category. We need to be *clear and strong* in our nonconformity.

We're to renew our minds. Renewal means constant reinforcement. *We're to love ourselves but humbly, without arrogance. We're to have sound judgment. We're to use our gifts.*

All of this takes intentionality and dedication.

Item in the Backpack: Dedication

Romans 12:9–21
The Experiment

What if everyone on the whole planet conducted him/herself according to this list? If only. What if everyone loathed evil, had a spirit of you-before-me, served God, stood firm and hopeful during times of trouble, contributed to the needs of others, blessed people (even their own persecutors), associated with the lowly, and overcame evil by doing good?

There would be no war, no poverty, no evil.

If only.

But the flip side is the real side. Sometimes people "love" hypocritically. They cling to what is bad. There's little devotion. There's a "me first" attitude that's applauded by society. There's little restraint when it comes to paybacks and vengeance. And social climbing is more popular than social descending.

There's war, poverty, evil.

We can't control others, but we can control ourselves. Ultimately, we're the masters of our own destinies. Verse 18 is a great example: "If it is possible, *as far as it depends on you*, live at peace with everyone." We don't have to fuss over what others do. We can be peacemakers. We can forgive if we've been wronged. We can soothe hurt feelings. We can adopt a charitable attitude.

I think the only thing for us to do is to make it *personal.* To make these things so prevalent in our lives that they define us. And possibly, possibly, if enough of us do that, there just might be less war, poverty, evil.

It's certainly worth an experiment.

Item in the Backpack: Godly Behavior

Romans 13:1–7
Government Matters

Generally speaking, governments are set up for our good and they're to be accepted and obeyed. Now it's true that in Acts 5, Peter and the apostles stood before the full assembly of the elders of Israel. They had disobeyed orders to keep quiet about Jesus and said, "We must obey God rather than human beings!" Hmmm.

Generally speaking, rulers are not to be a cause of fear for good behavior. Now it's true that some rulers are bad to the bone. Some racially profile. Some persecute Christians. Some order the killings of innocents. Hmmm.

But generally speaking, we really *are* to be subject to our governing authorities. We're to pay taxes. If we do something against the law, we're going to get in trouble, because God established governing authorities to manage societies. There's a reason it's called law and order.

If we disobey, we're subject to the law, so we need to be *really* careful if we choose civil disobedience. Some of our heroes broke the law because they were *really* convinced the law was wrong. Take Nelson Mandela, for example. He led a sabotage campaign against the apartheid government and spent twenty-seven years in prison… and later became the president of South Africa.

As I write this, our country is going through political craziness. I remember the days when we believed in objective truth. Now we have to read original documents to understand truth because of spin. And let's face it, few of us are going to read a lot of five-hundred-page documents. We've needed to trust our rulers, but now we're on shaky ground. As the saying goes, one man's terrorist is another man's freedom fighter. Whom can we trust?

This is a big, big issue. We must pray for goodness to prevail.

Item in the Backpack: Order

Romans 13:8–14
Neighbor Matters

Neighbors are a big deal in the Bible. Half of the Ten Commandments address being a good neighbor. No killing, committing adultery, stealing, slandering, or coveting. We're to love our neighbors as ourselves, meaning we need to love ourselves sufficiently enough to love them, which is an interesting study in itself; but we'll stay outwardly focused for now.

"Love does no harm to a neighbor. Therefore love is the fulfillment of the law."

What does this mean exactly? I don't even know some of my neighbors. What does God mean by "neighbor"?

I think a neighbor can be defined as "anyone who isn't me." *All* people are candidates for our mercy. That might be a literal neighbor, even the one with the dog that barks all night. I'm not saying you shouldn't call that person up and deal with it. In fact, you *should* call that person up and deal with it before you want to do something un-neighborly, but with mercy in mind.

Verse 13 tells us to behave properly. Maybe this is why the Bible talks about neighbors so much. Neighbors are in our space. We see the less-than-perfect side of them. We hear them yelling at their kids. We don't like that new color choice for their front door. They are *such* convenient targets when we have a bad day.

If we can love our neighbors, even the unlovable ones, then we've fulfilled the law.

Which is a big deal.

Item in the Backpack: Neighborliness

Romans 14
Little Distinctions

"The kingdom of God is not a matter of eating and drinking, but of righteousness, peace and joy in the Holy Spirit."

Take caffeine consumption, for example. One Christian has no problem with drinking coffee; another shuns it. Both people answer to God. There's a boundary, but where is it? We would all likely agree that using heroin is out of bounds, but what about drinking coffee… or alcohol?

There's such a diversity of thought *within* the kingdom of Christ followers (e.g., views on politics, homosexuality, public schools, guns, immigration, use of tax dollars, foreign policy, plus so much more). We've rarely experienced it more wildly than recently, in politics—81 percent of US evangelicals voted for Trump in 2016 while 19 percent were stunned.

Is it possible both "sides" can have a clear conscience before God? Is it possible both sides can be 1,000 percent convinced that their stance is the correct one? Apparently so, at least in politics. People glom onto defining issues even though there are hundreds of issues. And at some point, you have to mark your ballot.

What does this passage say to do?

We're not to judge each other. (We'll all stand before the judgment seat of God.)

We're to give thanks to God. (Giving thanks tamps down anger.)

We're not to put a stumbling block in someone else's way. (Do no harm.)

We're to pursue peace. (We can learn the delicate dance of voting according to our conscience and simultaneously building community.)

We're not to destroy the work of God over little distinctions. (We're to avoid church splits over the color of the carpet.)

We're to stand our ground. (Happy is he who does not condemn himself in what he approves.)

This quote sums things up nicely: "In essentials, unity. In non-essentials, diversity. In all things, charity." We're to strive for unity and let go of little things that don't matter, but if we can't come to agreement, we're still to love each other.

Item in the Backpack: Charity

Romans 15 and 16
Closing Remarks

Paul seemed quite fond of the Roman Christians. He gave them a few last-minute teachings and praised their goodness. He admonished them to be wise and innocent. He warned them to keep tabs on people who caused dissension. He seemed particularly concerned about those who "deceive the hearts of the unsuspecting." He asked them to pray for him. He reminded them that God would crush Satan under their feet. He gave blessings and benedictions.

I love blessings and benedictions.

Here are two I often hear in church:

A. "The Lord bless you and keep you; the Lord make his face shine on you and be gracious to you; the Lord turn his face toward you and give you peace" (Num. 6:24–26).

B. "To him who is able to keep you from stumbling and to present you before his glorious presence without fault and with great joy—to the only God our Savior be glory, majesty, power and authority, through Jesus Christ our Lord, before all ages, now and forevermore! Amen" (Jude 24–25).

What if we prayed blessings and benedictions over each other more often? They can be simple with eyes wide open, like "I hope God shines on you today." I often break into prayer in the middle of a conversation. Do you? I may be having lunch with a friend, and one of us will just start, "So, Lord, we give you [the situation we've been talking about]." The other will "amen" it, and we move on. No missing a beat. Just the flow of life in Christ. Christ above us, around us, within us.

Prior to God's offer to the Gentiles, they had had an assortment of philosophies, mythologies, and beliefs (or a lack thereof). Transformation through Christ ushered in a new mind-set and heart-set. Paul was intent on instructing them and blessing them. Benedictions were part of it. Closing remarks. A parting touch.

Item in the Backpack: Life Touches

1 Corinthians 1
Bragging Rights

Paul used exactly nine verses to say hi to the Christians in Corinth, then wasted no time. They were quarreling and splintering already. They thought they had bragging rights based on who their preacher was. Reminds me of denominationalism today.

I once worked for a denominational ministry. It wasn't "my" denomination, so I didn't know its fine points. In my zeal, I started contacting the conservative branch, the liberal branch, the branch based in this region, the branch based in that region, thinking they were at least similar since they all bore the same name. But no. They weren't. Seems a number of denominations are that way.

Paul asked if Christ had been divided. Why were they boasting? Boasting reeks of fragile egos.

At the end of the chapter he said, "Let the one who boasts boast in the Lord."

Paul also mentioned another kind of boasting. Seems he, as a preacher, wanted to hold himself and all preachers to the same "no bragging" standard. He said Christ sent him to preach the Gospel, but not in cleverness of speech, that the cross of Christ should not be made void. Preachers' charisma and style should never overtake the message.

I grew up in the Bible Belt during the Jesus Movement of the seventies. Almost all my close friends were Christians, but now I live in the Wild West during the "post-everything" era. It's no longer cool to be a Christian. I understand verse 18: "For the message of the cross is foolishness to those who are perishing, but to us who are being saved it is the power of God."

Sometimes what I say about God sounds crazy to my humanist friends, but it holds such power to me. Christ is our wisdom and righteousness and sanctification and redemption. Our loyalty needs to be laser focused on him for a number of reasons. What a great reminder when we feel foolish and weak, or on the flip side, a little boastful and uppity.

Item in the Backpack: Loyalty to God

1 Corinthians 2
Hidden Wisdom

Note to believers: *You have the mind of Christ.* You speak God's wisdom in a mystery. You have hidden wisdom, things that no eye has seen and no ear has heard, things that have never entered into a human heart. You speak with words taught by the Spirit. Natural people don't understand this. You can appraise all things, yet no one can appraise you.

Man, do I need that hidden wisdom right now! I've been patiently waiting on a certain matter for over a decade, and it's time to shift from patience to action, not because I'm fed up but because the circumstances warrant it. I need spiritual words to address it. Believe me, I could spew a whole narrative of "natural" words, but they would do more harm than good. As I sit here, God is calming my spirit and giving me lovely, affirming, and life-giving words.

I would call those words spiritually appraised.

What makes Christ followers different from "natural" people? Well, we have the natural means of acquiring knowledge and wisdom like our senses, minds, consciences, news sources, and trusted friends; but *in addition*, we have the Spirit of God, our pipeline to the mind of Christ.

"The Spirit, not content to flit around on the surface, dives into the depths of God, and brings out what God planned all along. Who ever knows what you're thinking and planning except you yourself? The same with God—except that he not only knows what he's thinking, but he lets *us* in on it" (1 Cor. 2:11–12, *The Message*).

We have hidden wisdom. Remarkable.

Item in the Backpack: Information Pipeline

1 Corinthians 3
Firm Foundation

I looked up the order for building a house on www.howstuffworks.com. Here ya go:

"Grading and site preparation. Foundation construction. Framing. Installation of windows and doors. Roofing. Siding. Electrical. Plumbing. HVAC. Insulation. Drywall. Underlayment. Trim. Painting. Bathroom and kitchen counters/cabinets. Carpet and flooring. Hookups. Punch list."

My relatives in construction might tweak the order a bit, but grading and site prep certainly come first. After you smooth out the dirt, you lay the foundation. Paul said we need to make sure our spiritual foundation is on Christ.

I feel there are some wrong foundations out there, like Hinduism. A glance at Hinduism shows an exotic, colorful, interesting mythology; a deeper look shows people trying to appease millions of gods, many of them evil. And it means the caste system.

But it's never too late to dig up the wrong foundation and start over. Many Hindus, especially Dalits, are converting to Christianity, which means laying a whole new foundation based on being loved rather than despised. (Which foundation would you prefer?)

Paul and his colleagues laid the solid foundation, which is Jesus Christ. Then others built on it. I guess you could say I'm building on it in writing this book. My goal is to be 100 percent true to the text, with relatable language and emotion as a fellow pilgrim on this journey.

Item in the Backpack: Solidity

1 Corinthians 4
Paul's Rebuke

Paul was *not* pleased with the Corinthian Christians' arrogance, but apparently they were doing pretty well as a new church. They were prudent, strong, and distinguished. The apostles (Paul included), on the other hand, were suffering. Homeless even.

I wonder if the world looks at American Christians' arrogance in the same way, even though we appear prudent, strong, and distinguished. So many of the world's people are suffering. Homeless even. They would long to live in a space as warm and safe and clean as an American church *restroom.*

So Paul chastised the Corinthians. (And they were the friendlies!) He called them to a higher standard and petitioned them to be imitators. "When we're reviled, we bless. When we're persecuted, we endure. When we're slandered, we try to conciliate. We've become as the scum of the earth while you're prospering."

Have you ever been at odds with the friendlies? I have. I often feel like an outsider even within my own wealthy American-Christian communities. Don't get me wrong. Comfort is a lot more fun than discomfort, but we're so isolated from the needs of the world. I fear it comes across as arrogance. But I must be careful. Pointing a finger at the arrogant is also arrogant, especially since I'm part of those communities.

I think the key is to be aware of our own shortcomings. Arrogance is not just disgusting; it also blinds us to massive need all around us.

My life scripture is 1 Corinthians 4:1: "This, then, is how you ought to regard us: as servants of Christ and as those entrusted with the mysteries God has revealed." My goal is to be a servant. A true servant of Christ is *not* arrogant.

I have so far to go, but thankfully, Philippians 3:12 is coming up: "Not that I have already obtained all this, or have already arrived at my goal, but I press on to take hold of that for which Christ Jesus took hold of me."

Item in the Backpack: Awareness of Our Shortcomings

1 Corinthians 5
Immorality Exposed

Paul had heard about an incestuous situation within the ranks, so he called for church discipline. I've been part of churches that had to administer discipline. A member here, a pastor there. If the person is resolute in their sin, they're to be removed from the church. This strikes me as so sad. They could have repented…

Apparently, removal is necessary because a little leaven leavens the whole lump. A little sin pollutes the whole congregation. That sin might be too enticing to others. Or tolerating it might water down the extent of its immorality, leading to an "anything goes" church. Or maybe, simply letting unconfessed sin go unchecked was, and is, a really bad idea. For one thing, the unrepentant person misses the blessing and freedom of forgiveness.

Paul told the church to not even associate with this particular man. And he went on to say that he was going to deliver him to Satan for the destruction of his flesh in order to save his spirit. That's pretty gutsy, but Paul was adamant.

This brings us to a fine line. We *want* imperfect people in our churches, or there would be nobody in our churches, but "open and affirming" cannot mean affirming about sin. Which brings us to the definition of sin. The dictionary calls sin a "transgression of divine law." And the onus is on each of us to determine what's a transgression of divine law. Also, I believe there's a distinction between sinners. Some people sin and know it and are mortified. They confess it, repent, and ask for forgiveness. The church is for these folks, because everyone sins.

Other people sin but rationalize it and decide it's okay after all, then find a community that affirms the okay-ness of the sin.

Paul said they needed to remove the wicked man from their midst. I believe he was describing an un-confessing, unrepentant wicked man.

Item in the Backpack: Confession

1 Corinthians 6:1–11
Tough Issues

Paul called on the Christians to step it up. "Is it possible that there is nobody among you wise enough to judge a dispute between believers?" In other words, he was saying something like, "You guys should be able to settle disputes internally or why not just turn the other cheek and be wronged? You're above pettiness."

I see people making a big deal of small infractions all the time. It's like there's an obsession with personal rights. That driver cut me off, or that kid cut through my property! At minimum, I think Paul was telling people to get over themselves.

And as always, he held people to the highest standards. No fornication, idolatry, adultery, etc. There's an item or two in this passage that Jesus didn't address, but Paul did. You may or may not agree with his assessment, but the onus is on us not to erase the parts we don't like. We must deal with them, always remembering that God is merciful and wants the best for us.

What about Paul's point about lawsuits? I know a couple of men who financially defrauded friends, many of whom were Christians. These two ended up in prison. Was Paul saying that folks like the financially ruined friends should have just let it go?

I doubt it. I think we've seen both sides of the coin in scripture. *Some situations require fairness and judgment; others require forgiveness and mercy.* There are complexities in life. "We don't yet see things clearly. We're squinting in a fog, peering through a mist. But it won't be long before the weather clears and the sun shines bright! We'll see it all then, see it all as clearly as God sees us, knowing him directly just as he knows us!" (1 Cor. 13:12, *The Message*)

Honest grappling with the mysteries is part of the equation.

Item in the Backpack: Honesty

1 Corinthians 6:12–20
Expensive Bodies

Your body is a temple of the Spirit. Most temples are pricey. It's been said that the gold and silver alone used for Solomon's temple would be worth over $216 billion in today's market.

I remember the first time I saw a cathedral in a poor section of Oaxaca, Mexico. The altar was silver-plated. I marveled at the desire of the poor to make their temple so valuable.

So do we see our bodies the same way? I can't imagine mine is worth $216 billion. But maybe God sees it that way.

Paul tied the topic of immorality to the body. Our bodies shouldn't be joined to a harlot's because the two become one.

Food is also discussed in this passage about the body. I've heard verse 12 used as an argument against certain food-isms. "I have the right to do anything," you say—but not everything is beneficial. "I have the right to do anything"—but I will not be mastered by anything. I get that.

My tummy does best when I don't ply it with too much meat or junk food. Whether it be food or drink or work or something addictive or a certain desirable person, we're to be master over our desires, not vice versa.

Why? Because expensive things need to be taken care of. Can you imagine what that silver-plated altar would look like if somebody hadn't polished it regularly? Care takes discipline.

"For you have been bought with a price."

Maybe, when Jesus was agonizing in the Garden of Gethsemane before his excruciating murder, he could see you and me as valuable, well worth $216 billion each. And that was that. He got up and went to the cross to pay the price.

Item in the Backpack: Value

1 Corinthians 7
Marriage Matters

At the time I'm writing, the divorce rate in the United States is at 53 percent. It's 70 percent in Belgium; 3 percent in Chile.

Interesting. Paul had strong words about divorce. So did Jesus in Matthew 19. Paul thought it better to stay single, but he gave concessions because of self-control. He made the point that married people have divided interests and single people can be solely devoted to the Lord. He also branched out into the "stay the way you are" narrative. If married, stay that way. If unmarried, stay that way, but if you do get married, you're not sinning.

"'The man who hates and divorces his wife," says the LORD, the God of Israel, 'does violence to the one he should protect,'[a] says the LORD Almighty. So be on your guard, and do not be unfaithful'" (Mal. 2:16).

So much of the time with divorce, treachery is involved. Cheating on one's spouse, for example.

Most of these words are clear, but one part is unclear, at least to me, and that's verses 13 and 14 about the unbelieving spouse being sanctified through the believing spouse. Here again, because of individual choice, I just don't know, but here's one thing we can count on. God hates treachery. If a married couple is struggling and one of them is dealing treacherously, that needs to be addressed. *That* is clear.

Item in the Backpack: Sanctity

1 Corinthians 8
Idol Issues

An idol is anything that substitutes for God.

Hinduism has millions of gods (idols), and each household has a sort of patron god. Its picture is often on the wall. Millions of gallons of milk are sacrificed to idols in India. But Americans have idols too. We can't see God, so we sort of set up images to worship, many on our smartphones through games, social media, texts. Some people pay inordinate attention to these things.

Food as it relates to idols (dining in an idol's temple or eating things sacrificed to idols) is a bit lost on me, but doing something that causes someone to stumble is not lost on me. Paul said that if you do so, you sin against Christ. Yikes.

In other words, we have a great deal of liberty (including with our smartphones), but we need to take care with it. Love is the final word. "Knowledge puffs up while love builds up."

We've been bought with a price. We've received much. "From everyone who has been given much, much will be demanded; and from the one who has been entrusted with much, much more will be asked" (Luke 12:48).

Item in the Backpack: Liberty and Responsibility

1 Corinthians 9
Tempered Freedom

Freedom is to be tempered with discipline. Tempered steel has gone through a heat process to make it stronger. Our freedom isn't lazy; it's more like the freedom felt after winning a competition.

We're free in Christ. (All things are lawful.) Yet we're tempered. (All things are not profitable.)

In Paul's case, he *should* have been able to make a living by preaching the Gospel but he tempered himself, not charging for his work. He seemed tireless. You can see his fiery personality squeaking out, but you also see his zeal. "Though I am free and belong to no one, I have made myself a slave to everyone, to win as many as possible."

Free but tempered.

Then he launched into a race illustration, which also speaks to his tirelessness and discipline.

Run to win. Exercise self-control in all things. Keep your eyes on the prize. Buffet your body and make it your slave.

In today's language, he might have said, "Don't cheat. Don't use illegal performance-enhancing drugs, lest after you win and become everyone's hero, you're disqualified."

There are no shortcuts. We've got to keep at it in this race called life. We've got to stay controlled and disciplined. Coach Paul is at our heels, urging us on.

Then when all is said and done, we'll receive a victory wreath—an imperishable one.

Item in the Backpack: Self-Control

1 Corinthians 10
Israelites' Example

Paul made a fascinating point in saying that the cloud the Israelites had been under in the Old Testament, and the sea they passed through, and the rock they drank from...was *Christ.* He tied the whole story together.

"In the beginning was the Word, and the Word was with God, and the Word was God. He was with God in the beginning" (John 1:1–2).

The Word was *Christ*...there from the beginning, there through the sea, there through his time on earth. And he's presently alive and well and will be forever. The Alpha and the Omega. The continuum, from the beginning throughout eternity.

However, backing up a bit, God wasn't pleased with the Israelites. Paul reminded his Corinthian audience that things happened as examples so they wouldn't crave evil like the Israelites did. Consequences of disobedience were severe—twenty-three thousand died in one day, some were destroyed by snakes, and so on.

I wonder if we would change our ways if we knew we would be destroyed by snakes "just" for trying God's patience. I feel like we try God's patience every day. This makes Jesus's sacrifice on our behalf even more compelling because of what had happened to sinners pre-Jesus. But, as we've seen before, grace doesn't give us license to sin. We're to pay attention to the Israelites' example and to our *own* sin.

Then Paul essentially said, "About that potential sin of yours, know that you won't be tempted beyond what you're able to withstand. Your temptations are common to humanity, immorality included, but God is faithful. With the temptation, he'll provide the escape route so you'll be able to endure it."

I find it fascinating that he said *with* the temptation he'll provide the way of escape also. Temptations will come but so will the escape routes. We just need to find them because they're there.

Item in the Backpack: Escape Routes

1 Corinthians 11:1–22
Church Matters

There's a big debate about what's cultural and what's universal in the Bible. This passage has examples of this conundrum, especially regarding church matters. For example, verse 13 says, "Judge for yourselves: Is it proper for a woman to pray to God with her head uncovered?"

So I'm judging for myself. "Sure." Having my head uncovered has no bearing on my prayer life. Although if my uncovered head caused offense to someone else, I would cover my head, just like I cover my ankles when I'm in India, because that's proper in India.

And on the topic of headship, I've led Christian ministries during a period when most were led by men. I led right alongside them. No one was higher. No one was lower. (I won't make a pronouncement for roles within the church, because I'm still processing that myself.)

Paul started off with "Follow my example, as I follow the example of Christ." Here's a quote (edited) in the Matthew Henry Commentary on this passage: "Paul encouraged neither implicit faith nor obedience. He would be followed himself no further than he followed Christ. Christ's pattern is a copy without a blot. We should follow no leader further than he follows Christ."

I wonder if this is a model for the headship issue. We'll dig into this more in Ephesians regarding marriage. Here are Ephesians 5:22 and 25, respectively: "Wives, submit yourselves to your own husbands as you do to the Lord." "Husbands, love your wives, just as Christ loved the church and gave himself up for her." Sounds like mutual submission, and submission is good for our selfish streaks, just like tithing is good for our greedy streaks.

But back to church matters. The church has historically been a place where people turn for meaning. It has been the keeper of the flame of morality and uprightness, in spite of some downfalls on the parts of its humans. It is a pillar of society, so church matters *matter*. In Corinth, a big church issue was head coverings. When I was a teen, a big church issue was whether girls should wear pants to church. Now, big church issues include women in leadership, whether to take political stances on important topics, etc.

We each need to judge for ourselves, before God, with assent to his will, on issues facing the church and our lives. Wrestling might be required.

Item in the Backpack: Wrestling with Tough Issues

1 Corinthians 11:23–34
Lord's Supper

Apparently, some people were misappropriating the Lord's Supper. Did that have to do with divisions among them or shaming the poor or drunkenness or people partaking in an unworthy manner or all of the above? Again, I'm not sure. The Communion practices of today are symbols of a meal, not a meal in itself. Some are open to any believer, and others are open only to the members of that particular church. Hmmm.

Several passages like this one are subject to interpretation, so I'll leave those to the experts. But here are some thoughts on the sacraments, *outward signs of inward grace*, particularly the Lord's Supper and baptism.

Baptism involves water. It symbolizes dying to the old self and rising to new life in Christ. That's graphic in a powerful way in immersion baptisms. It's also a statement to the world—"I have decided to follow Jesus."

The Lord's Supper (Communion) involves bread and wine. It symbolizes Christ's body broken for us and his blood shed for our forgiveness. That's graphic in a powerful way as you take them into your body. It's also a statement of remembrance, proclaiming Christ's death until he returns. (If you're new to Christianity, here's some news. Christ is coming back to earth. Stay tuned!)

In addition, the Lord's Supper is a statement of the unity of the Body of Christ. We all partake of one loaf and cup. The issue of unity is crucial in this section of chapter 11.

In the Old Testament book of Joshua, God instructed the Israelites to set up twelve memorial stones after they safely crossed through the Red Sea. Sometimes I set up little cairns to memorialize something important in my walk with God. Cairns of remembrance.

Item in the Backpack: Sacraments

1 Corinthians 12:1–10
Spiritual Gifts

One of the things that has helped me most in life has been discovering my spiritual gifts. I took a Spiritual Gifts Inventory a number of years ago. Not only did it clarify my main gift; it released me from the angst of not being good at all of them! (I'm a bit of a type A, alas.)

For example, in the past, if a friend was in the hospital, I would volunteer to tidy up her house or take care of her kids but I would feel bad about not sitting for long periods at her bedside. After figuring out this gifts stuff, I realized I have a gift of service, not mercy. It doesn't mean I'm heartless. I just gravitate to service. Freedom!

Thank God (literally) that someone else *does* have the gift of mercy, to sit with her, weep with her, hold her hand…and someone else is praying for a miraculous healing while I'm cleaning up her kitchen. In the second half of this chapter, we'll muse on the different members of the body. It takes *all* of us to make a body…and that *body* gets the job done.

Spiritual gifts are over-and-above natural gifts, talents, and inclinations. They're given by the Holy Spirit.

For reference, the scriptures on spiritual gifts are Romans 12:6–8, 1 Corinthians 12, Ephesians 4:11, and 1 Peter 4:9–11. And here's a full list of the gifts, from all of these passages together: leadership, administration, teaching, knowledge, wisdom, prophecy, discernment, exhortation, faith, evangelism, apostleship, service/helps, mercy, giving, healing, miracles, tongues, interpretation of tongues, and distinguishing between spirits. (Sometimes shepherding and hospitality are listed as well, rather than falling under one of the other categories.)

So there's your overview! I encourage you to take a spiritual gifts inventory through your church or online. Life-changing stuff. It makes you so much better at being *you.*

Item in the Backpack: Spiritual Gifts

1 Corinthians 12:11–31
One Body

We are all differently-abled. As you know, my friend, Randy, has cerebral palsy. He's in a wheelchair and unable to do a lot of things you and I take for granted, like putting on his socks. He's not "able-bodied," but Paul said that the parts of the body that seem weaker are *indispensable* and are given more honor.

My friend is so far ahead of most other Christians I know. He's agonized over his inability to play sports and get married, but you know what? He's come out on the other side victorious. God has elevated this "weaker" member to a position of strength.

God has a way of balancing the scales for the members of the body. He wants there to be unity and community, not divisions. He wants each of us to pull our load according to our gifting.

Everyone struggles. One of my wealthiest friends struggles with depression. One of my poorest friends lights up rooms with her laughter. They're both Christians. They're from different races.

They, plus my friend in the wheelchair, plus you and me, plus Christians all over the world make up the body of Christ. Isn't that an amazing thought? We're a global family.

I encourage you to get to know members of the body that are different from you. Randy tells stories in his book, *Lessons Learned from the Bottom of the Stairs*, about feeling superior to street people until he got to know them. My wealthy friend hangs out with the poor. My poor friend hangs out with the rich. I have a fair number of ex-gang member friends, some of whom have become Christians and are powerful members of the body.

One body (unity) with many members (diversity) = community.

Item in the Backpack: Unity

1 Corinthians 13
(A) Love Stories

I want to take the next four entries to muse about love. (I hope you have lots of love musings too!) These are glimpses, but there will come a time when we'll be in the presence of pure love for eternity. It will be heaven.

Love is patient. Jacob loved Rachel, so he worked for her dad seven years in order to marry her. The only problem was that at the end of seven years, the dad gave him her sister, Leah. The "payment" for Rachel? Another seven years (Gen. 29). That's patience. That's love.

Love is kind. My stepmom is probably the kindest person I know. She'll *pshaw* when she reads this, but it's true. She tended to our dad so lovingly before he passed away, wiping his face, trimming his nails, rising above when he was cranky, always leading him to a happier place. She could have defaulted to being a martyr or becoming depressed or falling into anger. But no, she chose kindness. That's love.

Love does not envy. Girl was over-the-moon-in-love with Boy, or so she thought. It turns out that Boy was the flirty type and Girl got jealous. She felt awful about her jealousy because it didn't fit within this 1 Corinthians 13 "love list." But neither did Boy's provocations to jealousy. (See "love is kind" above.) Love means emotional safety. Girl wasn't safe. So maybe it wasn't love after all.

These stories are about the love between a man and a woman. Later in the New Testament, we'll read about the church being the bride of Christ, so it's no wonder that we regard this kind of love so highly.

But this chapter also speaks of love for humanity. "If I give all I possess to the poor and give over my body to hardship that I may boast, but do not have love, I gain nothing."

"And now these three remain: faith, hope and love. But the greatest of these is love."

Item in the Backpack: Faith, Hope, Love

1 Corinthians 13
(B) Love's Selflessness

Love does not boast. It is not proud. Jim and Prudy adore each other in that wink-across-the-room kind of way. They're fun conversationalists, chatting about current events or opera or kids or whatever. It took me a long time to discover that Prudy had won over seventy-five first places in major races around the United States in her age bracket. In fact, she is the only runner of any age or sex who placed three straight years in the top seven places at the *Boston Marathon*. Prudy doesn't brag, nor is she arrogant.

I've found that as people mature, really mature, they don't need to brag or swagger. They're secure in who they are. They can love without everything having to be about them.

Love is not rude. In the New American Standard version of the Bible, the wording is that love does not act unbecomingly. What does acting unbecomingly look like to you? I think of sarcasm directed toward the "loved" one. Did you know that the word "sarcasm" means "ripped flesh"? Ugh. I would also include merciless teasing, cruelty, put-downs, lying, backstabbing, passive-aggressive behavior, frequent "coming against" rather than choosing to be on the same page, not listening.

Just thinking about this is depressing, so let's visit some examples of acting *becomingly*. Speaking the other's love language, elevating the other privately and in front of others, helping each other, doing activities together…ah, this feels better already. Wouldn't it be a lovely goal to try to outdo each other in the love department?

Love is not self-seeking. Kim and Brian loved each other. As they were driving to the mountains for a lovely day trip, they were in an accident. Kim injured her knee. Brian became a quadriplegic.

But their love endured, and three years later, they got married. Then they went through the process of adopting a little girl from overseas. Kim flew to pick her up, but before she and the baby could return, Brian got sick. They made it to the hospital in time, but due to the infection risk, Brian couldn't see his daughter. A short time later, he died. Kim's love transcended her own desires and needs, but she would be quick to point out how blessed she was as well.

Item in the Backpack: Selflessness

1 Corinthians 13
<u>*(C)* Love's Strength</u>

Love is not easily angered. My friend Paul is not easily angered. He's a retired pediatrician. His wife, Belle, was a nurse. They raised four children of their own and fostered nearly a hundred babies. Many were crack babies, so we're talking many sleepless nights. Belle passed away a few months ago. She had suffered horribly from cancer for nearly two years. They had so looked forward to retirement years filled with family, music, travel, and fun; but now Paul is alone.

Still, he's not easily angered. He's devoted to the Lord. He's sad, yes, but filled with so much quiet love, I just don't think there's any room for anger.

Love keeps no record of wrongs. This verse has been quite instructive to me over the years. See, sometimes I *want* to keep a running tab of wrongs suffered. I want to build my case. I want God and the offending person to understand just how bad things are. You know, keep score.

But God says to not keep a record of wrongs, which keeps things from building up, so I guess he's on to something wise. And then, of course, there's the Golden Rule. I really don't want people to keep a running list of *my* shortcomings.

Love does not delight in evil but rejoices with the truth. True love wants the very best for our loved ones. I think this is particularly poignant when it comes to parenting. We won't concede a single inch if evil is getting near our kids. And nothing makes us happier than when truth and wholeness win the day for them.

Item in the Backpack: Rejoicing

1 Corinthians 13
(D) Love's Completeness

Love always protects, trusts, hopes, and perseveres. My friend Gregg was piloting a plane in 2004. It encountered a severe wind shear upon landing, and Gregg hit the ground, nose gear first, at 130 knots. Over 90 percent of the bones in his body were severely broken, his right foot broken completely off. He's had seventeen surgeries. Ten years later, he summited the treacherous Grand Teton peak with his friend, Gary. Gary is a cancer survivor who lost his son to a hunting accident and a year later, his wife, also to cancer.

These men love Jesus Christ, and no amount of tragedy has deterred that. They have borne more things than most of us will ever bear. They still believe in God's overcoming love. They hope. They endure.

One of Gregg's life verses is Colossians 3:17: "And whatever you do, whether in word or deed, do it all in the name of the Lord Jesus, giving thanks to God the Father through him." Giving thanks. Amazing. Why? Because of love. Gregg knows God loves him. And Gregg loves God.

Love never fails. In the Old Testament book of Job, we read about an encounter between God and Satan. Satan asked God about the immensely blessed, immensely dedicated Job. "Does Job fear God for nothing?" Then, essentially, "Aren't the blessings the reason he's dedicated to you? Touch all he has and surely he'll curse you."

So God permitted it with the caveat that Job would survive. It was horrible, but Job was faithful, and eventually God restored him and increased all he had twofold.

Why did Job stay faithful? Because of love. Job was right about God. "Weeping may stay for the night, but rejoicing comes in the morning" (Ps. 30:5). God allowed Job's testing not out of anger but partly to help *us* know that God is love. And love never fails.

The difficulties of this life are not the end of the story. Life on earth is full of tribulations and tests mixed in with blessings, but at the finishing line, all will be complete and we'll be in the presence of pure love.

"He will wipe every tear from their eyes. There will be no more death or mourning or crying or pain, for the old order of things has passed away." He who was seated on the throne said, "I am making everything new!" Then he said, "Write this down, for these words are trustworthy and true." He said to me: "It is done. I am the Alpha and the Omega, the Beginning and the End. To the thirsty I will give water without cost from the spring of the water of life. Those who are victorious will inherit all this, and I will be their God and they will be my children" (Rev. 21:4–7).

Item in the Backpack: Final Victory

1 Corinthians 14:1–19
Superior Gifts

Chapter 14 begins this way: "Follow the way of love and eagerly desire spiritual gifts, especially prophecy." In the New American Standard version, prophecy is called a superior gift.

Prophecy has two meanings, one being foretelling (prediction) and the other, "forthtelling." The latter is the most common meaning and the one Paul used here. It's a word from God.

Paul made the point that prophecy is for hearers' (and readers') understanding about the things of God. He would rather speak five words with his mind to instruct others than ten thousand words in another tongue, a spiritual tongue not understood by others, unless there is interpretation.

Paul referred to musical instruments in this passage. If they don't produce a distinction of tones, how will that cacophony communicate? Ah, but *with* distinction of tones and a good dose of heart thrown in, the outcome can make people weep. I once sat at a symphony concert beside my son, listening to the Rachmaninoff No. 3. I looked over at him through my tears. It was one of the most glorious moments of my life. He was weeping too.

Like beautiful music, prophecy speaks. It speaks the deep things of God. In a sense, we're all called to speak these things for others' edification, exhortation, and consolation.

Item in the Backpack: Forthtelling

1 Corinthians 14:20–40
Wrestling Matters

Some of the most charismatic churches I know of have women in prominent leadership roles, and yes, they speak in church. So how does that square with the "let women keep silent in church" verse? As I've been saying a lot lately, I don't know. It's a wrestling matter similar to the one in 1 Corinthians 11, where Paul said that women who pray or prophesy in church need to have their heads covered.

It's curious that the love chapter (chapter 13) is in between. Hmmm.

Anyway, in Genesis 32, Jacob was distressed and wrestled with someone (a man? an angel? God himself?) through the night. At daybreak, Jacob wouldn't let him go until he blessed him, which happened. "Then the man said, 'Your name will no longer be Jacob, but Israel, because you have struggled with God and with humans and have overcome'" (Gen. 32:28).

In the Old Testament book of Amos, chapter 7, Amos the herdsman and prophet had quite a conversation with God. A couple of times, "the Lord relented."

Can we speak freely with God? Yes. Wrestle even? Absolutely.

We might wrestle with some things for a lifetime, but I believe that in this era of relativism and even nihilism, there *are* answers. We can wrestle, then go with what seems right according to the *whole counsel of the Bible*. We can ask God to confirm that position or keep our hearts restless. We must be willing to accept God's answer, God's best.

And one thing is clear in this passage regarding the church. "God is not a God of disorder but of peace." And "everything should be done in a fitting and orderly way." In our churches, there's not to be chaos, but we can wrestle, because our goal is peace.

Item in the Backpack: Whole Counsel of the Bible

1 Corinthians 15
Future Reality

This chapter is a matter of death...and life.

1. Because we're in the Adam League (human), we're all going to die.
2. Jesus, however, defeated death when he was resurrected.
3. Because believers are in the Jesus League in addition to the Adam League, we're going to be spiritually alive with him after our physical deaths.
4. There's an aspect of death that is daily. Paul said, "I die every day." We have to die to self in order to live to God. That's where the power is.
5. At the last trumpet, the dead will be raised imperishable.

Now, I don't understand the difference in the resurrection at death and the imperishable quality we'll take on at the last trumpet, but it sounds like a win-win to me. We will be immortal. Death will be swallowed up in victory. "With all this going for us, my dear, dear friends, stand your ground. And don't hold back. Throw yourselves into the work of the Master, confident that nothing you do for him is a waste of time or effort" (1 Cor. 15:58).

There's a saying about overly spiritual people that goes like this: "He's so heavenly-minded, he's no earthly good." But sometimes I wonder if we're missing out by not being heavenly-minded enough. I think Paul was encouraging the Corinthian Christians to live in the reality of resurrection. We're not *yet* resurrected, but that doesn't make it any less true.

Item in the Backpack: Immortality

1 Corinthians 16
Practical Matters

For most of us, the Christian life isn't a constant mountaintop experience, nor is it constant travail. Life just happens. We go to work, raise kids, do laundry. Paul closed this letter to the Corinthians with the common stuff of life, like instructions on handling some financial issues and his upcoming travel plans.

Even though this chapter seems mundane, we can draw a lesson from it. Life with a capital *L* can happen in the everyday stuff of life—doing laundry, dealing with financial matters, etc.

I sometimes slip into negative thoughts, frustration, even anxiety in everyday life; but Paul said, "Be on your guard; stand firm in the faith; be men of courage; be strong. Do everything in love." I believe this holds true for regular days as well as big days.

In Luke 16:10, Jesus said, "Whoever can be trusted with very little can also be trusted with much, and whoever is dishonest with very little will also be dishonest with much." In other words, doing the commonplace well when the stakes are small is training for doing well when the stakes are high. If we can stay positive and manage everyday life, we'll form habits to help us when "walking on water" is required.

And here's another practical matter. We have an adversary. This is likely another reason Paul said to be on guard and stand firm. "*Be alert and of sober mind.* Your enemy the devil prowls around like a roaring lion looking for someone to devour" (1 Pet. 5:8). There are about fifty references to our adversary/the devil/Satan in the Bible. He's a fallen angel, kicked out of heaven. Suffice it to say that he's real, just as real as God himself. He is evil personified.

Christianity is hard. G. K. Chesterton said, "Christianity has not been tried and found wanting; it has been found difficult and not tried." But we can do this. There is a way to follow Christ in good times and bad times, in heavenly matters and practical matters.

Item in the Backpack: Alertness

2 Corinthians 1:1–11
God's Comfort

Here's the bottom line. We're going to suffer unless we're freakishly out of touch. Aristotle said, "To perceive is to suffer," and most of us are pretty perceptive. Today's item in the backpack is "suffering." I hesitated about adding suffering to the backpack, because who wants to carry that around? But since the chances are pretty much 100 percent that you're going to suffer, it's better to be prepared. Think "first aid kit."

Paul started his second letter to the Corinthians talking about comfort. He essentially said, "God comforts us so we can comfort you with the same sort of comforting. The sufferings of Christ are ours in abundance, as is the comfort of Christ."

The curious thing about God's comfort is that it transcends death. Psalm 118:6 says, "The LORD is with me; I will not be afraid. What can mere mortals do to me?"

And Matthew 10:28 says, "Do not be afraid of those who kill the body but cannot kill the soul."

Man's inhumanity to man can be really bad, deadly even, but a person can't kill your soul.

In addition, we often have non-deadly suffering and affliction; and God brings comfort, eventually and always, in this life or in the hereafter. If you're suffering, I pray you'll be comforted, sooner than later. In the meantime, I pray your friends will quietly come alongside you and be with you.

Item in the Backpack: Suffering

2 Corinthians 1:12–24
God's Promises

Years ago, the head football coach at the University of Colorado was given a stellar opportunity to coach at another college. He could have jumped ship. However, a friend asked him if he had signed the

University of Colorado contract, which of course he had. The friend advised him to let his yes be yes, just like God's promises are to us.

He stayed.

Later, he started Promise Keepers, in Colorado. That coach was Bill McCartney. I wonder if things would have lined up the same way had he moved to the other university.

"For no matter how many promises God has made, they are 'Yes' in Christ." God doesn't vacillate. Neither should we.

Integrity was important to Paul. He didn't want to charge for his services. He didn't want to be an imposition. He didn't want the people to believe him to be wishy-washy, intending one thing but doing another (without a great reason). Maybe this was because his pre-Jesus life had been less than godly, so it was now extremely important to him to be a "promise keeper."

Paul wanted to communicate how confident we can be in God's promises. Biblegateway.com reports that there are 5,467 promises in the Bible, each one trustworthy.

Item in the Backpack: Confidence

2 Corinthians 2

<u>Sweet Aroma</u>

Paul had a sensitive side. He spoke of joy, tears of love, forgiving and comforting someone who had caused sorrow, and being a sweet fragrance. Lovely things!

Forgiveness is a shield against the schemes of Satan, and I believe it. Harboring unforgiveness is poisonous. Forgiveness opens up pathways for God to work. Paul advocated for restoration in this passage. Sin has its consequences, but Paul said that the punishment inflicted by the majority was sufficient for this particular person. Enough was enough. (Might excessive punishment also open us up to Satan's schemes?)

I'm not sure we should extrapolate a punishment-and-restoration model from this single situation, but I think it's generally a good idea to err on the side of love.

So back to the fragrance thing. I've always liked this little passage. I *want* the sweet aroma of Christ to be manifested through me. Wouldn't it be a fun exercise to ask people what aroma we "manifest"? Not literally, of course! But more like "What scent comes to mind when you think of me? Floral? Spicy? Stinky?"

I don't think Christ's aroma was always cotton candy sweet. You certainly wouldn't have thought that when he was driving the money changers out of the temple. Plus, he was a carpenter, so that clean, fresh sawdust smell comes to mind, as well as the scent of blood and sweat.

You know that feeling you get when you walk into a place that smells so good, like a bread shop? You take a deep breath. You have a sense of well-being. You might not even be able to identify why you like that place...you just do. That's how I want to manifest. I want people to *want* to be around the Jesus in me.

Item in the Backpack: Fragrance

2 Corinthians 3
<u>Unveiled Faces</u>

"And we, who with unveiled faces all reflect the Lord's glory, are being transformed into his likeness with ever-increasing glory, which comes from the Lord, who is the Spirit."

Those who read the Old Testament without the Christ lens have veils over their eyes. The understanding just isn't there. The Old points to the New. The Old is fulfilled by the New. The Old is incomplete without the New. I suppose it's like reading the first half of a book and stopping there instead of finishing it. But with *un*veiled faces, we can finish it, and in doing so, we can reflect the Lord's glory and be transformed into his image in an *ever*-increasing way with *ever*-increasing glory.

I believe contemplative practices open us up to a better understanding of God's glory. Martin Luther said, "I have so much to do that I shall spend the first three hours in prayer." Prayer and meditation are common traits of mystics, saints, and regular Christians I admire.

Glory is a God-trait, so to understand it, we must spend time with God—contemplating him, meditating on him, abiding with him. Being transformed into his image means becoming more like him. More loving, for example.

Item in the Backpack: Glory

2 Corinthians 4
Unseen Things

As Christ followers, we deal with unseen things.

1. Some unseen (hidden) things are to be shunned. "We have renounced secret and shameful ways." We're to walk in the light.
2. Some unseen (eternal) things are to be embraced. "So we fix our eyes not on what is seen, but on what is unseen, since what is seen is temporary, but what is unseen is eternal."

Paul had an eye on his future (i.e., the unseen things to come). He and his colleagues were often in dire straits—afflicted, perplexed, persecuted, struck down, always carrying about in the body the *dying* of Jesus. How could a person bear that without being completely convinced about the unseen things to come? Paul believed that momentary affliction was producing for them eternal glory *far beyond all comparison*.

Paul *knew*. So did his colleagues. They knew God would raise them (and the believers) to life after death.

Are you convinced of the unseen?

Item in the Backpack: Spiritual Eyes

2 Corinthians 5:1–9
Deep Groanings

Do you ever feel like life on earth is hell? "To live is to suffer, but to survive is to find some meaning in the suffering." You know who said that? Friedrich Nietzsche, famous for coining the phrase "God is dead."

Interesting. Both Paul and Nietzsche suffered massively.

Paul had eyes to see the unseen. He had taken the leap of faith, which changed his whole orientation to life. He knew that suffering was inevitable but temporary. He found meaning in it.

Plus, he had an unseen partner. "Now the one who has fashioned us for this very purpose is God, who has given us the Spirit as a deposit, guaranteeing what is to come." The Holy Spirit is a pledge, sort of like a down payment. The Spirit gives us a glimpse of things awaiting us. And the Spirit is a helper in getting us through this life until we can move on to the next.

But what about Nietzsche? Dr. Vernon Grounds once said, "Truth is sometimes spoken through false teeth." Maybe Nietzsche was on to something. We can only hope that at the very end, Nietzsche found the ultimate meaning.

So maybe we need a new view of suffering. We try to avoid it, but maybe we should seek the *meaning* of it when it happens. Why am I suffering? Is it because of evil on earth? Is it because of something dumb I did? Is there a lesson in it? Is it an opportunity to point people to Jesus? Is it to peel shallow layers off so I can better see the big picture? Is it a precursor to some sort of miracle? Is it to increase my faith or patience or love? Is it to remind me that this mortal life is temporary and heaven awaits? Or to remind me to live in that reality here and now?

Paul preferred heaven to the here and now, but he settled on this—whether here or there, we just want to be pleasing to God.

Item in the Backpack: Meaning

2 Corinthians 5:10–21
Christ's Ambassadors

Paul, as one of God's ambassadors, spoke to the citizens with a "first the bad news, then the good news" message, essentially saying, "You're going to appear before the judgment seat of God and you'll be recompensed for your deeds, good or bad. Christ died for you. We beg you to be reconciled to God."

The good news is verse 17. We first read it way back in entry number 2 of this book. "Therefore, if anyone is in Christ, the new creation has come: The old has gone, the new is here!"

Paul had spoken stern words to the Corinthians, but then inserted some diplomacy like a good ambassador, essentially saying, "Pay attention! All people will be judged, but can't you see that believers are new creatures?"

A new creature

- doesn't strive for perfection. He/she surrenders, or "let's go and let's God," as the saying goes.
- doesn't carry around the past. He/she surrenders to God's forgiveness.
- doesn't worry about the future. He/she surrenders to God's love and sovereignty.

In short, a new creature is healthy, whole, forgiven, reconciled to God, growing, and full of hope. Not yet perfect, but on the path.

Item in the Backpack: Newness

2 Corinthians 6
<u>Big Differences</u>

This passage is full of "but alsos." Yes, we experience beatings *but also* the power of God. Yes, there is dishonor *but also* glory. Yes, we're regarded as deceivers *but also* as true. Yes, we're sorrowful *but also* rejoicing. Yes, we have nothing *but also* possess all things.

I guess you could say Paul was an eternal optimist. Most people would falter under beatings, imprisonments, and hunger; but Paul focused on those two little words—"but also." His gaze was in the direction of the prize. He was different that way.

We can take a lesson. We'll face difficult things *but also* glorious things. We just need to keep the latter in sight as we do life.

In verses 14–15, Paul segued to another big difference between believers and nonbelievers: "Do not be yoked together with unbelievers. For what do righteousness and wickedness have in common? Or what fellowship can light have with darkness? What harmony is there between Christ and Belial? Or what does a believer have in common with an unbeliever?"(Belial was a demon considered to be the chief of all the devils.)

Paul cited Isaiah 52:11 with the words "Be separate." The difference between believers and nonbelievers may or may not be evident at first, but believers exist in a different realm. Jesus said in John 18 that his kingdom isn't of this realm. We're in the world but not of the world. We're not better than, just different from.

If we as Christians don't experience big differences between ourselves and nonbelievers, perhaps we should examine our lives. We exist in a different spiritual space. Keeping our eyes on the prize will help us through the downside of feeling different.

Item in the Backpack: Differentness

2 Corinthians 7
<u>Godly Sorrow</u>

Sometimes we have to discipline our children, and it tears us up inside. We don't want to cause them sorrow, but without it, their fate could be far worse. We wouldn't spare our kids that kind of sorrow even though it's gut-wrenching, and neither does God with his kids…us.

"Distress that drives us to God…turns us around. It gets us back in the way of salvation. We never regret that kind of pain. But those who let distress drive them away from God are full of regrets, end up on a deathbed of regrets" (2 Cor. 7:10, *The Message*).

Along the way, through God's discipline, we learn to repent. Repentance is turning 180 degrees away from our wrongdoing. Paul felt bad about his "parental" role with the Corinthians, but he knew it was necessary. Short-term pain, long-term gain.

So far, 2 Corinthians has been filled with things we don't like to think about—groanings, sufferings, afflictions, and sorrow—but doing a read through of the entire New Testament means we can't skip over unfun parts. Let's just try to find the gold in all that ore.

As we go through godly sorrow, let's seek the nuggets—the messages, the reasons, the outcomes. Paul pointed these things out to the Corinthians. "See what this godly sorrow has produced in you!" Things like zeal and the avenging of wrong.

I've never heard of a hero's journey that didn't include groanings and sufferings and afflictions and sorrow. Something to overcome. Something to learn and master. As Christians, our mastery comes through surrender. The question is, do we want the journey of an entitled, undisciplined soul or that of a godly hero?

Item in the Backpack: Learning

2 Corinthians 8
Equal Sacrifice

Basically, this chapter is about money. We can spiritualize it, but when it comes down to it, yeah, it's about money. Paul told the Corinthian Christians about the generosity of the Macedonian Christians. Their poverty overflowed in the wealth of their liberality. The Macedonian church wasn't wealthy, but the people wanted to participate in the support of the saints.

I love that.

Then Paul told the Corinthians to abound in the gracious work also, which sounds like a big ol' guilt trip…unless there's an understanding of giving.

Giving is good for us. It gets us out of our longing-to-acquire mind-set. Paul was stern with the Corinthians but seemed fond of them. He wanted them to have an experience equal to that of the Macedonians. "Not equal giving, but equal sacrifice."

As you may know, earlier in my life, I was the executive director of two ministries—one local and one global. A main task of a director is to raise funds, and that is *not* naturally my favorite thing to do. But Paul, in this passage, was wearing his fundraiser hat. Years ago, I learned fundraising lessons from him.

Here's the deal. Fundraising, as it turns out, is spiritual, particularly if the cause is for Christ's work. When we give, we grow. Sure, the people served through the ministry benefit, but it's a partnership of sorts. The givers benefit too.

When I sit in church, I look around and realize I helped build that church building. Lives are transformed there, so when that Capital Campaign team asked for money all those years ago, they did me a favor.

Item in the Backpack: Giving

2 Corinthians 9
Cheerful Giving

"Remember: A stingy planter gets a stingy crop; a lavish planter gets a lavish crop. I want each of you to take plenty of time to think it over, and make up your own mind what you will give. That will protect you against sob stories and arm-twisting. God loves it when the giver delights in the giving. God can pour on the blessings in astonishing ways so that you're ready for anything and everything, more than just ready to do what needs to be done. As one psalmist puts it, He throws caution to the winds, giving to the needy in reckless abandon. His right-living, right-giving ways never run out, never wear out" (2 Cor. 9:6–9, *The Message*).

I know people who give way beyond the 2.5 percent of income currently being given by American Christians. These folks even give way beyond the tithe (10 percent) taught in the scriptures. And they're not millionaires in return. But wait, maybe they are. How would I know? They just keep giving. The ones I'm thinking of are happy people—rich people in so many ways. Unencumbered. Free. Purpose-filled. Excited. Cheerful. Paul didn't want the Corinthians to miss that.

Item in the Backpack: Cheerfulness

2 Corinthians 10
Battle Plans

There are some seriously bad fortresses out there. Paul touched on a few—stray thoughts, disobedience, and boastful arrogance. Detractors were causing Paul and his mission a lot of trouble, so he reminded the Corinthians to use divine weapons against bad fortresses.

Notice how many war metaphors he used in this passage. It was time for battle tactics. "For though we live in the world, we do not *wage war* as the world does. The *weapons* we fight with are not the weapons of the world. On the contrary, they have divine power to *demolish strongholds*. We demolish arguments and every pretension that sets itself up against the knowledge of God, and we *take captive* every thought to make it obedient to Christ."

Are there any bad fortresses in your life? Is it time for spiritual warfare? Fortresses can be strongholds, like addictions or destructive thoughts. Things that control us. Things that can rarely be changed by trying harder. Things that demand all-out war.

Such internal things seem benign compared to racism, terrorism, abuse, and such; but maybe Paul was cutting to the source. Wrong thoughts and self-aggrandizement pave the way for racism, terrorism, and abuse. It's important to do war with the internal to *prevent* external harm to others. And our very souls are worth healing from addictions and other strongholds.

In our country, out-of-control egos are everywhere. We've seen boasting, self-commending, racism, sexism, and so much more. Those egos are diametrically opposed to the mental health and humility taught in the scriptures. So maybe Paul was making the point that such fortresses are so strong and wrong that they require spiritual weapons. We'll cover spiritual warfare more in Ephesians 6.

Item in the Backpack: Spiritual Warfare

2 Corinthians 11
<u>Persistent Paul</u>

Paul was mad, frustrated, and jealous, aka human. The charlatans had come to town to "preach." They were preaching an off-kilter message and deceiving people. And weirdly but not surprisingly, the people were licking it up! *The Message* says it like this: "You have such admirable tolerance for impostors who rob your freedom, rip you off, steal you blind, put you down—even slap your face! I shouldn't admit it to you, but our stomachs aren't strong enough to tolerate that kind of stuff" (vv. 19–20).

Have you ever tried to stay the course and do the right thing… and watch glitzier people pass you by on their way to fame? Grr, I hate that. And yes, you are seeing my humanity.

Paul dealt with it by talking like a fool. "Hey, if you, being so wise, bear with the foolish gladly," then I'll just act stupid, and maybe you'll listen since you listen to fools anyway. (Ugh, the frustration.)

The beauty of this chapter is that it's okay to feel angry and frustrated and insecure. We shouldn't stop short of our emotions, calling them un-Christlike. We should call 'em what they are and let God *use* them. Paul was watching the people he loved being led astray. He was *mad.* And that's a good thing. He was watching the boasters edge ahead, so he just went with it. "If I must boast, I will boast of the things that show my weakness."

Paul, however, didn't step aside and let the charlatans win. He fought for the people he loved. Yes, he was unskilled in speech, but he made up for it with sacrifice. This is a great lesson for me. Don't step aside and let the charlatans win. Fight!

P. S. I love the ending of this chapter. Paul essentially said, "And BTW, the ethnarch in Damascus wanted to seize me, but I was let down in a basket through a window in the wall and escaped."

Item in the Backpack: Embrace of our Humanity

2 Corinthians 12
<u>Paul's Thorn</u>

I have a feeling that Paul, before his encounter with God, was quite prideful. I hope that's not unfair. He just talked about boasting a lot. But in this chapter, he said this about bragging: "But I refrain, so no one will think more of me than is warranted by what I do or say."

Here's what I gain from this. Being appropriately happy with yourself in your Christ Life is a good thing. We're not to be doormats, but excessive boasting, *especially* when you're inflating the truth, is not a good thing. Boasting in your weakness is safe and healthy.

If my theory is true, that Paul had a propensity for pride, then God dealt with him. He allowed a thorn in the flesh. Some say it was likely his speech issue.

I once read an article about supermodels. They're so beautiful (especially when airbrushed), and therein lies the issue. They *are* airbrushed. All of them could cite an imperfection—hair that's too thin, thighs that are too big. Nobody's perfect. Nobody needs to get carried away with bragging.

Paul prayed three times that the thorn be removed, but God said nope. "My grace is sufficient for you, for my power is made perfect in weakness." (God sometimes says no.)

And Paul said okay. He didn't balk and pout. He accepted God's no and found the meaning in it. Here are verses 7–10 in *The Message*:

> Because of the extravagance of those revelations, and so I wouldn't get a big head, I was given the gift of a handicap to keep me in constant touch with my limitations. Satan's angel did his best to get me down; what he in fact did was push me to my knees. No danger then of walking around high and mighty! At first I didn't think of it as a gift, and begged God to remove it. Three times I did that, and then he told me, My grace is enough; it's all you need. My strength comes into its own in your weakness. Once I heard that, I was glad to let it happen. I quit focusing on the handicap and began appreciating the gift. It was a case of Christ's strength moving in on my weakness. Now I take limitations in stride, and with good cheer, these limitations that cut me down to size—abuse, accidents, opposition, bad breaks. I just let Christ take over! And so the weaker I get, the stronger I become.

This is so profound.

How does this relate to us? Well, is your life perfect? Mine is not. Do I go to God with my troubles every morning? Yes. Is he at work on them? Yes. Might he say no to me at times? Um, yes. If that would make me strong. God is *way* into the greater good. So the moral of the story is that my weaknesses can make me resentful and ineffective or they can make me strong. I get to choose my attitude.

Item in the Backpack: Acceptance of our Weaknesses

2 Corinthians 13
The Test

Paul said to test yourselves to see if you are in the faith. So what *is* the test?

I think it's this twofold question. "Do you understand that (a) you are weak and (b) God is strong?"

Paul had just finished a lengthy rant about boasting, so maybe some in his audience thought (a) they were strong and (b) God was weak.

Do you pass the test? Do you know people who would fail the test?

I'm well aware of my weaknesses in contrast to God's strength. A prerequisite for becoming a Christian is awareness of one's own sin.

We can tell others about the Christ Life and invite them to it, but at some point, we need to accept their responses. Paul was persistent because some had strayed (which broke his heart), but in the end, he gave them encouragement and a blessing. He knew they had all the information they needed, which included an always-open invitation.

Item in the Backpack: Outreach

Galatians 1
Paul's Reputation

Galatia was part of the Roman Empire along with Rome and Corinth. Rome was in Italy; Corinth was in the province of Achaia, in modern Greece. The Galatian churches were scattered in the province of Galatia, in modern Turkey. It was heavily populated by the Celts and Gauls, thus its name.

Paul started his epistle to the Galatians by defending his ministry and filling in some details. He had been "extremely zealous for his ancestral traditions," which puts it mildly. He had tried to *destroy* the church. But God met him on the Damascus road and changed his life. Paul put it this way: "He was pleased to reveal his Son in me."

After that experience, he went to Arabia, then three years later to Jerusalem, and later to Syria and Cilicia. In verse 1 of the next chapter, we'll see how after an interval of fourteen years, he returned to Jerusalem. Suffice it to say that he didn't immediately launch into evangelistic work.

However, his reviews preceded him. People kept hearing that the guy who had once persecuted them was now preaching the faith he had tried to destroy.

Think Hitler converting to Judaism. Incredulous. Maybe he needed fourteen years under his belt to prove the fortitude of his conversion.

This makes me think about reputation. What do people say about me? I know what they say *to* me. I've read people's reviews of my books. I get likes on Facebook! But what would people say about my walk with God? What's my spiritual reputation?

Like Paul, do people glorify God because of me?

Item in the Backpack: Good Reputation

Galatians 2:1–10
Beautiful Differences

Years ago, I found a fantastic house to buy. It was a refinished vintage Denver Square with polished-to-a-sheen woodwork throughout, a second-floor deck, a lovely kitchen, and updated systems. It was in a 90 percent black neighborhood…and we're white. So I decided to visit the neighbor next door to ask her about my situation. I knocked on her door, introduced myself, and asked her what she thought about having a white neighbor. It was awkward, but she was gracious and said, "Hey, as long as you keep your yard looking nice, it's fine with me."

That story reminds me of this passage. Paul was called to preach to the Gentiles, which was a diversion from the original outreach of going to the Jews. And there was that issue about circumcision. Should the Gentile converts be circumcised like the Jews? It was awkward. So, with fear and trepidation, he visited the pillars of the church. Would he be accepted?

Drumroll…

Yes! They extended the right hand of fellowship to him. It was awkward, but they were gracious and said, "Hey, as long as you remember the poor, it's fine with us."

Some things are so important. Keeping our yards looking nice. Remembering the poor. Treating each other with deep respect.

Which reminds me of another story. A friend of mine tells about watching her husband iron his shirt. He was using the big end of the ironing board. She pointed out that he's supposed to use the small end. Then he pointed out the merits of the big end. They laughed and realized that neither end was wrong, just different.

Ah, equality. How often is one side or the other not wrong, just different?

Item in the Backpack: High Regard for Others

Galatians 2:11–21
<u>Crucified People</u>

"If I rebuild what I destroyed, then I really would be a lawbreaker." Paul had, in a sense, destroyed prejudice and inequality between the Jewish and Gentile believers. If he had allowed Cephas and the other leaders to revert back without calling them out, he would have been rebuilding what he had once destroyed.

And he didn't mince words. "When Cephas came to Antioch, I opposed him to his face, because he stood condemned."

Yikes.

I wonder why Peter (Cephas) and Barnabas reverted back. I find that so strange, but they were human. Maybe they felt peer pressure from the circumcised believers or just subconsciously slipped back to the familiar.

Do we ever do that? It seems that every people group thinks it's better than some other group. And there's even stratification within each group!

Paul didn't preach an "I have a dream" sermon. He just said something like the ground being level at the foot of the cross. It's about the man who was crucified for us. And if we're believers, *we* have been crucified with him. We're not our own. We have been bought with a price.

Item in the Backpack: Death to Old Thinking

Galatians 3
<u>Faith Leaping</u>

Yesterday, I had one of *those* conversations with a friend who said, "I won't believe unless you can prove the existence of God to me." I talked about how I'll go to the death for love and God is love, but my friend said, "How do you know God is love? Prove it." I talked about life change in mutual acquaintances, but my friend said, "So? That could be attributed to other things." I mentioned several things from my own life, but not one could prove God.

So I got up and started walking off with the statement "I can't prove it." I felt like the blind man in John 9. People were pressuring him about the credentials of the man who had healed him, and he essentially said, "I don't know. All I know is that once I was blind, but now I can see." (I suppose my friend might pay attention if I had been healed from blindness, but I haven't.)

Faith is so unproveable. It's the assurance of things hoped for, the conviction of things not seen (Heb. 11:1).

My friend would really be rolling his eyes at that definition. But here's what I've been thinking about since yesterday. Skydiving. A skydiver wouldn't take the leap of faith unless he or she trusted the process. I think that's as close as I can come to a picture of faith.

Here are a few nuggets about faith from Galatians 3:

a. Faith brought righteousness.
b. Faith unlocked the promise to Abraham.
c. Faith wipes out the law curse.
d. Faith does what the law couldn't do.

Faith makes us children of God.

And here are verses 6–14 from *The Message*. It's a bit long, but too good to pass up.

> He [Abraham] believed God, and that act of belief was turned into a life that was right with God. Is it not obvious to you that persons who put their trust in Christ (not persons who put their trust in the law!) are like Abraham: children of faith? It was all laid out beforehand in Scripture that God would set things right with non-Jews by *faith*. Scripture anticipated this in the promise to Abraham: "All nations will be blessed in you." So those now who live by faith are blessed along with Abraham, who lived by faith—this is no new doctrine! And that means that anyone who tries to live by his own effort, independent of God,

> is doomed to failure. Scripture backs this up: "Utterly cursed is every person who fails to carry out every detail written in the Book of the law."
>
> The obvious impossibility of carrying out such a moral program should make it plain that no one can sustain a relationship with God that way. The person who lives in right relationship with God does it by embracing what God arranges for him. Doing things for God is the opposite of entering into what God does for you. Habakkuk had it right: "The person who believes God, is set right by God—and that's the real life." Rule-keeping does not naturally evolve into living by faith, but only perpetuates itself in more and more rule-keeping, a fact observed in Scripture: "The one who does these things [rule-keeping] continues to live by them."
>
> Christ redeemed us from that self-defeating, cursed life by absorbing it completely into himself. Do you remember the Scripture that says, "Cursed is everyone who hangs on a tree"? That is what happened when Jesus was nailed to the cross: He became a curse, and at the same time dissolved the curse. And now, because of that, the air is cleared and we can see that Abraham's blessing is present and available for non-Jews too. We are *all* able to receive God's life, his Spirit, in and with us by believing—just the way Abraham received it."

Okay, I've taken the leap and I'm glad I did, although I can't prove why. (Can skydivers?)

Item in the Backpack: Leap of Faith

Galatians 4:1–20
God's Kids

The last verse of chapter 3 says that if you belong to Christ, you're an heir. In fact, you're a fellow heir with Jesus himself. Like…a sibling. Mind-boggling. "The Spirit himself testifies with our spirit that we are God's children. Now if we are children, then we are heirs—heirs of God and co-heirs with Christ, if indeed we share in his sufferings in order that we may also share in his glory" (Rom. 8:16–17). People born pre-Christ were like child heirs (i.e., slaves). Under guardianship. They were under the Law. Even Jesus's mother was under the Law. All were in bondage to the Law and the elemental things of the world.

So what about those of us born post-Christ? We can stay stuck in bondage and try to be good enough for God, or we can opt for adoption. That's the way to become a child of God, fully vested as an heir.

If you're a believer in Christ, do you feel chosen? Special? Wanted? Worth dying for? Worthy of a massive inheritance?

I don't always, but I can muster a thank-you, even on days I feel unlovable. Rather than reverting back to the weak and worthless elemental things, we can live out *strong and worthwhile* things and, in that way, say thanks.

It's so easy to fall back, but as God's kids, we have the power to be better than that.

Item in the Backpack: Adoption

Galatians 4:21–31
Free People

I am a barren woman. I did not bear my children. I adopted them.

Now fast forward thirty-five years. I'm writing this two days before my son's wedding. I've been busy with family gatherings and errands and a hundred cheek kisses and a thousand details. It's now midnight, and I'm weary, but that's not stopping me from the beautiful task of pondering these things in my heart. My children are children of the promise. I am a free woman.

Back a couple thousand years ago, being barren was like being cursed. Bearing children was the pinnacle of life, yet I've never experienced the flicker of life in my belly. Have I missed the pinnacle of life?

Absolutely not. My children were conceived in my heart, where the flickers occurred. They grew through happy-times galore and in-spite-of-mistakes galore. Somehow, together, we've made it this far, and it's good. Messy, but *really* good.

So I can identify with the barren woman and her children of promise in this passage. In other words, it's not about being born into a Jewish family rather than a Muslim family or coming into a family by birth or adoption or via privilege or poverty or whatever. It's spiritual. The playing field is level. Every human on the planet faces the *exact same* scenario (i.e., that becoming a child of God is by adoption).

So women who can bear children, take heart! Women who can adopt children, take heart! Women who are childless, take heart! Men who can never bear children in the first place, take heart! Be free! Let God be your Father...and your Mother. May he give you a child in some form, if that's what your heart desires. God has the master equation for cutting through our circumstances and giving us what we need for a really good life.

It might look single and childless or married with a houseful of kids. It might look like a niece or nephew or a young person to mentor or sponsor. Maybe our challenge is to discover the children God is putting right in front of us.

Item in the Backpack: Discovery

Galatians 5:1–18
<u>Power Walking</u>

Galatians 5:1 says this in *The Message*: "Christ has set us free to live a free life. So take your stand! Never again let anyone put a har-

ness of slavery on you." What is your harness of slavery? One of mine is an incessant default to enabling, taking on responsibility that's not mine to own. You know... codependency. I just seem to jump right back into that harness.

God's remedy? Walking. (Stay tuned.)

"Harness of slavery" is an apt visual. I think of iron chains on the ankles of slaves and inmates, memory chains in the souls of the traumatized, habit chains in the synapses of people like me.

Hard to break. In fact, some of those harnesses might take a lifetime to break, but we have a lifetime. After all, it was for freedom that Christ set us free.

Do you ever have moments of victory though? Progress on the prison tunnel that leads to freedom? I think this passage is saying, "Don't backfill that progress! Keep going. You were running well. Who hindered you from obeying the truth? *Walk by the Spirit and you'll not carry out the desire of the flesh.*"

It takes all-out battle to tackle my propensity for codependency. My tactics are to tell myself the truth, use healthy psychology, hang out with healthy people, and create new habits. To walk by the things God has taught me to do and to use the Spirit as my walking stick.

But here's the hard part. I always thought of codependency as godly—selfless, sacrificial, other-oriented. God's had his work cut out for him to change me, but he hasn't let me stay stuck. If we let God do his Spirit work in us, we can eventually shift. And over the past ten years or so, that harness no longer holds nearly as much power over me as it once did.

What does walking by the Spirit look like to you?

Item in the Backpack: Walking Stick

Galatians 5:19–21, 24–26
<u>Dirty Deeds</u>

This Deeds of the Flesh list is not a happy one. Let's dissect it here and dedicate the "Fruit of the Spirit" list to the next entry.

The dirty deeds include sexual immorality, impure thoughts/actions, hedonism, prioritizing stuff over God, dabbling in the dark side, hatred, strife, jealousy, angry outbursts (notice that anger itself isn't necessarily a dirty deed), dysfunctional lack of cooperation with others, drunken revelry, and, if you throw in verse 26, boasting.

Notice that the passage doesn't suggest that those who have *ever done* such things shall not inherit the kingdom of God. It says that those who *practice* such things shall not inherit the kingdom of God. Practice implies "intentional pursuit in order to become proficient." God doesn't want us to intentionally pursue the dirty deeds so we can become proficient at them.

In remedy, God says to walk by the Spirit. To grab that walking stick if we're tempted to get dirty. There's even mention of crucifying our passions and desires.

Think about these words from the hymn "Come Thou Fount of Every Blessing." "Prone to wander, Lord I feel it, prone to leave the God I love. Here's my heart, oh, take and seal it, seal it for thy courts above." In other words, sometimes fleeing the temptations of the dark side takes all-out war.

We can practice fleeing and saying no when the stakes are small, like saying no to that second cookie. Then when the stakes are big, like saying no to impurity, we'll be better equipped. Practice, practice, practice.

Here's a homework assignment. Practice saying no to a dirty deed, small or large, today. I will too.

Item in the Backpack: Practice

Galatians 5:22–23
Juicy Fruit

Fruit grows by being connected to the tree, vine, or plant. *Only* by being connected. A piece of fruit can't grow without a source. It's the same with the fruit of the Spirit. We can't strain hard to produce fruit apart from our source. We can't fake fruit. We can't be practicing the dirty deeds and still yield love, joy, peace, patience, kindness, goodness, faithfulness, gentleness, self-control. Dirty deeds and self-control are mutually exclusive.

Billy Graham once said, "Mountaintops are for views and inspiration, but fruit is grown in the valleys." So yeah, if we're willing to do some valley time, we can bear fruit.

Here are a few quotes/scriptures about each piece of fruit.

Love: "Hatred paralyzes life; love releases it. Hatred confuses life; love harmonizes it. Hatred darkens life; love illuminates it" (Martin Luther King Jr.).

Joy: "I sometimes wonder whether all pleasures are not substitutes for Joy" (C. S. Lewis).

Peace: "A heart at peace gives life to the body, but envy rots the bones" (Prov. 14:30).

Patience: "Waiting in prayer is a disciplined refusal to act before God acts" (Eugene Peterson).

Kindness: "But he's already made it plain how to live, what to do, what GOD is looking for in men and women. It's quite simple: Do what is fair and just to your neighbor, be compassionate and loyal in your love, and don't take yourself too seriously—take God seriously"(Mic. 6:8, *The Message*).

Goodness: "Do your little bit of good where you are; it's those little bits of good put together that overwhelm the world" (Desmond Tutu).

Faithfulness: "You can trust us to stick to you through thick and thin—to the bitter end. And you can trust us to keep any secret of yours—closer than you yourself keep it. But you cannot trust us to let you face trouble alone" (J. R. R. Tolkien in *The Fellowship of the Ring*).

Gentleness: "I choose to be gentle. If I raise my voice may it be only in praise. If I clench my fist, may it be only in prayer. If I make a demand, may it be only of myself" (Max Lucado).

Self-Control: "You can control yourself if you really want to. I'll tell you how I know...if you were in a full-fledged emotional temper tantrum in your house and I knocked on your front door...Come on! Let me tell you what, you would get control of yourself, and it would only take a few seconds" (Joyce Meyer).

Item in the Backpack: Fruit

Galatians 6
Self Work

Maturity is being able to determine "Whose issue is this?" and taking responsibility for your own work. Sometimes the lines are fuzzy between one's own work and that of others, but Paul ends his letter to the Galatians with an "own your own stuff" message.

Accordingly, the following things are within one's own control. To

> restore a trespasser gently,
> look to yourself less you be tempted,
> bear one another's burdens,
> be humble,
> examine your own work,
> not boast,
> bear your own load,
> reap what you sow,
> not lose heart or grow weary,
> do good to all, especially fellow believers,
> know that it's not about the externals, and
> know that you're a new creation.

We're responsible for our decisions, actions, self work. We're not to procrastinate or brag or even use weariness as an excuse. You can figure out Paul's mind-set here. He wasn't saying to be superhuman, like beyond the need for rest. He just seemed tired of human frailty. Here's Galatians 6:17 in *The Message*: "Quite frankly, I don't want to be bothered anymore by these disputes. I have far more important things to do—the serious living of this faith. I bear in my body scars from my service to Jesus."

In short, "Grow up. Own your stuff. Get over petty issues. We've got work to do. And I don't know about you, but I'm only going to boast in the cross of Christ. The world's been crucified to me anyway, and I to the world."

That was Paul's reality, and he desperately wanted the same for us, even though it takes a lot of depth to give oneself to crucifixion that way. We have to believe it's worth it.

Surrender is the height of self work.

Item in the Backpack: Self Work

Ephesians 1:1–12
<u>Mystery Revealed</u>

We get a breath of fresh air in Ephesians 1. Galatians ended with a "get with the program" message. Ephesians starts with a "because you're on the winning side" message.

In this passage, Paul listed some traits of redemption for the Ephesian saints (and for us as believers). We have been blessed with every spiritual blessing in the heavenly places. God has chosen us, predestined us, adopted us. He has freely bestowed grace on us, forgiven us, and provided us with an inheritance. He has made known the mystery of his will to us (which is flat-out remarkable).

What *is* the mystery of God's will? The word "mystery" is used twenty times in the New Testament (NIV), seven of those times in this little book of Ephesians. In verse 10, he reveals the mystery.

It's to bring unity to all things in heaven and on earth under Christ.

Frankly though, I still have a couple of questions, details that are still mysteries to me. One is the notion of election and predestination, that God chose us in him before the creation of the world and predestined us for adoption. The second is that he chose us to be holy and blameless in his sight (vv. 4–5).

I don't always feel holy and blameless...and to think that God knew me and chose me before he even created the world? Mind-boggling.

But as Billy Graham said, "I've read the last page of the Bible. It's all going to turn out all right." The mystery has already been revealed, but we're still operating somewhere in the middle pages of the book. There are still depths to plumb, experiences to experience.

In short, the war has already been won but our task is to stay in the battle. Or in book speak, the mystery has already been solved but our task is to keep reading.

Item in the Backpack: Knowledge

Ephesians 1:13–23
News Report

In musing on this passage, I noticed I had circled the word "heard" in my Bible (v. 15). There are magnificent phrases in the passage, like "the riches of the glory of his inheritance" and "the surpassing greatness of his power," but I circled one little word, "heard."

Paul had heard of the Ephesian Christians' faith and love. I wonder what Paul or better yet, Jesus, has heard about my church, my Christian friends, *me*?

Since Paul had gotten good reports about the Ephesian Christians, he shared his prayer with them. Here's a condensed version of it from *The Message*, vv. 16–23:

> I couldn't stop thanking God for you...but I do more than thank. I ask (God) to make you intelligent and discerning in knowing him personally, your eyes focused and clear, so that you can see exactly what it is he is calling you to do, grasp the immensity of this glorious way of life he has for his followers, oh, the utter extravagance of his work in us who trust him—endless energy, boundless strength! All this energy issues from Christ: God raised him from death and set him on a throne in deep heaven, in charge of running the universe, everything from galaxies to govern-

> ments, no name and no power exempt from his rule. And not just for the time being, but *forever.* He is in charge of it all, has the final word on everything. At the center of all this, Christ rules the church. The church, you see, is not peripheral to the world; the world is peripheral to the church. The church is Christ's body, in which he speaks and acts, by which he fills everything with his presence.

Um, wow. Paul had fiery passion about this message. Some people operate out of emotion and passion; others, out of intellectual assent. Either way, it's good to examine how we're doing in the faith and love department from time to time. We want to be people of character.

Item in the Backpack: Character

Ephesians 2:1–7
<u>New Life</u>

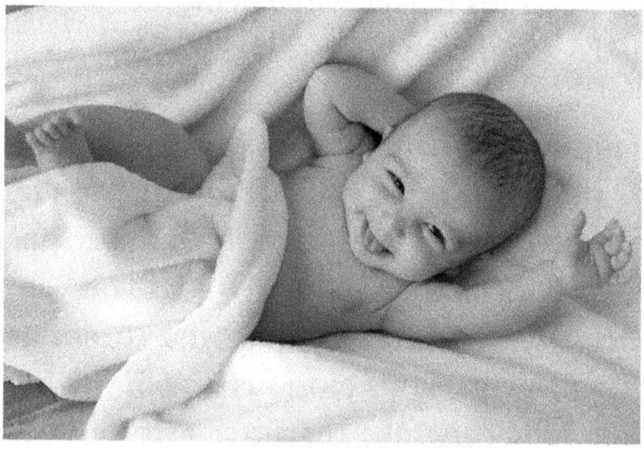

When a person is born physically, everybody knows. There's hospital buzz, the newborn's cry, and massive joy at the sight of that little wrinkly miracle. The baby has arrived! Everything is different now. And later, hopefully many, many years later, the physical body dies.

Life, then death.

With spiritual life, however, the order is reversed. "Because of his great love for us, God, who is rich in mercy, made us alive with Christ even when we were dead in transgressions."

Death, then life.

What are the markers of spiritual birth? For a lot of us, they're minor compared to the arrival of a baby. I accepted Christ when I was six. I prayed the prayer and felt happy inside. Then we drove home from church, and life went on.

What does spiritual birth even mean? "How can someone be born when they are old?" Nicodemus asked. "Surely they cannot enter a second time into their mother's womb to be born!"(John 3:4).

Here's a visual that helps me. Maybe "being made alive in Christ" is like becoming a naturalized citizen in a new country as a refugee from a country where you would die if you stayed. There may or may not be fanfare, but positionally, you're different. You have new privileges and responsibilities, plus the power of that country's government behind you. But after that naturalization ceremony, you just drive home, and life goes on.

Over time, however, everything is different. Being a citizen of the country (kingdom) of God means listening to God himself as the leader, turning from the old and dead ways, and adapting to his ways, which are the ways of new life and new love. Positionally changed in an instant; experientially changed over a lifetime. And according to verse 7, also for the ages to come.

Item in the Backpack: New Life

Ephesians 2:8–22
His Handiwork

The difference between Christians and humanists is that Christians are God's workmanship. Humanists feel they are their own workmanship. That's quite a distinction, because I know some pretty wonderful humanists. But God said that our transformation is *his* gift, not a result of *our* works.

He must want us to transcend our humanity.

My nephew is a woodcarver. He creates spoons—all beautiful, all different. Those spoons are his handiwork. Maybe God sees the "spoon" in each of us while we're still slabs of wood. Verse 10 says that "we are God's handiwork, created in Christ Jesus to do good works, which God prepared in advance for us to do."

What do you think God sees in you? What good works does he want you to do? The handiwork theme continues in verses 11–22, about the building Carpenter God is constructing. It's made up of both Jews and Gentiles. It's full of peace. It has kicked out enmity—hostility, hatred, and ill will. Its foundation has been built on the apostles and prophets. Its cornerstone is Jesus. It's growing into a holy place.

If we are believers, we are God's handiwork, both individually and collectively.

What do you think God sees in your community of believers? What good works does he want you, collectively, to do?

I think he wants us, collectively, to transcend our humanity as well. To not fall prey to petty arguments. To kick out hatred and ill will. To figure out our tasks based on his blueprints. To live out our calling as God's creations or if you will, his spoons.

Item in the Backpack: Willingness

Ephesians 3
Filled Up

There's that word "mystery" again! This mystery is that the Gentiles are fellow heirs and fellow partakers in the body of Christ, should they accept the invitation.

Think women being allowed to vote…on steroids.

And Paul seemed ecstatic about it. He asked God for several things on their behalf—that they would be strengthened inwardly, that they would be able to comprehend the depth of Christ's love, and that they would be filled up to all the fullness of God.

What does it mean to be filled up to all the fullness of God? When I first started musing on this, I assumed that filling the bucket meant filling it with *blessings*. Yay! Bring 'em on! And maybe that's right, but I sense there's more to the fullness of God than blessings. Stuff like courage, insight, an overcoming spirit, endurance, keen awareness of others' needs, wisdom, power, and spiritual gifts, to name a few. Supernatural things.

Paul certainly needed his bucket-full. His life was hard. Then he died by decapitation. He needed the supernatural to endure and thrive in life, much less at his death.

So do we. Fortunately, through faith we can approach God with freedom and confidence (v. 12), and that makes all the difference between a filled life and an empty life.

Item in the Backpack: Bucket

Ephesians 4:1–16
<u>Worthy Walking</u>

Remember the graphics in the "Why I Believe" section of my introduction? Here's a recap.

Hinduism: There are infinite manifestations of God. (Arrows pointing in all directions)

New Age: We ourselves are God. (Arrows following each other in a circle)

Buddhism: There is no God. (No arrows—just a circle with a line through it)

Islam: There is one powerful, transcendent, strict God. (Arrow pointing up)

Christianity: There is one God and he is loving and personal. (An arrow pointing down and one meeting it pointing up)

I'm drawn to that "loving and personal" part. To me, this whole passage fits the down-arrow and up-arrow picture. The down arrow is God drawing us, calling us, loving us. The up arrow is us saying yes and walking the walk in response.

Paul implored us to walk in a manner worthy of our calling. We're to be humble, gentle, patient, tolerant, unified in the Spirit, bonded in peace, full of grace, operating within our part for the sake of the whole, mature, truthful, loving, and growing.

Verses 4–10 reiterate that God is everything—God and Father of all, over all, through all, in all. Since God is everything and is loving, we can respond by walking in that remarkable reality.

Item in the Backpack: Godly Traits

Ephesians 4:17–32
<u>Life Lists</u>

This passage has two parts—an "old life" list (vv. 17–22) and a "new life" list (vv. 23–32).

List 1: futile of mind, dark of understanding, excluded from the life of God, ignorant, hard of heart, callous, given over to sensuality, impure, greedy, and corrupted by the lusts of deceit

List 2: truthful, appropriately angry when the situation calls for anger (but without sin), not prone to getting close enough to evil to give the devil opportunity, not stealing, performing good work, speaking wholesome words, not grieving the Spirit, putting away bitterness and the like, and being kind, tenderhearted, and forgiving

We're supposed to lay aside the former, but sometimes we don't see our old lives as *that* bad. And sometimes we get confused between our old selves and our new selves. It's easy for me to slip into, say, callousness. I can be callous one minute, catch myself, then choose to turn 180 degrees toward sensitivity and compassion. It can be somewhat of a revolving door.

Paul provided a solution to the revolving door dilemma. *We're to put off our old selves, which are being corrupted, and put on the new selves, created to be like God.*

"Put off" and "put on" are action phrases. Living according to the new-life list isn't something that's done unto us; it's something we *do.* If we slip back to the old-life list, we can always, *always* grab the new-life list…and be made new.

Item in the Backpack: Renewal

Ephesians 5:1–21
<u>Danger Zones</u>

The lists continue, adding a few new items. They have to do with speech and imbibing. Danger zones.

There must be no filthiness and silly talk or coarse jesting, which are not fitting, but rather giving of thanks. And do not get drunk with wine, for that is dissipation, but be filled with the Spirit.

Sounds like fraternity parties are out.

Do I mean that literally? Of course not. A person can go to a fraternity party without spouting filth and getting wasted. Dissipation means "a wasting by misuse."

There is a line when it comes to alcohol or for that matter, a lot of legit things that can become addicting. For some, the line is at point zero. Zero alcohol (or whatever). Others know their own lines. Still others step over the line, and too often, bad things happen. These lists are for our gut-level honest introspection. I'm reminded of this quote: "Don't judge someone just because they sin differently than you." To some, drinking is up there with ax murder; but something like, say, prejudice is not. To others, it's the other way around.

Being an imitator of God is not for the fainthearted. It's easy to slip into silly talk and all sorts of hedonism, even little bitty versions of it. You know, the harmless versions. (Can't we have a little bit of fun?)

I sure hope we can have fun! I just worry about those who can't without getting drunk. There is a higher plane of existence for us. We can rise above base things. "Wake up, sleeper, rise from the dead, and Christ will shine on you."

Item in the Backpack: Higher Call

Ephesians 5:22–33
Marital Issues

What a loaded passage…loaded with beauty and, yes, controversy.

For example, are wives really supposed to be subject to their husbands? What if their husbands are abusers or cheaters? (I'm not picking on husbands. Wives can be abusers or cheaters as well.)

I think it's answered in verse 25. "Husbands, love your wives, just as Christ loved the church and gave himself up for her." Loving on that level is a tall order for husbands. We all know what that kind of love meant for Jesus.

And what about wives? Verse 33 says, "And the wife must respect her husband." I think it would be hard not to respect a husband willing to die for you.

That being said, how many couples live at that level day in and day out? I once heard an illustration about a couple who went to their marriage counselor with the news that they planned to divorce. The counselor asked them to hold off for a month so they could go out on a high note, so to speak. During the month, the husband was to be unselfish and sacrificial and the wife, respectful.

You can guess the end of the story. No divorce.

I like that story. We can aspire to it, but what are couples to do in the midst of abuse or severe personality disorders or harm to the kids? I can't answer that, but if we believe that God is personal, we can ask him. My go-to prayer in matters requiring a "what to do" decision is this: "Lord, make it unmistakable."

Controversy and difficulty aside, the point is that we have a picture of enormous love here. We (Christians) are the bride of Christ, and he died for his bride.

Item in the Backpack: Sacrificial Love

Ephesians 6:1–9
Mutual Respect

God set up the perfect plan for relationships, and in my opinion, here's the key: mutuality.

In other words, if parents are pretty cool, the kids are more likely to obey. If masters are pretty cool, the slaves are more likely to obey. (In fact, if masters are pretty cool, they'll likely set their captives free.)

God doesn't want us to show favoritism in our relationships, giving greater importance to one person/side over another. There are different roles, yes, but they are of equal value. We *all* need love, honor, respect, mutuality. We *all* need to feel like we're the most important person on the planet, whether we're parent, child, master, slave, black, white, woman, man, rich, poor, disabled, or able bodied. In your heart of hearts, don't you agree?

The problem with this theory is that it's about the *perfect* plan for relationships, and I haven't met perfection yet. So since that's the case, does the whole thing fall apart?

Well, we can only be responsible for ourselves. If our kids are rebellious, we can still try not to provoke them. If our parents are dysfunctional, we can still find ways to honor them. If our masters (maybe bosses?) are horrible, we can still do our work with integrity.

And maybe with mutuality, relationships would improve. It's hard to treat someone badly who's being good to you.

Item in the Backpack: Mutual Respect

Ephesians 6:10–24
Battle Prep

Do you ever feel spiritually attacked? Like something evil is targeting you beyond the usual ebbs and flows of life? The attack might be depression or illness or grief or an abusive relationship or anything else that holds you back from feeling spiritually alive.

I believe the battle is real, not imaginary or even poetic. Real. There's an enemy to our souls. Here are some of his aliases in the Bible: ruler of the demons, god (little *g*) of this world, devil, accuser, prince of the power of the air, roaring lion, serpent, dragon, adversary, tempter, wicked one.

Fortunately, "the one who is in you is greater than the one who is in the world" (1 John 4:4).

Fortunately! And not only that, but God has given us armor to resist the enemy and then stand firm. Sounds like war…because it is.

When we find ourselves naked on the battlefield, we're to put on full armor. We need to gird our loins with truth. (I've read that to gird one's loins meant to hoist and tuck one's tunic, or as one author said, to "man up" to get ready for battle.) We need to don the breastplate, footwear, shield, and helmet. And we need to take up the sword.

When I'm having a particularly troublesome day, I like to visualize putting on the armor. Spiritual armor for spiritual battles, because the battles are real.

As are the victories.

Item in the Backpack: Armor

Philippians 1
<u>Win-Win</u>

The most compelling reason to follow Christ is that it's a win-win. Paul said, "For to me, to live is Christ and to die is gain." He was ready to die, but he was also willing to live on for the sake of the believers. Either way, he was okay.

I see the Christian life as a win-win like this: I'll have eternity in the presence of love no matter what life throws my way. There will be ultimate victory over evil. My prayers are answered in the affirmative even if the answer is no, as expressed so beautifully in this Confederate soldier's prayer:

> I asked for strength that I might achieve; I was made weak that I might learn humbly to obey. I asked for health that I might do greater things; I was given infirmity that I might do better things. I asked for riches that I might be happy; I was given poverty that I might be wise. I asked for power that I might have the praise of men; I was given weakness that I might feel the need of God. I asked for all things that I might enjoy life; I was given life that I might enjoy all things. I got nothing that I asked for but everything that I had hoped for. Almost despite myself my unspoken prayers were answered, I am, among all men, most richly blessed.

Following Christ might mean hardship. It might not always be politically correct. It could even result in persecution. It is said that 255 Christians are killed for their faith every month.[1] So how can this be a win-win?

You have to take the long view. You have to believe in ultimate victory. You have to believe in the reality of spiritual things. And you have to believe that love wins.

Item in the Backpack: Ultimate Victory

---

1 www.opendoorsusa.org

Philippians 2
Jesus Attitude

Philippians 2:6–11 pretty much summarizes the whole Jesus story. Here it is in *The Message*:

> He had equal status with God but didn't think so much of himself that he had to cling to the advantages of that status no matter what. Not at all. When the time came, he set aside the privileges of deity and took on the status of a slave, became *human*! Having become human, he stayed human. It was an incredibly humbling process. He didn't claim special privileges. Instead, he lived a selfless, obedient life and then died a selfless, obedient death—and the worst kind of death at that—a crucifixion. Because of that obedience, God lifted him high and honored him far beyond anyone or anything, ever, so that all created beings in heaven and on earth—even those long ago dead and buried—will bow in worship before this Jesus Christ, and call out in praise that he is the Master of all, to the glorious honor of God the Father.

And we're to be like him: unselfish, humble, regarding others as more important than self and looking out for their interests, obedient, blameless, innocent, above reproach in this perverse world, true to the scriptures, lights in the darkness.

Because that's how Jesus was.

I would love it if my friends said of me, "She reminds me of Jesus."

Jesus had a certain attitude, essence, vibe. One of these days, we'll be in the presence of that vibe. And in the meantime, we're to give off his same light-in-the-darkness essence when we interact with others.

"Your attitude should be the same as that of Christ Jesus."

Item in the Backpack: Light in the Darkness

Philippians 3
Pressing On

It's not about how you start; it's how you finish.

Paul started off "perfect," a Hebrew of Hebrews, but he left that all behind for the *surpassing* greatness of knowing Christ. My friend Randy, on the other hand, started off fairly miserably. He's had to grind his way through loneliness, addictions, and extreme pain. However, he's also left all that behind for the *surpassing* value of knowing Christ. Sure, he might face more pain before he dies, but he's not turning back now. The goal is too compelling, the prize too great.

It's so easy to live in the past, whether the past was glorious or gut-wrenching. We can be paralyzed by things like shame, regret, fear, or guilt; but Paul said to *forget* what lies behind. "All of us who are mature should take such a view of things." So I'm taking it to heart for myself. Letting go of the past. Embracing the present. Reaching for the prize.

And what is the prize? Heaven with the Savior, in bodies transformed from their humble state into their glorious state. Imagine.

Hebrews 11:13–16 (*The Message*) says,

> Each one of these people of faith died not yet having in hand what was promised, but still believing. How did they do it? They saw it way off in the distance, waved their greeting, and accepted the fact that they were transients in this world. People who live this way make it plain that they are looking for their true home. If they were homesick for the old country, they could have gone back any time they wanted. But they were after a far better country than that—*heaven* country. You can see why God is so proud of them, and has a City waiting for them.

Heaven is beyond our wildest imaginations, but the reality of letting go of the past and living life in fullness is pretty heavenly in itself.

Item in the Backpack: The Prize

Philippians 4:1–9
Happy Thoughts

This passage is full of encouraging phrases, like "Be anxious for nothing," "Let your requests be known to God so the peace of God can guard your hearts and minds," and "Dwell on lovely things."

Let's explore those lovely things a bit, because dwelling on lovely things is good for the soul. It beats dwelling on unlovely things, like horror movies or fake news or damaging gossip.

Paul said to dwell on whatever is honorable, right, pure, lovely, and of good repute.

> Honorable = upright
> Right = proper and just

Pure = uncontaminated
Lovely = beautiful, appealing
Reputable = respectable

You might say God had some insight into cognitive behavioral therapy, which is "a form of psychotherapy that treats problems and boosts happiness by modifying dysfunctional emotions, behaviors, and thoughts. CBT focuses on solutions, encouraging patients to challenge distorted cognitions and change destructive patterns of behavior." He is the Great Physician, after all.

Change your thoughts. Change your life.

Is it time for your life to start dwelling on different things? Lovely, honorable things?

Homework: Name five lovely, honorable, pure things to dwell on today.

Item in the Backpack: Healthy Thoughts

Philippians 4:10–23
Inner Transformation

God provided for Paul. Sure, sometimes Paul went hungry and suffered, but God provided. Are you beginning to see a pattern here? It's not about circumstances; it's about inner transformation. It's about transcendence, not in a transcendental meditation sense (four monthly payments of $125!) but in an affordable-for-all sense. God can provide. No payment required.

This transcendence is based on more than "recharging your mind and body and creating a brighter, more positive state of mind," per the Transcendental Meditation website. This transcendence is based on God.

Paul said in Philippians 4:12–13, "I know what it is to be in need, and I know what it is to have plenty. I have learned the secret of being content in any and every situation, whether well fed or hungry, whether living in plenty or in want. I can do all this through him who gives me strength."

Are you with me here? The transcendent life is possible. Paul called it a secret. He ended his letter with an invitation to enter into the secret. "And my God will meet all your needs according to his glorious riches in Christ Jesus."

What are your needs?

Pray for God's clarity on wants vs. needs. I believe our deep needs may be different than our superficial needs. Deeply, we need transcendence to thrive within our circumstances.

Item in the Backpack: Contentment

Colossians 1
<u>Growth Spurts</u>

Christ gives us redemption and forgiveness. Christ is the image of the invisible God (God-con-carne, if you will). Christ is the first-born of creation. All things have been created by him and for him. Christ is before all things and in him all things hold together. Christ is the head of the church. Christ inhabits all fullness of deity. Christ made peace through his blood. Christ reconciled us to God so we can be holy and blameless and beyond reproach…

If we continue in the faith.

In other words, we need to keep growing. "We instructed you how to live in order to please God, as in fact you are living. Now we ask you and urge you in the Lord Jesus to *do this more and more*" (1 Thess. 4:1). We need to keep growing.

Paul reminded the Colossians of another mystery (there's that word again!) among the Gentiles, which is "Christ in you, the hope of glory." Then he discussed his efforts toward their growth. "To this end I labor, struggling with all his energy, which so powerfully works in me."

The theological term for this kind of lifelong growth in the faith is "sanctification."

Item in the Backpack: Sanctification

Colossians 2
Fake Teachings

Paul wanted to make sure the Colossian Christians were rooted in Christ himself, in whom are hidden all the treasures of wisdom and knowledge.

All the treasures of wisdom and knowledge.

Not surprisingly, there are detractors. This chapter describes an assortment—philosophies that go against Jesus's teachings, empty man-made traditions that focus on foods or festivals, self-abasement strategies, worship of created things (rather than the creator), or people who have inflated ideas about their own importance. In today's language, these detractors might be things like fascination with the "hip" side of dark religions or fad diets or assigning godlike status to someone who's anything but.

Paul had sharp warnings, essentially saying, "Let no one defraud you of your prize." "Why do you submit yourself to (such) decrees?" "These are matters that have the appearance of wisdom but are of no value."

People can find all sorts of delicious distractions—exotic travel, the latest gadgets, protein shakes. There's nothing wrong with any of these things; but sometimes, at least with the people I know who are incessantly searching, I wonder if they're just looking for home.

Jesus said, "Come to me, all who are weary and burdened, and I will give you rest" (Matt. 11:28).

The fake teachings distract and defraud. The true teachings lead us home.

Item in the Backpack: Home

Colossians 3:1–11
New Habits

This passage is about "putting on the new self," which reminds me of putting on new habits, which reminds me of nuns' clothing, which are called habits. (Yeah, sometimes my mind works that way, but stay with me. I think there's a good analogy here.)

"Since, then you have been raised with Christ, set your hearts on things above, where Christ is seated at the right hand of God." The raising up happens once. The sanctification means we *keep setting our hearts on things above*, and that requires forming new habits.

So here's the nun part. Traditionally, a nun wore the same tunic and headpiece every day. Her habit became her habit. It represented setting her mind on things above and putting away her old self.

In *Hamlet*, Polonius said to his son, "The apparel oft proclaims the man."

Coco Chanel said, "Dress shabbily and they remember the dress; dress impeccably and they remember the woman."

I think that if we put on the new self every day, like we put on clothing, we'll look more and more like Christ.

Stay tuned for verses 12–25 for a peek at that impeccable new clothing.

Item in the Backpack: New Habits

Colossians 3:12–25
<u>New Clothes</u>

Hmmm, what should I put on today? We're to put on a heart of compassion, kindness, humility, gentleness, and patience. We're to bear with one another and forgive each other. We're to put on love. We're to let the peace of Christ rule in our hearts. We're to be thankful. We're to let the word of Christ dwell within us. We're to teach and admonish each other. ("Admonish" means to reprove in a good-willed way.) We're to do all in the name of Jesus with sincere hearts, standing in awe of him. We're to do our work heartily as for the Lord.

There are consequences if we keep on wearing the old clothes (habits) rather than the new ones, so let's get practical. These traits/habits sound lovely on good days when we feel gentle and patient anyway, but what about bad days, when we just don't feel it? Well, we can walk over to our closet, stand there until we can name the old stuff for what it really is, then choose to put on the new.

You may laugh at me, but I just did this. As you know, I've had a frustration lately, and since I'm working from home, I literally went to my closet and stood there until I could name the old pain. Then I figuratively took it off and figuratively put on something new from the list above.

And felt better.

Sometimes putting on the new self requires hard soul-searching work.

Item in the Backpack: Hard Work

Colossians 4
Wise Words

"Be wise in the way you act toward outsiders; make the most of every opportunity. Let your conversation be always full of grace, seasoned with salt, so that you may know how to answer everyone." Think about your day today. Who are you encountering? Do those people's belief systems align perfectly with yours? Not likely, unless you live in a very closed system. So Paul provided us with a mini-course on speech. It's to be with grace and seasoned with salt. Why? Because gracious, salty speech leads to wisdom in our dealings with people.

What does salt do? It creates thirst, preserves, and seasons.

I want my words to create thirst for God. My network of friends and family and the people I encounter (grocery store employees, librarians, fellow choir members, and so on) is very diverse. I want my life and my words to interpret my relationship with God. I want to use everyday language to try to steward the mysteries of God. George Washington Carver said, "When you can do the common things of life in an uncommon way, you will command the attention of the world."

Common words with a dash of salt have power.

Look people in the eye today. Ask them how they're doing, and wait for their answer. Season their day with something good.

Item in the Backpack: Seasoning

1 Thessalonians 1:1–4:18
Pure Love

Paul, Silvanus, and Timothy wrote to the church at Thessalonica with affection. Since we're sort of eavesdropping on them in chapters 1–3 without much applicability to us, I've chosen to pick up in chapter 4.

In this chapter, Paul reiterated the concept of sanctification, specifically around sexuality. Sexuality is discussed a lot in the Bible, maybe because it's so ever-present and ever-important. "You know the guidelines we laid out for you from the Master Jesus. God wants you to live a pure life. Keep yourselves from sexual promiscuity. Learn to appreciate and give dignity to your body, not abusing it, as is so common among those who know nothing of God" (1 Thess. 4:2–5, *The Message*).

I've heard it said that love is affection with patience and lust is affection with impatience.

God wants our love and our sexuality to be as pure as possible. He *is* love, and he created sex. He wants what he made to be highly regarded.

Paul concluded chapter 4 with some new material (i.e., the fate of those who die as Christians). When a person dies in Christ, the rest of us aren't to grieve like people who have no hope. That person has eternal life with Christ.

Then there's the part about the Lord descending from heaven at some future point with a shout and trumpet and so forth and the dead in Christ rising first and those still alive being caught up together with them in the clouds to meet the Lord in the air.

All righty then. Count me in.

The second coming of Christ and eternity in the presence of Christ are natural extensions of the pure love offered to us in the here and now.

Item in the Backpack: Anticipation

1 Thessalonians 5
Day People

Okay, so the Lord is coming back and nobody knows when. However, we're not to be slackers in the meantime. We're people of the day, so we need to act like it, even in this long in-between time. We're to be sober and faithful and loving and hopeful, encouraging one another and building each other up. We're to appreciate our coworkers and leaders. We're to live in peace. We're to admonish the unruly, encourage the fainthearted, help the weak, and be patient with all. We're to avoid repaying evil for evil, instead seeking what's good for one another. We're to rejoice always, pray without ceasing, give thanks in everything. We're not to quench the Spirit or despise prophecies. We're to examine everything carefully. We're to hold fast to what is good and abstain from every form of evil.

Because that's what people of the day do.

Daunting? Absolutely, but we can count on verse 24: "*The one who calls you is faithful and he will do it.*" God will sanctify us entirely. He'll preserve our spirits, souls, and bodies without blame at the coming of Jesus.

God could have told us that being a Person of the Day is entirely on us, by our own power, and one slipup means failure, but God's not like that. He sets the bar really high and then says something like, "Tell you what. I'll do this through you."

Deal.

Item in the Backpack: Excellent Conduct

2 Thessalonians 1
Dark Things

In my view, afflictions seem to be sort of a fitness test. Not a pass/fail test but more of a victory-is-sweeter-if-you-have-to-fight-for-it kind of thing. Iron ore doesn't become steel unless it's smelted in furnaces where the impurities are removed.

Chances are you've gone through a good bit of tough stuff, holding God's hand so tightly you thought you might die, but coming through on the other side. Persecutions and afflictions are temporary. Relief will come when the Lord is revealed from heaven. I think this means that at that time, all the persecution and affliction toward believers will cease forever.

We must hold on to the long view.

Retribution. Penalty. Eternal destruction. Now these are different. They're for people who don't know God or obey the Gospel of Jesus. Eternal destruction equates to being away from the presence and power of the Lord, which would be hell. Literally.

Hell, at least the fire and brimstone variety, is not a popular topic these days. I really don't know what to say, except that these scriptures are part of the equation. Some people choose against God. God, therefore, doesn't force himself into their lives. At death, they will be away from God's presence and power.

I wish all would be saved. God wishes all would be saved. "The Lord is not slow in keeping his promise, as some understand slowness. Instead he is patient with you, not wanting anyone to perish, but everyone to come to repentance" (2 Pet. 3:9). Some, however, opt out.

Item in the Backpack: Understanding

2 Thessalonians 2
Lawless Man

The Thessalonian Christians were getting ahead of themselves about the second coming of Christ. Paul set them straight, telling them that the apostasy and man of lawlessness had to come first. It is likely that 2 Thessalonians was written around AD 51 or 52, so to my knowledge, this man hasn't shown up for a long time.

Apostasy means a total desertion of or departure from one's religion, principles, party, or cause. So that's coming up, unless it's already here.

And who is this man of lawlessness? We can get some info by referencing Daniel 7:25, 1 John 2:18, and Revelation 13:5ff. He will oppose and exalt himself above every so-called god. He will display himself as actually being God. He'll deceive many with his fake power, signs, and wonders. God will allow the delusion among those who don't receive the truth of salvation.

This man will work in accord with Satan. I'm guessing even some believers might be tempted to follow him. Satan deceives, so this man might come across as something wonderful. The truth, however, is this: "Your enemy the devil prowls around like a roaring lion looking for someone to devour" (1 Pet. 5:8).

In the end, God will kill him.

Paul told the Thessalonians and, by extension, Christians alive during the reign of lawlessness to stand firm. We can be so tuned into God that we can recognize the un-God, even if he appears as the god of this world and people all around are singing his praises.

Item in the Backpack: Discernment

2 Thessalonians 3
Unruly Friends

"Keep away from every brother who is idle and does not live according to the teaching you received from us." "If anyone does not obey our instruction in this letter, take special note of him. Do not associate with him, in order that he may feel ashamed. Yet do not regard him as an enemy, but warn him as a brother."

This is interesting counsel. Paul wrote so much about loving each other. Is not associating with certain people loving?

Maybe it's one of the most loving things we can do.

We're not to judge unfairly, but we *are* to admonish.

There are times when our brothers and sisters in Christ get unruly, like being too lazy to work or drinking too much or being mean to their kids or gossiping or having an affair or whatever. We're to admonish each other. We need each other.

It would be easy to look the other way or just let the unruliness continue. Admonishing takes a lot of work and managing our own lives is hard enough. Maybe that's why Paul added this sentence: "And as for you, brothers, never tire of doing what is right."

Item in the Backpack: Tough Love

1 Timothy 1
Misguided Teachers

Paul wrote to his young protégé, Timothy, to stay in Ephesus because wrong teachings were afoot.

Have you ever heard wrong teaching under the guise of right teaching? Man-made stuff that sounds sort of on point? Forays into side topics that deflect attention from the main topic? Underemphasis on the Law? (The Law was given to us to point out wrong from right. Underemphasis blurs the lines between the two.) Or overemphasis on the Law, which reminds me of the Pharisees who kept the letter of the Law but missed the point, the point being grace.

Or maybe those teachings that ignore certain Bible passages because they just don't fit one's worldview?

The goal of Paul's instruction was love from a pure heart, a good conscience, and sincere faith. Maybe this gives Bible teachers guidance. If a teacher can teach assured of the correctness of his/her motives and of the message, that's good.

If a teacher has a check in his/her spirit, maybe it's best to wait for clarity. "Not many of you should become teachers, my fellow believers, because you know that we who teach will be judged more strictly" (James 3:1).

And Paul reminded Timothy to fight the good fight. What an excellent, clarifying reminder for each day.

Item in the Backpack: Clarity

1 Timothy 2
Equal Rights

We need to be clear about one thing: "There is neither Jew nor Gentile, neither slave nor free, nor is there male and female, for you are all one in Christ Jesus" (Gal. 3:28). This chapter is about roles, not levels.

There are a few places where Paul expresses his opinion, such as "I want women to dress modestly, not with braided hair or gold or pearls" and "I do not permit a woman to teach or have authority over a man. She must be silent." Are these commandments or Paul's instructions that addressed a particular situation in Ephesus at the time?

At first glance, this chapter seems quite sexist, which has bothered me terribly for years. (Ain't gonna lie.) But many of the traits in this chapter and the next are common to *both* genders—temperance, faithfulness, love, sanctity, self-restraint, modesty, discretion, good works, and dignity.

Women and men do have different roles in much the same way that they have different roles in society in general. Women bear children. Eighteen-year-old males, at least in the United States, are required to register for the draft, which could mean being called up for combat.

(I wonder if they would rather trade for the childbirth role?)

Proverbs 31:10–31 says this about wives:

> An excellent wife, who can find? For her worth is far above jewels. The heart of her husband trusts in her, and he will have no lack of gain. She does him good and not evil all the days of her life. She looks for wool and flax and works with her

> hands in delight. She is like merchant ships; she brings her food from afar. She rises also while it is still night and gives food to her household and portions to her maidens. She considers a field and buys it; from her earnings she plants a vineyard. She girds herself with strength and makes her arms strong. She senses that her gain is good; her lamp does not go out at night. She stretches out her hands to the distaff, and her hands grasp the spindle. She extends her hand to the poor, and she stretches out her hands to the needy. She is not afraid of the snow for her household, for all her household are clothed with scarlet. She makes coverings for herself; her clothing is fine linen and purple. Her husband is known in the gates when he sits among the elders of the land. She makes linen garments and sells them and supplies belts to the tradesmen. Strength and dignity are her clothing, and she smiles at the future. She opens her mouth in wisdom, and the teaching of kindness is on her tongue. She looks well to the ways of her household and does not eat the bread of idleness. Her children rise up and bless her; her husband also, and he praises her, saying: "Many daughters have done nobly, but you excel them all." Charm is deceitful and beauty is vain, but a woman who fears the Lord, she shall be praised. Give her the product of her hands, and let her works praise her in the gates.

The great equalizer is that *each person*, male or female, is called to the highest of standards.

Item in the Backpack: Equality for All

1 Timothy 3
<u>Above Reproach</u>

This passage is about church leaders, elders (overseers), and deacons (servants who care for the members). Here again, the standards are quite high, much, *much* higher than the standards for holding political office. Paul gave specifics that boil down to the church leaders being people with character (i.e., having the moral qualities of honesty, courage, integrity, and the like, even before they become leaders). They need to be people who manage their own lives and families well. (The pot of applicants seems relatively small.)

I like to think of these lists, however, as character goals for *all* of us: above blame, temperate, wise in practical affairs, hospitable, not addicted (to anything), not quarrelsome, free from the love of money, good household managers, good parents, of good reputation in the public eye, and having a clear conscience.

We all have spheres of influence, so in a sense, we're all leaders. It's never too late to turn toward higher character.

Item in the Backpack: Leadership Qualities

1 Timothy 4
<u>Godly Discipline</u>

Paul told Timothy to discipline himself. He knew the task ahead was great, so he cut to the chase.

> Let no one look down on your youthfulness.
> Show yourself an example.
> Give attention to scripture.
> Don't neglect your spiritual gift.
> Take pains with these things.
> Be absorbed in them.
> Pay close attention.
> Persevere.

Paul pointed out that bodily discipline is of less profit than godly discipline, but we can draw analogies between the two. Trying to get one's body into shape requires dieting, exercise, goals, regimens, and willpower. There are activities for getting one's spirit into better shape too, like Bible studies, prayer journals (noting the prayer and when/how it's answered), going to church, fasting from time to time, etc.

If we take pains with these things, become absorbed in them, pay close attention to them, and persevere in them, we'll see results.

Item in the Backpack: Regimens

1 Timothy 5:1–16
Honoring Widows

In my work with the Dalit Freedom Network, I once took a leader from India to speak at a gigantic retirement center here in the United States. He was shocked that so many of our elderly don't live with their children. In India, they do, and woe to a widow who doesn't have family.

Maybe the situation was similar in the Middle East in Paul's time. The church was destined to carve out new norms, so Paul laid out the plan. Families were to make some return to their own parents. Older widows were to be cared for through the church. Younger widows were to remarry. Maybe Paul wanted to avoid welfare for able-bodied young women when "widows indeed" needed to be priority.

(Another practice in India is that the kids call their elders Auntie and Uncle, even if they're not relatives. They're terms of endearment. Reminds me of verses 1 and 2.)

Paul wanted to make sure the church was holistic, not just a collection of creeds. The church was to be a community of care. Family.

Do we honor our widows enough?

Do we honor our elderly enough?

Item in the Backpack: Community Care

1 Timothy 5:17–6:21
Miscellaneous Instructions

I'm struck by how much Paul had to say to Timothy about elders, sinners, slaves, conceited people, rich people, empty chatterers, and wine. Maybe there's a theme, but maybe these verses were Paul's "sticky notes." A few of them stand out to me as particularly relevant.

> Honor your hardworking elders.
> Pay people what they're due, even if they're working for the church.
> Verify accusations with witnesses.
> Don't be too hasty.
> Do your homework.
> Rebuke repeat offenders.
> Operate without bias or partiality.
> Stay sin-free.
> Call out those who brew up controversies.
> Flee from the love of money.
> Instruct the rich not to be conceited or to pin all hope on their wealth.
> Avoid worldly chatter and fake knowledge.

One of the most compelling is the one about fleeing from the love of money. The downsides to excessive love of money are temptations, snares, foolish and harmful desires, ruin, destruction, many a pang. Really negative stuff.

Note, however, that money isn't the culprit—it's the *love* of money. Money can be used in spectacular ways, but idolizing it can snare us. We need to be intentional regarding our feelings about it.

Item in the Backpack: Intentionality

2 Timothy 1
No Timidity

People on the front lines of something new must feel exhilarated! Think: colonists planning the Revolutionary War or black Americans planning the Selma marches or new followers of this radical Jesus planning the church. These people knew there was great risk. The outcomes were uncertain. They were writing the playbooks as they went along. They suffered setbacks. They were persecuted and put down.

But they knew they were right.

Paul was often in dire straits. The powerful people tried to discredit him, making him look foolish. Maybe it was hard for the early Christians to stand strong behind him, but Paul told Timothy to not be ashamed of the Lord or of him. Paul was like a general or head coach or movement leader. Outspoken. Undeterred. And 1,000 percent convinced.

One of the tasks of a leader is to amass the troops. Paul did that but focused his fatherly attention on a few, like Timothy. Timothy had been vetted. He had the character and unwavering commitment to lead, but he needed boot camp. That's why these letters are so full of instructions and pep talks.

One of my favorites is verse 7: "For God did not give us a spirit of timidity, but a spirit of power, of love and of self-discipline." This verse has girded me up when I've felt shy or embarrassed or fearful.

When we're on the cutting edge, we *must* remember that God has given us the spirit of boldness, power, love, and discipline. It is enough. We're on the front lines…of the winning side.

Item in the Backpack: Boldness

2 Timothy 2:1–13
Personal Training

In this passage, Paul continued his Timothy Lessons. He told him to be strong and focused like a soldier or athlete or farmer.

The soldier stays single-minded. The athlete competes according to the rules. The farmer works hard.

What do these have in common? The soldier, athlete, and farmer give their all to the task. They're disciplined.

Paul wanted to instill the concept of personal discipline in Timothy; but he never failed to *also* let him know that the Lord would be with him, giving him insight, staying faithful to him. Forgive this limited comparison, but it's sort of like having a personal trainer at the gym. The discipline and hard work are one's own, but the trainer is there to encourage and support.

Item in the Backpack: Help in Time of Need

2 Timothy 2:14–26
Cleaned Up

We can come to the Lord dirty and utterly messy. We don't have to clean up our acts before God will accept us into his home. Afterward, though, we *get* to go through transformation into an honored vessel.

"If a man cleanses himself from [ignoble purposes], he will be an instrument for noble purposes, made holy, useful to the Master and prepared to do any good work."

Everyone who names the name of the Lord is to abstain from wickedness. To be wicked is to be evil in principle or practice. Specifically, Paul targeted stuff like lust and a quarrelsome spirit. According to Christian tradition, the seven deadly sins are pride, greed, lust, envy, gluttony, wrath, and sloth. It's thought that these sins are abuses or excessive versions of one's natural faculties. For example, lust is a misuse/abuse of sexuality; gluttony, of eating; etc.

But we don't need tutoring on what wickedness is. We know in our hearts when we're screeching to a halt at the precipice. That very thing is addressed in Ephesians 4:27: "Do not give the devil a foothold." Or put another way, stay far away from that precipice. The edge is way too tempting.

So that in itself is a way to clean up our acts. We can stay away from the edge. For example, if you're tempted to gossip, cancel that coffee date where you planned to do so.

When we abstain from mud puddles, we don't get muddy. God helps us get washed and clean, but we have to cooperate.

Item in the Backpack: Soap

2 Timothy 3:1–4:4
Haters Ahead

The "last days" folks in this passage don't sound pleasant. The adjectives are obvious—boastful, arrogant, irreconcilable...but there are a couple of things that are a little surprising.

1. They will hold to a form of godliness but will deny its power. I think this is interesting. They might present as spiritual, maybe even religious, but will miss the mark.
2. They will always be learning but will never be able to get to the truth. Also interesting. They might present as scholarly, intelligent, or wise, but, again, will miss the mark.

They'll proceed from bad to worse. They won't endure sound doctrine. They'll find teachers who will tell them what they want to hear. But I have a feeling they'll look really hip and politically correct and admirable. It's already in vogue in some circles to be self-absorbed, way into money, and shamelessly arrogant.

Fortunately, they won't progress indefinitely. Their folly will be obvious to all.

What are we to do in the midst of it all? Stay the course. Hold to the scriptures. "All Scripture is God-breathed and is useful for teaching, rebuking, correcting and training in righteousness, so that the servant of God may be thoroughly equipped for every good work."

We have the tools we need to operate in this world.

Item in the Backpack: Scripture

2 Timothy 4:5–22
Finish Line

I look forward to the time when I can say these words: "The time of my departure is near. I have fought the good fight, I have finished the race, I have kept the faith. Now there is in store for me the crown of righteousness, which the Lord, the righteous Judge, will award to me on that day—and not only to me, but also to all who have longed for his appearing."

Can there be any better words, knowing that Jesus will be cheering me on at the finish line as I cross over? I don't feel anywhere near worthy of a crown of righteousness. Truth is, I'm *not* worthy, but God's point is that he's worthy. He made up the rules. He loved the world so much that he gave his only Son for us. He sent him not to judge the world, but to save the world.

The Peace Corps once had this slogan. "It's the toughest job you'll ever love." That's how I feel about my journey with Christ. All it takes is obedient belief, but life is tough. If we're in the last days, opposition and persecution could become severe, even to the point of death.

We just need to hold on to a mental image of Jesus at the finish line, holding a crown in just our size.

Item in the Backpack: Mental Image

Titus 1–3
Added Emphasis

When my son was about four years old, I picked him up from Sunday school one Sunday and asked him which Bible story had been taught. He said, "The one about Noah, but I already know that one." (I chuckled.)

Don't we wish we could grasp every story or instruction after one hearing?

In Titus, it seems like Paul reiterated instructions he had already given. It's true that this letter went to Crete and others to other cities, but for us as Bible readers, we're reading the same stuff over and over.

Maybe it's because we just can't always grasp instructions after one hearing. Maybe we need added emphasis. So although the following instructions are for church overseers or people of different ages, many apply to all of us. I'll list them here because they bear repeating. I'll emphasize the ones he used multiple times in Titus alone. (He must have felt *really* strongly about those.) We're to be...

Above reproach. Not accused of dissipation or rebellion. God's stewards. Not self-willed. Not quick-tempered. *Not addicted to wine.* Not combative. Not fond of sordid gain. Hospitable. *Loving and teaching what is good.* Just. Devout. *Sensible.* Self-controlled. Holding fast to God's word. Not paying attention to myths. Temperate. *Dignified.* Sound in faith, love, perseverance, and speech. Reverent. Not gossip-y. Pure. Kind. Not argumentative. Denying ungodliness and worldly desires. Subject to authorities. Obedient. *Engaging in good deeds.* Maligning no one. Uncontentious. Gentle. Considerate. Shunning foolishness.

He also reiterated that our salvation isn't based on our worthiness. "He saved us, not because of righteous things we had done, but because of his mercy." We need to be told that story over and over, partly because some still don't get it, and partly because it's so incredibly beautiful.

Item in the Backpack: Repetition

Philemon
<u>Showing Appreciation</u>

Out of the hundreds, maybe thousands, of sermons I've heard, I think I've only heard one on the Epistle to Philemon. It's a bit bland, sort of like reading an email from Paul to Philemon with the subject line: "Onesimus."

But at second glance, it's not so bland. Paul was giving his fellow worker kudos. Sure, he had a question to ask him, but he still gave him lots of good words.

Do we do that enough with our network of friends, family, coworkers?

Paul was sending Philemon's slave back to him with the request that he be set free. Furthermore, if Onesimus had wronged Philemon or owed him anything, Paul wanted that charged to his account. He felt sure that Philemon would grant or exceed his request.

That's the essence of the "email," but let's talk about the kudos. Paul had heard of Philemon's effectiveness. He wanted to approach him man to man out of love instead of ordering him around. He honored his goodness. He was confident in his obedience. Philemon seemed like a fine person.

So often in my communications, I cut straight to the "subject line" topic. I could do more in the way of kudos. There are some very fine people in my life.

As straightforward (and even off-putting) as Paul was at times, he was pretty good about starting his letters with positives and compliments. Their lives were often on the line because of their faith, so no doubt those affirmations carried a lot of weight.

Item in the Backpack: Appreciation

Hebrews 1
<u>God's Masterpiece</u>

The letter to the Hebrews (Jewish Christians living in Jerusalem) has disputed authorship. Maybe the author was Paul. Maybe it was someone else, such as an associate of Paul. At any rate, Hebrews is one of my favorites because it's *so* rich.

Chapter 1 is like a work of art. The author paints Jesus in such lovely terms. The radiance of God's glory, the exact representation of God's being, sustainer of all things by his powerful word, seated at the right hand of God, worshipped by angels, holder of the scepter, and anointed with the oil of joy. (Can you visualize it?)

Jesus is God's masterpiece, like those wall-sized paintings with thrones and winged cherubim and such in the Louvre in Paris.

The author gave us a visual of angels. They are winds and flames of fire, God's ministering spirits. They've been sent to render service to all of us who will inherit salvation. This is *amazing*. (See why Hebrews is one of my favorites?)

Are angels real? Absolutely. They are beyond natural, but so are the virgin birth, miracles, the resurrection, etc. We live in a physical *and* spiritual world.

Take a moment to soak this up. Jesus is real. Angels are real. May God give us the eyes to see and the hearts to understand the beauty of his masterpiece and his ministering spirits. Sometimes the intentions of our enemies block our view, but God is greater than our enemies.

Item in the Backpack: Eyes to See

Hebrews 2:1–9
Paying Attention

It's so easy to drift away. "We must pay more careful attention, therefore, to what we have heard, so that we do not drift away."

Why do people drift? Maybe they were never moored in the first place. Maybe they get tired. Maybe they get fed up with that constricting anchor.

Or maybe they quit paying attention, drifting just a little bit, but still having the shore in sight, each drift being "no big deal." After a while, they're in the open ocean, wondering how they had gotten so far away from God.

My friend Randy wrote a poem entitled "A Ship Adrift." Here's an excerpt:

> There is a ship adrift on a dark and stormy sea.
> But there is a lighthouse of hope calling all ships
> to come in. One ship could be you and another
> could be me.

Your mind could be tangled in a lie from what the world wants its residents to believe. Are you haunted by worry but thirsty and wanting to be free? You could be ensnared by your anger or the wounds of your past.

Maybe you feel hopeless and when you look down you see that you are going nowhere because you just discovered that what you built your house upon is really sinking sand.

There is a man known as a lighthouse calling to lead you out of the darkness who says, "Whoever follows me will never walk in darkness but will have the light of life."

Do you know him? Are you hungry? Are you thirsty? Are you looking for security? Are you looking for a home? Come! Bring it all to him and leave it there. Because…one ship could be you and another could be me.

Item in the Backpack: Moorings

Hebrews 2:10–18
High Priest

For a little while, Jesus was lower than the angels, just like us. Since he had to die for us, he had to become one of us first. He became very attached to us. He had to suffer, because it took his death to disempower the devil. In dying, he paid the penalty for our sins. But there's more. Since he was one of us, he understands our temptations. He is able to come to our aid.

I'm not Catholic. I've never sat in a confessional booth. I grew up believing we have direct access to God without going through a human intermediary. The doctrine is called the priesthood of all believers. But I love that priests declare forgiveness and, from what I understand, can also offer counseling onto the path to repentance so the sin/temptation can take a 180-degree turn.

In a sense, *we* are priests. "But you are a chosen people, a royal priesthood, a holy nation, God's special possession, that you may declare the praises of him who called you out of darkness into his wonderful light" (1 Pet. 2:9). And we're to be priests to each other. "Therefore, confess your sins to each other and pray for each other so that you may be healed" (James 5:16).

But there's only one High Priest. We're not God. We're not even gods. We are people the High Priest loves. We are his brothers and sisters. "Both the one who makes people holy and those who are made holy are of the same family. So Jesus is not ashamed to call them brothers and sisters."

Item in the Backpack: Priesthood of the Believer

Hebrews 3
Hard Hearts

It makes sense that the author would compare Jesus to Moses. Moses was faithful to his people as a servant; Jesus was faithful to his people as a Son. The author quoted from Psalm 95, bringing to memory how the Israelites had hardened their hearts and weren't able to enter the Promised Land for forty years.

But eventually the Israelites *were* able to enter the Promised Land under Joshua's leadership. "If serving the Lord seems undesirable to you, then choose for yourselves this day whom you will serve, whether the gods your ancestors served beyond the Euphrates, or the gods of the Amorites, in whose land you are living. But as for me and my household, we will serve the Lord" (Josh. 24:15). And the people answered. "We will serve the Lord our God and obey him" (Josh. 24:24). They were able to enter because they understood the peril of unbelief.

They returned to softheartedness.

In Moses's day, the consequence of hard-heartedness was forty years of wandering around. When Jesus arrived, he paid the price. No more wandering. "We all, like sheep, have gone astray, each of us has turned to our own way; and the LORD has laid on him the iniquity of us all" (Isa. 53:6).

Yet hard-heartedness continues to this day.

Have you ever known someone who refused to be loved? Who pushed others away before they had a chance to get close? Who chose their own lonely path because they misunderstood love? God longs for us to believe his love.

Item in the Backpack: A Soft Heart

Hebrews 4:1–11
Blessed Rest

"For if Joshua had given them rest, God would not have spoken later about another day. There remains, then, a Sabbath-rest for the people of God."

The primary Greek words for "rest" in the New Testament are *anapausis* (cessation of motion, business, or labor; rest from weariness), *katapausis* (the heavenly blessedness in which God dwells and of which he has promised to make persevering believers in Christ partakers after the toils and trials of life on earth are ended), and *sabbatismos* (the blessed rest from toils and troubles looked for *in the age to come* by true Christians). The latter is the one used in Hebrews 4:9. This rest is referring to our heavenly rest. All our strivings will cease when we attain it. Readers need to persevere in the faith, for only then will we get to this rest.

"Let us, therefore, make every effort to enter that rest…"

Sometimes I have a sense of unrest in my spirit. I pay attention when that happens. It means something's not right. I need to ask God about it and wait for his answer. And sometimes, of course, I experience peace and rest. It doesn't necessarily mean that all is right with my relationships or circumstances. It's just the sense that God's bigger than my relationships and circumstances. There's a big plan that I can't see. And it's good. I just need to rest in it.

But again, the rest discussed here is the rest of heaven.

Item in the Backpack: Rest

Hebrews 4:12–16
Living Words

The spiritual realities keep on coming.

1. The word of God is living and active.
2. Nobody is hidden from God's sight.
3. We can draw near to God for help in time of need.

Notice that these realities aren't past tense. They're living and active *today*.

I want to focus on verse 12. What does it mean that the word of God is *living, active, piercing, and judging?* For me, it means (a) I can expect literal outcomes.

Consider this passage. "But those who hope in the Lord will renew their strength" (Isa. 40:31). When I truly wait for the Lord, I expect a literal outcome. Renewed strength.

It also means (b) I can expect epiphanies.

As I read scripture, I can count on the living God to get through to me. You know that feeling when something suddenly becomes clear? That.

And (c) I can expect ongoing clarity about the big picture.

As we've discussed, many prophecies have already come to pass or are coming to pass before our eyes. This ancient book has predicted the future. The author is eternally alive and active in the here and now of humanity, and he's not finished yet. There's more unfolding to come.

Some people regard the Bible as a work that contains some great ideas. Great ideas meaning *concepts*, but if Hebrews 4:12 is true, then those concepts literally have power. Isn't that mind-boggling?

God has transcended ordinary limits to be alive and active, this very moment, for you and me.

Item in the Backpack: Transcendence

Hebrews 5:1–10
Indescribable Gift

"Although he [Jesus] was a son, he learned obedience from what he suffered." Wait. What? I know *we* learn obedience from what we suffer (at least I hope we do), but Jesus had to learn that way too? That means he *really* understands what we go through.

"And once made perfect, he became the source of eternal salvation for all who obey him."

Human priests can deal gently with the ignorant and misguided because they're also weak. Jesus is different, however. He understands our pain and temptations, but he also has the power to do something about them.

Years ago, I went to the Lord in tears about a situation. God's message was "Watch me work." (Now one thing I've noticed about God is that he doesn't necessarily operate on the American I-want-it-and-I-want-it-now time frame. Watching him work can stretch over long periods of time. It's not a "one and done" thing.)

Anyway, a couple of decades later, I'm seeing the fruit of that "Watch me work" message and it's indescribable in its beauty. "Thanks be to God for his indescribable gift" (2 Cor. 9:15).

I really think he understands me.

Item in the Backpack: Assurance of God's Understanding

Hebrews 5:11–14
Solid Food

Babies need milk. Their little systems are too immature for solid food, but as they grow, they get to try out tasty stuff like strained beets.

"Anyone who lives on milk, being still an infant, is not acquainted with the teaching about righteousness. But solid food is for the mature, who *by constant use have trained themselves* to distinguish good from evil."

Maturity takes practice. Repetition. Taking the narrow road, over and over. "Enter through the narrow gate. For wide is the gate and broad is the road that leads to destruction, and many enter through it. But small is the gate and narrow the road that leads to life, and only a few find it" (Matt. 7:13–14). "Two roads diverged in a wood, and I—I took the one less traveled by, And that has made all the difference" (Robert Frost).

To me, the road less traveled is the narrow one.

Apparently, some readers had become dull of hearing, maybe cutting over to the wide path, so they needed to go back to their training. Sometimes I've had to do that too.

And that has made all the difference.

Item in the Backpack: Training

Hebrews 6
<u>Better Things</u>

The author was convinced that these believers weren't going to fall away, but what about those who *do* fall away? It does not look good. "Once people have seen the light, gotten a taste of heaven and been part of the work of the Holy Spirit, once they've personally experienced the sheer goodness of God's Word and the powers breaking in on us—if then they turn their backs on it, washing their hands of the whole thing, well, they can't start over as if nothing happened. That's impossible. Why, they've re-crucified Jesus! They've repudiated him in public!" (Heb. 6:4–6, *The Message*)

I have friends who have fallen away. Maybe they had never tasted of the heavenly gift in the first place. Maybe they felt coerced to make a decision for Christ before they were ready. Maybe they are just incredulous and want proof.

But with God, all things are possible, even the impossible. "With man this is impossible, but with God all things are possible" (Matt. 19:26).

The author again made a throwback to the Old Testament, this time about the promise to Abraham: "I will surely bless you and give you many descendants." Then he tied together the two unchangeable things, the second being the promise of Jesus.

In the Old Testament tabernacle, the Holy of Holies was covered by a veil, and no one was allowed to enter except the high priest. Even he could only enter once a year on Yom Kippur (the Day of Atonement), to offer the blood of sacrifice and incense before the mercy seat. When Jesus died, the veil was literally torn in two, from top to bottom. The symbolism is that there is no longer a veil separating believers from God. The author was citing the double promise for Jews who become Christians, but the veil has been torn in two for Gentiles as well. Everyone in the whole wide world has direct access to God.

Item in the Backpack: No Separation between God and Humanity

Hebrews 7
New Covenant

Melchizedek was mentioned twice in the Old Testament, in Genesis 14:18 and Psalm 110:4. Once again, the author of Hebrews was connecting dots for the Jewish believers.

The former priests were prevented from continuing because, well, they died. Jesus became the guarantee of a better covenant. He holds the priesthood permanently. He's able to save those who draw near to God through him. He makes continual intercession for them/us. He is holy, innocent, undefiled, separated from sinners, and exalted above everything, even the heavens. He is perfect.

The sacrifices in the Old Testament were birds or animals that were as perfect as possible, but in essence, they were place holders until *the* sacrifice came on the scene.

As we've seen, there are many pointers from the Old to the New. The writer of Hebrews worked diligently to explain the new covenant to these believers (i.e., that Jesus came not to abolish the Law or the Prophets but to fulfill them) (Matt. 5:17).

Item in the Backpack: New Covenant

Hebrews 8:1–10:18
Better Ministry

Under the Old Testament sacrificial system, blood had to be shed all the time. Animal sacrifices were endless. Blood symbolizes life, the ultimate sacrifice. "Without the shedding of blood there is no forgiveness" (Heb. 9:22).

Jesus shed his blood. We are forgiven. "And where these have been forgiven, sacrifice for sin is no longer necessary" (Heb. 10:18). No more animal sacrifices. As Jesus said at the end of his life, "It is finished."

Jesus set up Communion with bread and wine symbolizing his body and blood. Communion isn't the sacrifice; it's about remembering the sacrifice.

The detail in these chapters was essential for the Hebrews. The author had to drive home the point that the Old Covenant was over. The Messiah had arrived.

Here's Hebrews 10:16–18 in the words of *The Message*: "This new plan I'm making with Israel isn't going to be written on paper, isn't going to be chiseled in stone; This time I'm writing out the plan *in* them, carving it on the lining of their hearts." He concludes, "I'll forever wipe the slate clean of their sins." Before leaving these chapters, there's another important concept to highlight. Verses 9:27–28 negate the concept of reincarnation found in other religions: "Everyone has to die once, then face the consequences. Christ's death was also a one-time event, but it was a sacrifice that took care of sins forever" (*The Message*).

Item in the Backpack: Completion

Hebrews 10:19–25
New Mind-Set

After verses and verses about the New vs. the Old, the author essentially said, "Okay, let's move on. Because there's a new covenant and because Christ's sacrifice is sufficient, let's give the plan more substance. Reality is one thing. Operating in it is another. New mind-sets are needed."

As a comparison, when the slaves were emancipated after the Civil War, they probably couldn't comprehend it at first and didn't know what to do. I'm not inferring that the Old Covenant was like slavery, just that the New was a bit mind-boggling.

As another comparison, as our children age, we parents have to take on new mind-sets every few years, like during the terrible twos, the mid-teens, and as they marry and have their own kids. Each time, they're declaring, "I want to do it myself!" It's hard for them and hard for us. We all have to take baby steps into the new realities.

The Hebrew Christians had to unlearn hundreds of years of protocol, like animal sacrifices and many points of the Law. Then they had to take on new beliefs and lifestyles. The Old was just a shadow of good things to come, but sometimes people prefer the lesser if it's known rather than the greater if it's unknown.

They had to step out in faith.

We do too.

Item in the Backpack: Baby Steps

Hebrews 10:26–39
Staying Strong

Here's a tough passage. "If we give up and turn our backs on all we've learned, all we've been given, all the truth we now know, we repudiate Christ's sacrifice and are left on our own to face the Judgment—and a mighty fierce judgment it will be! If the penalty for breaking the law of Moses is physical death, what do you think will happen if you turn on God's Son, spit on the sacrifice that made you whole, and insult this most gracious Spirit? This is no light matter. God has warned us that he'll hold us to account and make us pay. He was quite explicit: 'Vengeance is mine, and I won't overlook a thing' and 'God will judge his people.' Nobody's getting by with anything, believe me" (Heb. 10:26–31, *The Message*). There's just no way to soft pedal it.

So the author said, "Do not throw away your confidence; it will be richly rewarded. You need to persevere so that when you have done the will of God, you will receive what he has promised" (Heb. 10:35–36).

Like soldiers on the front lines, we're to not shrink back. How would wars be won if soldiers pulled back at the first sign of hardship? (They don't pull back. They have mettle.)

Likewise, we need to endure.

"Consider it pure joy, my brothers and sisters, whenever you face trials of many kinds, because you know that the testing of your faith produces perseverance. Let perseverance finish its work so that you may be mature and complete, not lacking anything" (James 1:2–4).

"But the one who stands firm to the end will be saved" (Matthew 24:13).

The author made it *very* clear that we're to take the salvation of Jesus *very* seriously. Perseverance is the key ingredient to being perfect and complete, lacking in nothing.

And in the end, there will be great reward.

Item in the Backpack: Mettle

Hebrews 11:1
<u>Faith Examined</u>

"*Now faith is being sure of what we hope for and certain of what we do not see.*"

Here again, the author of Hebrews instructed his readers using Old Testament patriarchs and other Jewish folk, this time about the concept of faith.

By faith, Noah built a boat before the world had even gotten a hint of a flood. By faith, Abraham and Sarah started the Jewish nation on the basis of a promise alone, even though Sarah was too old to conceive. By faith, Abraham was willing to kill his son Isaac because he believed God's words (i.e., "In Isaac your descendants shall be called."). Those descendants are the Jews. By faith, Moses gave up the riches of Egypt to lead the Jews out of slavery. By faith, the Jews encircled the walls of Jericho for seven days, at which point the walls fell down and progress was made toward the Promised Land. By faith, others conquered kingdoms, obtained promises, received their dead back by resurrection, and were generally people of whom the world isn't worthy.

All died in faith without receiving what had been promised, because the promise was for the life to come. (This is the "rest" mentioned in Hebrews chapters 3 and 4.) We live by faith as well. Like those in this Hall of Faith list, we won't see the *complete* reward until we reach heaven, unless the second coming of Christ occurs in our lifetime.

Why do we believe even though we don't have proof? It flies in the face of everything rational.

I believe because of God's promises. I take them personally. I believe because God has answered so many of my prayers. I believe because I'm "betting all the marbles" on love…and God is love. In the NASB version of the Bible, Hebrews 11:1 reads like this: "Now faith is the assurance of things hoped for, the conviction of things not seen." I guess I have that conviction.

Item in the Backpack: Conviction

Hebrews 12:1–3
Putting Aside

Picture yourself at the starting line of a race, carrying a pack full of rocks and wearing tire chains around your neck and steel-toed boots on your feet. Look up at the stands. The witnesses are incredulous. You're so weighed down! Picture them *wanting* you to be free so you can win, but at a loss as to what to do.

Now picture Jesus walking over to the finish line and turning to face you, just standing there with a big smile on his face. Imagine pure love, all for you. No going back. You have arrived. Almost.

Just lay aside the pack of rocks, the chains, and the boots. (They're symbols of sin.) Fix your gaze on Jesus. The race will be long, but with the goal in sight and the sin left behind, you can do it. Don't lose heart. Keep your eyes on the prize.

The story of Little Much Afraid in *Hinds' Feet on High Places* by Hannah Hurnard has a similar theme. It's an allegory about the Christian's journey. Little Much Afraid leaves the Valley of Humiliation accompanied by Sorrow and Suffering and eventually reaches the High Places. The tests along the way are extreme. It seems the Shepherd is not helping her, but as it turns out, he is allowing her to find peace and answers. Her pain purifies her. She receives a new name, Grace and Glory, and is then able to return to the valley with compassion.

Putting one foot in front of the other, she was able to do it.

Putting one foot in front of the other, we're able to do it too.

Item in the Backpack: Eyes on the Prize

Hebrews 12:4–17
<u>Discipline Fruit</u>

"No discipline seems pleasant at the time, but painful. Later on, however, it produces a harvest of righteousness and peace for those who have been trained by it."

I feel like I'm wading through dark waters in these passages, waters full of suffering and sorrow. Honestly, I'm poring through these passages looking for silver linings. I want happy endings sooner than later. Nevertheless, we're to take God seriously, which means facing his high standards and the discipline to get us there. We're sons and daughters, so the expectations are high.

Do you experience his discipline?

If you're tempted to stray, does he turn into the "hound of heaven" to bring you back? If you're training hard, does he turn into "head coach" to push you even further? If you're full of shame or confusion, does he turn into "master teacher" to get you to a better place?

Discipline is doled out by someone who knows the better way. We have to trust God and trust the process. Our job is to find the lesson.

If we do, we win. That's a happy ending.

Item in the Backpack: Acceptance of God's Discipline

Hebrews 12:18–29
Another Contrast

Mount Sinai was where Moses received the Ten Commandments. It's mentioned in the book of Exodus as well as in the Qur'an. Fire and clouds signified God's presence on the mountain. Moses was full of fear.

That was the old mountain.

The new is Mount Zion—the city of the living God, the heavenly Jerusalem, the general assembly of the firstborn.

The former mountain was shakable; the latter, unshaken.

Once again, the author created a contrast for the readers, yet the contrast seems confusing. There are so many warnings in these passages about God's judgment. The confusing part is how those warnings square with God's grace.

Well, here's the deal. Coming to Mount Zion is coming to God the Judge *and* to Jesus the Mediator. If our hearts want to stop sinning, there's hope.

"*But because of his great love for us*, God, who is rich in mercy, made us alive with Christ even when we were dead in transgressions—it is by grace you have been saved" (Eph. 2:4–5).

"But because of his great love for us…" Those words change everything.

Item in the Backpack: Reverence for the Truth

Hebrews 13
Pleasing Sacrifices

The author gave his readers some parting instructions:

Keep loving each other.
Show hospitality to strangers. You might be entertaining angels.
Remember prisoners and the ill-treated. We're all in this together.
Let marriage (and the marriage bed) be held in honor.
Be free from the love of money.
Be content with what you have.
Remember your spiritual teachers. Imitate their faith.
Don't be carried away by other teachings.
Go outside the camp where Jesus died, to identify with him.
Offer a continual sacrifice of praise and good works.
Obey your leaders.
Pray.

Then he gave them his benediction, asking God to equip them in every good thing to do his will.

God equips.

And therein is the victory. People failed to keep the Old Covenant. The onus was on them, and it was too much. No number of animal sacrifices could pay the price for their sins. And animal sacrifices couldn't achieve the added blessing anyway, which is life transformation.

Jesus became the sacrifice, and now we, in turn, can offer a different kind of sacrifice back, that of praise. Praise means adoration and overwhelming appreciation…an eternal standing ovation.

One of the reasons I praise God is because I don't have to strive through life alone. I *literally* find that he equips me for what needs to be done.

Item in the Backpack: Sacrifice of Praise

James 1:1–16
Downside Up

The Epistle of James is attributed to the brother of Jesus (James the Just) and was written to Hebrew Christians dispersed outside Palestine. James exhorted them to stay strong as they faced injustice and poverty. "Consider it pure joy, my brothers, whenever you face trials of many kinds." "The brother in humble circumstances ought to take pride in his high position."

Don't these seem paradoxical? I mean, who can be happy when they're going through trials, and how is a poor person supposed to see him/herself in a high position? These are a few of the "downside up" realities of the Christian life. Things may look bad in the natural world; but those things can bring upsides, like endurance, perfection, completion, the crown of life, and clarity about God's nature.

Right now, I'm going through a trial in life. (Have you noticed that I'm *often* going through a trial in life? I think I'm a slow learner.) Well, anyway, I'm to consider the experience of trials as something to rejoice over. It'll produce endurance in me, which in the end will make me perfect and complete, lacking in nothing. This testing might last a while, so I'll need endurance. I'll have to keep calling on God's faithfulness. I've been obedient to him, but the price is very high. I could easily despair. I need wisdom. I need patience.

God wants good to come out of this trial. I get to watch his answer unfold, which frankly opens up a little speck of joy in me.

Item in the Backpack: Beautiful Paradoxes

James 1:17–27
Action Figures

There are a lot of action words here, like "be," "put," "receive," "prove," "abide," "bridle," "keep," and "*do*."

"Do not merely listen to the word, and so deceive yourselves. *Do* what it says." "But whoever looks intently into the perfect law that gives freedom, and continues in it—not forgetting what they have heard, but *doing it*—they will be blessed in what they do."

James put a lot of emphasis on works, which on the surface seems to put him at odds with the doctrine of justification by faith alone (*sola fide*). He put a lot of merit in the *outer manifestations of inner faith*. He defined religion as bridling the tongue, visiting orphans and widows in their distress, and keeping oneself unstained by the world. You know, being an action figure.

For James, only a working faith saves.

Here's another action-packed verse: "My dear brothers and sisters, take note of this: Everyone should be quick to listen, slow to speak and slow to become angry." That's a short course on healthy relationships, Communication 101.

Be quick to listen.

Listen for content and feeling, accurately reflecting back what the speaker said, making sure the speaker felt heard rather than jumping in to fix things. Being quick to listen means the focus is on the other person, not self.

Be slow to speak.

Take time to value the other person before voicing an opinion.

Be slow to becoming angry.

Take time to evaluate. We can get anger wrong…or we can get it right.

I like action, but taken to an extreme, it can get in the way of deep faith and understanding. It's easy to substitute action for the centering work of hearing God in the first place. Motion is not the same as progress. In short, we need faith *and* works.

Item in the Backpack: Works

James 2:1–13
Dalit Freedom

When I think of people who have been massively dishonored, I think of the Dalits of India. Traditionally, they were called "untouchables." They weren't even part of the caste system. They were outcasts, lower than cows in the pecking order. Lower even than the insects under one's feet. They were not allowed to use their village's well. If their shadow crossed an upper caste member's body, the latter became "polluted." They were relegated to menial jobs, such as manual scavenging, which is cleaning the feces from floors of toilet-less bathrooms. They number over 250 million people.

People God loves.

"Listen, my dear brothers and sisters: Has not God chosen those who are poor in the eyes of the world to be rich in faith and to inherit the kingdom he promised those who love him?"

Here's the good news. Christian ministries have joined forces with Dalit Freedom movements in India. English-medium Dalit schools are being built so the children can become educated. (English is the language of commerce in India.) Economic development programs like sewing classes are popping up everywhere. Microloans enable people to buy vegetable carts or flocks of chickens. Community medical workers are being trained, and mobile clinics are offering vaccinations. Christianity is presented as an alternative to Hinduism, and Dalits are converting in massive numbers. They are sometimes severely persecuted. I know of a pastor who was killed by Hindu extremists, yet many, *many* Dalits are undeterred.

Why? Because they are treated as equals in church. They are given places of honor. They are not judged because of their status. In fact, they are elevated for the first time in three thousand years.

We *must* give equal honor to all people. If we find ourselves showing partiality to a rich acquaintance, we should drop everything and find a person of low status and heap honor on them. We can make equal honoring a way of life.

Item in the Backpack: No Partiality

James 2:14–26
Faith Works

I could look at a particular chair and have faith that it would support me; but unless I were to sit down on it, that faith would be dead, being by itself.

The pastor of Colorado Community Church once said, "Faith without works is dead, but works without faith is empty." I think that sums up this passage. It takes both.

Protestant reformer Martin Luther denied that the book of James was the work of an apostle and termed it an "epistle of straw." He thought it conflicted with Paul on the doctrine of justification by faith alone. On the other hand, I know people who think they can earn their way into God's favor by being really, really good. Works alone.

God has relieved us of having to be really, really good (i.e., earning his favor). How would we ever know if we made the cut? All we have to do is sit down on the chair, so to speak. Believe. Trust. Commit.

Item in the Backpack: A Chair

James 3:1–12
Tongue Taming

It's easy to let the tongue slip a bit. It might not even be *that* bad, but in the words of the bunny, Thumper, in *Bambi*, "If you can't say something nice, don't say nothin' at all."

James felt strongly about the dangers of the tongue. "It is set on fire by hell." Yikes.

My wise brother-in-law sometimes says, "You can't unflush a toilet." Once something is said, you can't unsay it. If it's hurtful or negative, you can apologize or just watch it do its damage, but you can't make it unsaid. If it's life-giving, you can watch the positive ripples bless and transform.

I'm not always in touch with what's going on inside my heart. I may have a vague feeling of this or that, but I might not be able to identify it. But what comes out of my mouth identifies it. If I'm at peace, my words bless. If I'm angry, my words are angry, even if they're on a totally different subject. If I use my words as a gauge, as in "Wow, something's going on inside me," then I can look inside to find it.

James said that no one can tame the tongue. I think he meant "in general." The human condition will always require restraint, but fortunately, we have a particular piece of fruit of the Spirit that can help, and that is self-control.

Today, notice your words and let the Spirit guide you to blessing, not cursing. Freshness, not bitterness.

Item in the Backpack: Restraint

James 3:13–4:17
Strong Strategy

James gave us a cause-and-effect list.

Cause	Effect
jealousy and selfish ambition	disorder and every evil thing
lust and not having	murder
envy and not obtaining	quarreling
praying with wrong motives	not receiving
friendship with the world	hostility toward God
pride	opposition by God
humility	grace, God's exaltation
resisting the devil	the devil flees
drawing near to God	God drawing near to you
speaking against or judging a brother	speaking against/judging the law
boasting in arrogance	evil
knowing the right thing to do but not doing it	sin

"Resist the devil, and he will flee from you." (I think that one is particularly powerful.)

I believe there are spiritual forces lurking about. "For our struggle is not against flesh and blood, but against the rulers, against the authorities, against the powers of this dark world and against the spiritual forces of evil in the heavenly realms" (Eph. 6:12). When we resist oppression or temptation, the forces flee. When we succumb, they stick around.

Paired with resisting evil is drawing near to God. He rewards people who earnestly seek him. These aren't just interesting ideas. They're real strategies for life.

Item in the Backpack: Resistance to Evil

James 5
<u>More Exhortations</u>

Exhortations (admonitions) are urgent advice. Here are James's parting ones:

> Don't misuse riches.
> Be patient.
> Don't complain.
> Endure. Endure. Endure.
> Let your yes be yes and your no, no.
> If you're suffering, pray.
> If you're cheerful, sing praises.
> If you're sick, call the elders of the church to pray over you.
> Confess your sins to one another.
> Pray for each other.
> If anyone strays from the truth, turn that person back.

I want to focus on a couple of these. One is "Let your yes be yes and your no, no." What practical wisdom. Don't lie. Don't be passive-aggressive. Don't manipulate. Don't swear when you really mean it, but otherwise fudge a little. Just say what you mean and mean what you say.

Sometimes we might feel pressured to say yes when we really want to say no. We might need time to get clarity. We might need to check our motives. In short, we might need to wait until our yes is firmly yes or our no, no.

The other one I want to focus on is the last one, about turning a person back if they stray from the truth. If a friend strays, we're to speak the truth in love. That will save his/her soul from death and cover a multitude of sins.

Item in the Backpack: Admonitions

1 Peter 1:1–12
Suffering Lessons

The Apostle Peter is the most likely author of this letter to dispersed Christians in Asia Minor. The Dispersion was partly intentional (for the spread of the Gospel) and partly a result of persecution. These readers needed encouragement. Persecution, trials, sufferings, and testing were major themes in the writings of Paul and James and now, Peter.

Peter spoke of their inheritance—imperishable, undefiled, unfading, protected, and sure—but in the meantime, there would be a downside. I never realized how much suffering was addressed in the New Testament until I undertook this project, but such is life in general. Suffering's part of the equation. Do you know anyone who hasn't suffered?

So what does suffering actually accomplish? Hmmm. Well, it helps us relate to others who suffer, including Jesus himself. It makes us more tenderhearted. It refines the shallowness out of us. It even refines the sin out of us (1 Pet. 4:1). It makes us focus on what's really important. It's inevitable, so we might as well find the lessons, the good.

Helen Keller said, "Character cannot be developed in ease and quiet. Only through experience of trial and suffering can the soul be strengthened, ambition inspired, and success achieved."

Martin Luther King Jr. said, "Human progress is neither automatic nor inevitable…Every step toward the goal of justice requires sacrifice, suffering, and struggle; the tireless exertions and passionate concern of dedicated individuals."

Brennan Manning said, "Suffering, failure, loneliness, sorrow, discouragement, and death will be part of your journey, but the kingdom of God will conquer all these horrors. No evil can resist grace forever."

Suffering is temporary. Salvation is forever…and the envy of angels.

Item in the Backpack: Trials

1 Peter 1:13–25
Appropriate Fear

Peter called on the believers to focus so they wouldn't lose heart. To gird their minds for action. To keep sober in spirit. To fix their hope completely on Jesus's grace. Not to conform to their former lusts, but to be holy. To fervently love each other. To conduct themselves in fear. I always assumed "fear" in this context meant awe or reverence, but since I wasn't sure, I found out its meaning in Greek. The word for fear in verse 17 means "alarm" or "fright." Ugh. Who wants to conduct themselves in fright? What can this mean in relation to the whole counsel of the Gospel, which is all about love, mercy, and grace?

I think it means we're to take Jesus's mercy and grace seriously. "What then? Shall we sin because we are not under the law but under grace? By no means!" (Rom. 6:15).

But fearing God is so countercultural. Can you imagine saying to someone, "I'm not going to do this or that because I'm terrified of God?" I can imagine not doing those particular things for all kinds of reasons, but naming it "fear" just sounds uncomfortable.

We've dumbed down the Gospel to get away from fear-based fire-and-brimstone preaching, so nowadays, many of our churches have become happy-at-all-costs rock concerts. (Yes, I'm one of *those* people.) Don't get me wrong. I like happy messages! (And I like rock concerts.) I just think we sometimes take for granted the great price that was paid. Had it not been paid, you better believe we should be fearful.

Item in the Backpack: Gravitas

1 Peter 2:1–12
Solid Rock

Peter's writing was full of word pictures: gold, fire, blood, a lamb, seeds, grass, milk, and now stones. Peter painted both Jesus *and* believers as living stones.

Jesus was a stone rejected by people but choice and precious in the sight of God—the very cornerstone. A cornerstone is the first stone set in the construction of a masonry foundation. All other stones are set in reference to it, determining the position of the entire structure.

We, as living stones, are used to construct a spiritual house.

When I think of cornerstones, I'm reminded of my childhood church, which had an inscribed cornerstone. (Funny how those things come to mind decades later.) Church was a safe haven for me, full of people I loved. It was my sanctuary, a strong place of learning and protection and refuge and guidance and fun. Seems to me it was made of stone. It was definitely built on the Chief Cornerstone, spiritually speaking. Maybe that's why it took such a strong stand for integration, just a few blocks from Central High School in Little Rock, Arkansas, in 1957. And why it took care of latchkey kids and the homeless elderly before that was cool. And why it takes unpopular stands even today, after its members search God's heart on tough issues.

There's another point about Jesus being a living stone in this passage. He was (and is) a "stone of stumbling and a rock of offense" to some. Maybe that's why my home church suspiciously burned down during World War I. Church leaders had received anonymous phone calls and threatening letters for ministering to those unsavory figures called soldiers. (The events including dancing.)

God wants us to build our lives on solid rock, on *the* living stone. My parents introduced me to Jesus and took me to this rock-solid church. That firm foundation has made all the difference in my life.

Item in the Backpack: Firm Foundation

1 Peter 2:13–25
Honoring Authority

Question: Do you ever disagree with a leader, no matter who it is? I hope so. We're humans led by humans, yet we're to submit ourselves for the Lord's sake to every human institution. Kings and governors are set up to punish evildoers and praise those who do right.

But what about our *leaders* who don't do right themselves?

"For it is God's will that by doing good you should silence the ignorant talk of foolish people."

I believe that on occasion, it's good and right to disobey the government. Take those who protected slaves in the South or Jews during World War II as examples. They had to obey God rather than people and as a result, the slave owners and Nazis were defeated.

Generally-speaking, however, governments are set up for our good. We must discern three things relating to very flawed governments, however. We need to determine (a) which things to engage in (maybe even running for office), (b) which things are worthy of civil disobedience, and (c) which require us to quietly endure with patience and prayer, just like Jesus did. He was murdered by the government, and that was *not right.* He could have resisted, but he didn't.

And by his wounds, we're healed.

Our job is to do right. God's job is to silence the ignorant talk of foolish people.

Item in the Backpack: Right Behavior

1 Peter 3:1–12
Godly Living

The "do good" theme continues.

"You are [Sarah's] daughters if you *do what is right* and do not give way to fear."

"They must turn from evil and *do good*; they must seek peace and pursue it."

Who is the finest Christian you know? I'm guessing it's not someone who talks about how great they are but someone who *does good* from a place of faith. Someone who lives in harmony with others and is sympathetic, kindhearted, and humble.

Someone who blesses others.

Bless people as much as you can today. Do good from the heart. Experiment with that "actions speak louder than words" thing. It will be a reward in itself, but additionally, God will notice. "For the eyes of the Lord are on the righteous and his ears are attentive to their prayer."

Item in the Backpack: Goodness

1 Peter 3:13–22
Blessed Suffering

Recently, I was on the phone with someone who screamed at me for ten solid minutes. My infraction? Doing something gut-wrenchingly hard to support a mutual friend.

I did the right thing.

After shaking and getting my heart rate to settle down, I read this passage, because chronologically, that's where we happen to be in this journey. (Coincidence? I think not.) "Who is going to harm you if you are eager to do good? But even if you should suffer for what is right, you are blessed."

And it goes on: "Always be prepared to give an answer to everyone who asks you to give the reason for the hope that you have. But do this with gentleness and respect, keeping a clear conscience, so that those who speak maliciously against your good behavior in Christ may be ashamed of their slander. For it is better, if it is God's will, to suffer for doing good than for doing evil."

I've done my share of wrong things, but this "infraction" wasn't one of them. I knew the blowback would be severe. I'm suffering for doing what was right.

I'm using this as an example, not to puff myself up. It's an example of God being living and active. He knew my need in the here and now. He affirmed me with the scripture above. The word that pops out to me the most in the passage is "gentleness." I need something to do while giving this situation time. I can be gentle.

Item in the Backpack: God's Support

1 Peter 4
Fervent Love

"Above all, love each other deeply, because love covers over a multitude of sins."

I've done research on this verse and here's what I found. There seems to be consensus that we're not to sweat the small stuff. Proverbs 19:11 says, "A person's wisdom yields patience; it is to one's glory to overlook an offense."

But on the flip side, there's James 5:19–20. "My brothers and sisters, if one of you should wander from the truth and someone should bring that person back, remember this: Whoever turns a sinner from the error of their way will save them from death and cover over a multitude of sins."

Deep love must mean overlooking small offenses and calling out the big ones.

The following quote captures the issue well, in my opinion. It's by Leslie Vernick in an Association of Biblical Counselors blog post called "Does Love Cover a Multitude of Sins?"

> We ought to forgive and forbear, overlooking minor offenses, hoping others will do the same for us. And we are to speak up when someone's sin is hurting them, hurting others, or hurting us. Serious and repetitive sin is lethal to any relationship. We would not be loving the destructive person if we kept quiet and colluded with his self-deception or enabled his sin to flourish without any attempt to speak truth into his life (Ephesians 4:15).

Deep, fervent love means esteeming others as higher than self, caring for each other, praying for each other, restoring each other, and so much more. God loved us so much that he sent his Son to die for us, and in turn, we're to love each other. In a sense, it's a "pay it forward" kind of thing.

In Greek, there are six words for love. *Agape*, meaning God's love for man and man's love for God. *Philia*, meaning affectionate regard between equals or brotherly love. *Eros*, meaning sexual or passionate love. *Storge*, meaning love between parents and children. *Pragma*, meaning love demonstrated during a lengthy marriage. And *Philautia*, meaning self-love.

I would have thought that the word for love in this verse would have been *philia* (brotherly love), but as it turns out, it's *agape*. We're to love each other with the fervency of God's love for us.

Item in the Backpack: Fervent Love

1 Peter 5
<u>Leadership Lessons</u>

Peter wrote to the elders *and* the young about leadership.

To the elders: "Be shepherds of God's flock that is under your care, watching over them—not because you must, but because you are willing, as God wants you to be; not pursuing dishonest gain, but eager to serve."

To the young: "In the same way, you who are younger, submit yourselves to your elders. All of you, clothe yourselves with humility toward one another, because, 'God opposes the proud but shows favor to the humble.'"

Excellent leadership lessons.

I'm thinking of some of the top leadership authors/speakers of our time: John Maxwell, Jim Collins, Sheryl Sandberg, Peter Drucker, Stephen Covey, Dale Carnegie, Winston Churchill, Oprah… But leadership lessons found in the Bible preceded those of these folks by a long shot. Here are a few examples:

Be a servant leader. Seek wise counsel. Be willing to change. Serve with integrity. Forgive people (and self). Pay attention to injustices. Persevere. Use your weaknesses. Use your strengths. Use your influence.

(Speaking of influence, have you ever made a list of the people you influence? It might be bigger than you think.)

I think Peter was unique as a leadership author. After he instructed the elders and the "youngers," he left them with a promise: "And when the Chief Shepherd appears, you will receive the crown of glory that will never fade away."

Item in the Backpack: Influence

2 Peter 1
<u>Divine Formula</u>

> "For this very reason, make every effort to add to your faith goodness;
> and to goodness, knowledge;
> and to knowledge, self-control;
> and to self-control, perseverance;
> and to perseverance, godliness;
> and to godliness, mutual affection;
> and to mutual affection, love."

It's a great formula. There's a procedure. It unfolds. Peter said to *make every effort* to do these things. (The NASB version says to "apply all diligence." "Diligence" means persistent exertion.)

Persistent exertion.

It's a formula with a promise. If these qualities are yours and increasing, you'll be useful and fruitful, and entrance into the kingdom of Christ will be abundantly supplied to you.

It's not a menu. We can't choose, say, knowledge and mutual affection and ignore the rest. Entry into the kingdom begins with faith. Then, after the faith step, there's the unfolding. To your faith, *add* goodness, etc.

It's a lifetime pursuit.

Item in the Backpack: Divine Formula

2 Peter 2
Evildoers

Memo No. 1
To: False prophets, fallen angels, self-willed revilers, and repeat offenders
From: Peter
RE: Your bad behavior

Make no mistake! There are consequences to bad behavior, like swift destruction, pits of darkness, punishment, enslavement, and return to one's own vomit. Stop it!

Memo No. 2
To: You and me
From: Peter
RE: Your bad behavior

Make no mistake! There are consequences to bad behavior, like swift destruction, pits of darkness, punishment, enslavement, and return to one's own vomit. Stop it!

Although we would prefer not to think of ourselves as false prophets or revilers, we're vulnerable. We're vulnerable to heresies, because some are one degree off truth. Flat-out blasphemy is easy to spot, but those teachings that are close to truth are tricky. Well-meaning people can be tricked into following dictators or refusing to get medical help for their children by misunderstanding scripture. We need to ask God for insight that cuts through falsehood.

False prophets must have been prevalent in Peter's day just as they are now, so he devoted a chapter to strong words of warning, but he made two things abundantly clear.

1. The Lord knows how to rescue the godly from temptation.
2. The Lord knows how to keep the unrighteous under punishment for the Day of Judgment.

We need to take Peter's memos seriously.

Item in the Backpack: Insight

2 Peter 3
Coming Day

A day is coming when there will be new heavens and a new earth. Righteousness will dwell there. The current heavens will pass away with a roar. The elements will melt. The earth and its works will be burned up.

So far, nuclear wars and deadly fires have been contained, but Revelation 8:7 says this: "The first angel sounded his trumpet, and there came hail and fire mixed with blood, and it was hurled down on the earth. A third of the earth was burned up, a third of the trees were burned up, and all the green grass was burned up."

This was a vision of things to come and that day *will* come, unexpectedly. We can't predict when, but we should be at the ready. We're to conduct ourselves in holiness and godliness, peacefulness, spotlessness, and blamelessness.

We're also (and this is key!) to regard the patience of the Lord to be salvation. The scripture we've touched on before is found in this particular chapter, verse 9: "The Lord is not slow in keeping his promise, as some understand slowness. Instead he is patient with you, not wanting anyone to perish, but everyone to come to repentance."

If we knew the world would end tomorrow in one big fireball, we would get our acts together (if they weren't already together), but we don't know when, so Peter calls us to *everyday holiness* anyway.

I don't live in la-la land (and I don't mean Los Angeles). Nor do I live in hell-on-earth. But I live on "unrighteous earth." I long for injustices and cancers and meanness and evil to be gone...and that day is coming.

Day 1 of our journey through the New Testament was titled "Great Expectations." As we near the end of the New Testament, we're again reminded of the same. The first was the expectation of Jesus's first arrival. The second is anticipation of Jesus's second arrival.

Item in the Backpack: Forward Thinking

1 John 1
<u>Light Effects</u>

The three Epistles of John as well as the Gospel of John and the Revelation to John were written by Jesus's best friend. John was called "the one whom Jesus loved" no less than five times in the Bible (John 13:23, 19:26, 20:2, 21:7, 21:20).

The first chapter of 1 John reminds me of the first chapter of the Gospel of John. John called Jesus the Word of Life and spoke of him being "light" in both writings.

God is light, and in him, there is no darkness at all. If we say we have fellowship with him but walk in darkness, we lie. If we say we have no sin, we lie. But here's the good news. "If we confess our sins, he is faithful and just and will forgive us our sins and purify us from all unrighteousness."

Then we can walk in the light.

"Your word is a lamp for my feet, a light on my path" (Ps. 119:105). The lamp was likely a small oil lamp, just big enough to illuminate one step at a time.

Sometimes light is brilliant and blocks out all darkness. Sometimes there's just enough light to get from point A to point B, which is enough.

Do you have enough light? If not, is something inside blocking it? It's worth a gut check. "If we claim to have fellowship with him and yet walk in the darkness, we lie and do not live out the truth."

Item in the Backpack: Lamp

1 John 2:1–14
<u>Great News</u>

Okay, time for some self-deprecation or more accurately, truth. As much as I long to be strong and faultless, I need an advocate. I've made progress toward the light. I'm not as stuck as I used to be. There are people who would call me a strong believer, but I have so far to go.

Fortunately for people like me, there's great news. "My dear children, I write this to you so that you will not sin. But if anybody does sin, we have an advocate with the Father—Jesus Christ, the Righteous One."

Jesus is not only an advocate; he's the atoning sacrifice for my sins and, as a matter of fact, for yours as well. (Theologically, atonement is the doctrine concerning the reconciliation of God and humankind through Jesus.)

Nobody's holding a gun to my head to make me believe that. A lot of people don't believe it. But if we *do* believe, the evidence is that we'll keep his commandments.

But I fall short in even keeping his commandments! We all fall short of perfection.

So here's the summary.

God is God. I'm not. I don't even come close, but…there's atonement. Jesus. In response, I'm to keep his commandments, but if I fail…there's atonement. Jesus. And so on.

It's not about me. It's about him. For that, I'm eternally grateful. And in the end, completely at peace.

Item in the Backpack: Peace

1 John 2:15–29
Last Hour

The world and its lusts are passing away, but the one who does the will of God abides forever. The last hour has arrived. We know this because antichrists have risen up, but again…the one who does the will of God abides forever.

We don't really know what the "last hour" means. Seems it's lasted over two thousand years. But it's not so hard to figure out antichrists. They are "against Christ." Might some be the Stalins or Osama bin Ladens of the world? Or maybe less notorious people? Antichrists deny the Father and the Son. That could be a lot of people.

That's frightening, but John gave a simple solution. *Abide.*

To be a little more graphic, it's like knowing that enemies are attacking all around us, but we're to stick close to Jesus. That's all we need to do—stick close. Porch-sit with. Dwell with. Nest, lodge, perch, roost, settle, stay with.

When we abide with someone, we get to know them. And this is Jesus we're talking about. Abiding with him means learning the character of pure love. It means knowing he has our backs. We won't shrink away in shame when we see him coming. In fact, I picture breaking out into a flat-out run when I see him.

Abiding starts now.

Item in the Backpack: Abiding

1 John 3:1–13
Maturing Children

What are the traits of God's children?

Loved by the Father
Hated by the world
Moving toward purification
Moving toward righteousness
Loving one another
Sinless

Okay, about that last one. We've discussed the positional aspect of Christianity, that we're like naturalized citizens. For example, if I were to become a citizen of China, I would have all the rights and responsibilities thereof, but it might take me a lifetime to start acting Chinese.

To me, that's like the "sinless" aspect of verses 6 and 9. We move toward sinlessness. In fact, verse 9 says that no one who is born of God practices sin. "Practices" implies repetitive, intentional action.

If someone practices sin, they'll get really good at it. The one who practices righteousness will, likewise, get really good at it.

Maybe it's more than coincidence that John referred to believers as children four times in this passage. Children have to mature, or they stay stuck as…children.

My children weren't little robots, happily and automatically doing whatever I said to do. They had their own wills. They balked. Sometimes they had to learn the hard way, but they matured. They figured it out.

If we're believers, we *want* to mature, moving toward righteousness and sinlessness. Maybe we won't always be little children.

Item in the Backpack: Maturity

1 John 3:14–24
Four *C*s

If our hearts don't *c*ondemn us, we have *c*onfidence before God. We can *c*all out to God and receive what we asked for, because we keep his *c*ommandments.

Ever wonder why your prayers aren't answered? Have you put them through the "four Cs" first? Does your heart condemn you? If not, go for it. You can have confidence before God.

I think the four *C*s are a start, but there's another letter to think about, taking into consideration the whole counsel of the Bible. It doesn't start with a *c* but with a *y*. In Matthew 26:39, Jesus was praying in the Garden of Gethsemane before being apprehended. He fell on his face and prayed, "My Father, if it is possible, may this cup be taken from me. Yet not as I will, but as you will."

The word is "yet."

Jesus passed the four *C*s. His heart didn't condemn him. He had confidence before God. He called on God. He had kept the commandments. But in the end, he submitted to God's will, not his own, essentially saying, "This is what I want, but I'll submit to your greater wisdom."

Elisa Morgan in her book *The Prayer Coin* calls it praying with honesty and abandon.

Item in the Backpack: Submission

1 John 4:1–6
Spirit Testing

Don't believe everything you hear.

Have you ever been swayed by the latest and greatest parenting technique or someone who came on a little too strong, but they've been shams? False preachers can be in this category. We're to test ideas and even people because they could be fakes.

John said we can be victors over the world's falsehoods. "The one who is in you is greater than the one who is in the world." I've relied on that verse a lot over the years. I can shake my fist in the face of evil and claim it.

Here are verses 4–6 from *The Message*:

> My dear children, you come from God and belong to God. You have already won a big victory over those false teachers, for the Spirit in you is far stronger than anything in the world. These people belong to the Christ-denying world. They talk the world's language and the world eats it up. But we come from God and belong to God. Anyone who knows God understands us and listens. The person who has nothing to do with God will, of course, not listen to us. This is another test for telling the Spirit of Truth from the spirit of deception.

Do you ever have a catch in your spirit about something? Maybe it's one of God's ways to get us to pause for a gut check (i.e., spirit testing).

Item in the Backpack: Gut Checks

1 John 4:7–21
<u>Love Tests</u>

Here's a summary about love in chapters 2–4 with the scripture address.

1.	Keep God's word.	1 John 2:5
2.	Love one another.	1 John 2:10
3.	Don't love the world.	1 John 2:15
4.	Love one another.	1 John 3:16
5.	Love one another.	1 John 3:17
6.	Love one another.	1 John 3:18
7.	Love one another.	1 John 3:23
8.	Love one another.	1 John 4:7–8
9.	Love one another.	1 John 4:11
10.	Love one another.	1 John 4:12

Summary of the summary: If we truly love, we'll keep God's commandments, we won't love the world, and we'll love each other. Heavy on the "loving each other" part.

To me, the crux of the whole Bible is 1 John 4:16: "*And so we know and rely on the love God has for us. God is love. Whoever lives in love lives in God, and God in them.*"

Item in the Backpack: Love for Each Other

1 John 5:1–12
Beyond Infinity

"And this is the testimony: God has given us eternal life, and this life is in his Son."

If we have the Son, we're immortal.

What an enormous truth. Humans are different from animals or even angels. God could have chosen animals or angels to invest himself in, but he chose humans…and he chose to give us eternal life if we believe in his Son. Our pets may mean a lot to us, but I'm not sure they're immortal. (However, Billy Graham once said, "God will prepare everything for our perfect happiness in heaven, and if it takes my dog being there, I believe he'll be there." I love that.)

Anyway, this passage also touches on a second huge truth.

If we have the Son, we've overcome the world.

Think about this. *If we have the Son, we have eternal life and we have overcome the world.* Who can really comprehend the enormity of those fifteen words?

Item in the Backpack: The Magnitude of Reality

1 John 5:13–21
Truth Reiterated

The Bible is drawing to a close. John, in a way, had the last word. Here's a closing concept about sin (i.e., there is sin leading to death and sin not leading to death). What does this mean?

John Piper said that "the sin that does not lead to death and damnation is any sin that we commit that, by God's grace, we are capable of truly confessing and repenting from."

A Japanese proverb puts it this way: "Fall seven times, stand up eight."

And here's the opinion of Craig Blomberg, Distinguished Professor of New Testament at Denver Seminary: "The assurance John offers is always for those who are presently believers (1 John 5:13), not for those who have repudiated their professions of faith.

But as long as the breath of life remains in a person, repentance unto eternal life is always possible. The only unforgivable sin is the sin of unwillingness, in the final analysis, to repent and come to Christ."

Here are verses 18–21 from *The Message*:

> We know that none of the God-begotten makes a practice of sin—fatal sin. The God-begotten are also the God-protected. The Evil One can't lay a hand on them. We know that we are held firm by God; it's only the people of the world who continue in the grip of the Evil One. And we know that the Son of God came so we could recognize and understand the truth of God—what a gift!—and we are living in the Truth itself, in God's Son, Jesus Christ. This Jesus is both True God and Real Life. Dear children, be on guard against all clever facsimiles.

In some churches, the altar call includes the opportunity to rededicate one's life to God, because sometimes we feel the need. If you've drifted slightly or massively but genuinely want to come back, you can.

Item in the Backpack: Rededication

2 and 3 John
Truth Walking

John wrote a short letter to the chosen lady and to Gaius. Scholars believe that the chosen lady was a metaphor for a local church. He encouraged both to walk in truth, keep the commandments, and love one another. Nothing new there, but a message they could never hear enough. We can take note. What if we woke up every morning with those words as our guiding lights for the day?

> Today I will...
> walk in truth,

keep the commandments,
love.
Tomorrow I will…
walk in truth,
keep the commandments,
love.
The next day…

You get the picture.

In addition, John reminded them to watch out for deceivers. In 2 John, he said to not even allow such a person to come into one's home. In 3 John, he singled out Diotrephes. Sounds like this guy was a bit narcissistic. (He loved to be first.) He unjustly accused John and his colleagues and he put people out of the church.

We can take note about this too. I'm guessing Diotrephes was a larger-than-life person who spoke wicked words so often and so convincingly that people were tempted to follow him.

The early church had to rely on visits and letters from the likes of Paul and John for instruction, beyond that of local leaders. We now have blogs and phone calls and e-mail and conventions and books and videos and so on and so on. There are many ways to disseminate information, both correct and incorrect. We need to be careful with what we let in. We need to walk in truth, keep the commandments, love one another…and watch out for deceivers.

Item in the Backpack: Keen Perception

Jude
Ungodly People

Jude wrote to the believers about the ungodly in their midst. He quoted from the book of Enoch, which was probably written in the century before Christ. (It may have useful historical information, but isn't regarded as part of the biblical canon by Christians.) He also paraphrased an incident (in text that has been lost) about Satan and Michael the Archangel quarreling over the body of Moses.

He warned about grumblers, faultfinders, lust-followers, the arrogant, flatterers, mockers, the divisive, the worldly minded, and those devoid of the Spirit. Unsavory characters, but they might not have looked that different from people we know or see on TV. Our culture celebrates some of these traits.

To stand against these folks takes courage, because it makes us look out of touch, judgmental, or, at best, uncool.

Jude, for whatever reason, admonished them to have mercy on some. He said to save others, snatching them out of the fire. And lastly, he recommended having mercy-with-fear on others, likely meaning that they were so corrupt and polluted that they (the believers) needed to be careful.

We too can be merciful…and cautious.

The last two verses have become one of the most used benedictions in the church. Here it is from *The Message*:

> And now to him who can keep you on your feet, standing tall in his bright presence, fresh and celebrating—to our one God, our only Savior, through Jesus Christ, our Master, be glory, majesty, strength, and rule before all time, and now, and to the end of all time. Yes.

Item in the Backpack: Caution

Revelation 1
<u>Last Prophecy</u>

We've arrived at the last leg of our journey, but it's a doozy of a leg. It's so cryptic that I'm not even going to attempt to comment on most of it. The first three chapters are John's messages to the seven churches in Asia, the recipients of the book. Chapters 4–22 are his visions regarding how God will bring this age to its conclusion…and what lies beyond. We'll take a look at the church messages and do a quick overview of the rest.

(I recommend taking a course on the book of Revelation.)

In AD 95, John was banished to a Greek island called Patmos as punishment for his Christian activities. It was a place of exile for convicts. This was under the Roman emperor Titus Flavius Domitianus. Little did Domitian know that God would speak to John there. (It reminds me of the Mexican proverb, "They tried to bury us. They didn't know we were seeds.")

John was in the Spirit on the Lord's Day and heard a loud voice behind him. He turned around and saw…all the things you'll read in his book. And when he saw Jesus, he fell at his feet as a dead man but Jesus touched him and said to not be afraid. Jesus made this clear: "I am the First and the Last, the Living One. I was dead, but now I'm alive forevermore." And…

"I have the keys of death and of Hades."

Backing up a bit to verse 7, John set the stage for his book by quoting Daniel 7:13. (Daniel, an Old Testament book, is also apocalyptic.) Here's verse 7 from *The Message*: "Yes, he's on his way! Riding the clouds, he'll be seen by every eye, those who mocked and killed him will see him, People from all nations and all times will tear their clothes in lament. Oh, Yes."

In other words, we're on the victory side of things. The Revelation to John gives us a sneak peek into the rest of the story. It's been said that most of the prophecies in the Bible have already been fulfilled. Who knows? We may see the rest come to pass in our lifetimes, but whether we do or don't, we need to be informed.

Item in the Backpack: Information

Revelation 2:1–11
<u>Ephesus, Smyrna</u>

The people of the church at Ephesus were known for working hard and separating themselves from the wicked. They called out false prophets. They hated the deeds of the Nicolaitans. (The Nicolaitans were possibly followers of a heresy that the saved weren't bound to follow moral law. Jesus was not okay with that.)

But these Ephesians were admonished for forsaking their first love, losing their passion, or taking their loved one for granted. It takes work to keep the flame alive. Most folks who have been married for quite a while know that, but it's also true of the Bride of Christ, the church. We need to keep the flame alive for our Groom.

If the Ephesian Christians turned things around, they would be granted the ability to eat of the tree of life in the paradise of God. What a graphic promise that goes all the way back to Genesis.

The people of the church at Smyrna were acknowledged for their sufferings but were forewarned about more persecution to come. Ten days' worth, specifically. The promise? "Be faithful, even to the point of death, and I will give you life as your victor's crown." I believe the messages and promises apply to all of us. Renew your vows to your first love and hang on during persecution, and you'll receive the crown of life. Amen.

Item in the Backpack: Renewing and Persisting

Revelation 2:12–29
<u>Pergamum, Thyatira</u>

Pergamum was where Satan's throne was. Maybe this was a reference to a major Greek temple there, symbolized by the figure of a snake. Another explanation is that it's where Antipas, possibly the first Christian martyr in Asia, was killed; so his killers were labeled "Satan." At any rate, the people of the church were praised for holding fast to Jesus, but they needed to repent for allowing false teachers in. The teachings were similar to those of the Nicolaitans, which encouraged believers to abandon moral codes.

The promise for overcomers? To receive some of the hidden manna as well as a white stone. (I told you this was cryptic.) Manna was a wafer-like food provided supernaturally by God for the Israelites in the wilderness. Jesus was known as "the bread of life." See John 6:48–51 for a comparison.

The white stone? I believe it's something special given to believers, personalized, meaning we each have a unique personal relationship with Jesus.

The people of the church at Thyatira were known for their charity. They seemed to be maturing because their recent deeds were greater than their first deeds, but they held to the teachings of a false prophetess. The falsehoods were eating food sacrificed to idols and sexual immorality. Maybe eating food sacrificed to idols meant stepping onto the slippery slope of worshipping the idol, but sexual immorality is clearly a slippery slope. Our best bet is to avoid step one.

The promise for overcomers? To rule over the nations and receive the morning star. It's thought that the period we live in, between Jesus's ascension and his second coming, is called night. The morning star heralds the dawn.

Item in the Backpack: Morality

Revelation 3:1–13
Sardis, Philadelphia

Most of the people of the church at Sardis had soiled their garments. Not a pretty picture. "Wake up! Strengthen what remains and is about to die, for I have found your deeds unfinished in the sight of my God."

The promise for overcomers? To be clothed in white garments and to be in the Book of Life.

As we near the end of our journey, I'm once again struck by our responsibility in the Christian life. We're to obey and endure. There are consequences for slacking and sinning. I'm going out on a limb here, but it seems that our churches are lukewarm. (Spoiler alert: That's the message to the seventh church, at Laodicea.)

But back to my point. A huge takeaway for me, after spending many months immersed in the New Testament, is God's *seriousness*. Jesus told the church at Sardis to wake up and get with the program.

The people of the church at Philadelphia were steadfast. They kept the commandments and didn't deny Christ. He didn't have an issue with them, so he chose to keep them safe from the testing to come.

In general, though, we'll be subject to testing and discipline from time to time, just as children are disciplined so they'll grow up healthy and wise. It's just the way things work. The promise for overcomers? To become a permanent pillar in the temple of God and to be marked with God's name.

Item in the Backpack: Reward

Revelation 3:14–22
<u>Lukewarm Laodicea</u>

"Here I am! I stand at the door and knock. If anyone hears my voice and opens the door, I will come in and eat with that person, and they with me."

This verse is used a lot as a picture of salvation, but it could mean Jesus knocking on the doors of lukewarm Christians. Maybe richness breeds lukewarmness. Riches can mask truth. The rich say, "I have need of nothing."

Maybe the rich wear the emperor's new clothes.

Jesus gave some advice to the rich: "I counsel you to buy from me gold refined in the fire, so you can become rich; and white clothes to wear, so you can cover your shameful nakedness; and salve to put on your eyes, so you can see."

Jesus reproves and disciplines those he loves. Maybe he's knocking on our door.

The promise to overcomers? To sit down with Jesus on his throne, because he also overcame and sat down with his Father on his throne.

Summary: Do the needful, even to the death, and you will be rewarded. Opening the door means life and love, no matter how hard the journey. And lest we ever forget, Jesus promised in Matthew 28:20 that he would be with us always. *Always.*

Item in the Backpack: Opening the Door

Revelation Chapters 4–21
The Future

I recently took a course on Revelation. I happen to love symbolism and connecting historical dots, plus, I'm curious. Revelation ties the big picture together, from the beginning of the Old Testament to the end of the New. Studying the symbols (seals, horses, queens, the beast, and such) was fascinating, but as I've said, this is all *way* beyond me.

Frankly, I think it's way beyond most people. We'll understand it as it unfolds, or at least shortly after it unfolds, just like Jesus's disciples quickly figured out the big picture after the resurrection.

Here's a summary of chapters 4–21: The throne of God is discussed. The seven seals are opened. The seven trumpets are sounded. The seven spiritual figures are introduced. The seven bowls are poured onto earth. Aftermath. Marriage supper of the Lamb. Judgment of the two beasts, the dragon, and the dead. New heaven and earth, New Jerusalem.

May our hearts be open to the enormity, power, rightness, truth, and holiness of the things to come.

Item in the Backpack: Awe

Revelation 22
Alpha and Omega

"He has made everything beautiful in its time. He has also set eternity in the human heart; yet no one can fathom what God has done from beginning to end" (Eccles. 3:11).

How am I supposed to summarize God and bring this journey to a conclusion? Who can fathom what God has done from the beginning to the end? Love has no end point.

This chapter contains quite a message. When the time comes, there will no longer be a curse or the darkness of night. We'll be able to see the faces of God and Jesus. We'll be able to serve them without any impediments. The name of Jesus will be on our foreheads. It will be a time of unlimited fruitfulness and healing.

"Look, I am coming soon! My reward is with me, and I will give to each person according to what they have done. I am the Alpha and the Omega, the First and the Last, the Beginning and the End. Blessed are those who wash their robes, that they may have the right to the tree of life and may go through the gates into the city."

"Let the one who hears say, 'Come!' Let the one who is thirsty come; and let the one who wishes take the free gift of the water of life."

Even at the very, very end, he's still telling us how much he loves us. Still offering us the water of life without cost. For those who haven't yet accepted, the offer holds, right here, right now. For those of us who have said yes, eternity with pure love awaits.

So I can't bring this journey to an end…because it's only the beginning.

Post-Trip Debriefing

When I returned from my European trip, I took some time to ponder it. I reread my journal. I celebrated a thousand memories. I took to heart some lessons learned. I thanked people who had helped me along the way. And of course, I unpacked the stuff in my backpack. I treasured each item, because it had sustained me or had given meaning to my life.

Since then, I've gone back to Europe, which was an even sweeter journey.

Maybe this is a good way to think about our trek through the New Testament. To ponder it, celebrate it, and treasure each item in the backpack. To go back and do it again.

In 1 Corinthians 2:9, Paul quoted from Isaiah: "As it is written: 'What no eye has seen, what no ear has heard, and what no human mind has conceived'—the things God has prepared for those who love him."

I can't wait.

Acknowledgements

I heartily thank the people who first brought the Bible to my attention, like my parents, my pastor, Dr. Dale Cowling, and my church family. I don't take this early learning for granted!

I also thank my later-in-life friends, like a whole host of coffee-drinking buddies (my "Inklings" of sorts), my family for their patience and even their hard theological questions, my Fabs, my colleagues, my fellow hikers who introduced me to backpacking journeys in the first place, and all who have been with me through thick and thin.

I thank Dr. Bill Klein and endorsers Luis Villarreal, Cindy Smith, Karl Wheeler, and Adrian Miller for their friendships and very kind words.

I thank Covenant Books for their professionalism and excellence and Pixabay and Pexels for the use of photographs. I thank the influential people whose stories appear in the book.

It would take a long time to list <u>all</u> the people who have given me glimpses of Jesus over the years. I'm just so happy to be on this journey with all of you.

About the Author

Debbie Johnson has a passion for stewarding the scriptures with a contemplative yet contemporary (and fun!) voice. Her personal mission statement is "to live an abundant life in Christ (John 10:10) and to motivate her fellow Americans and fellow Christians to become more involved in the world, making a difference both spiritually and practically." In 1995, she founded DenverWorks to equip the unemployed in her community. She led the organization for ten years before engaging in international ministry, first as the vice president of Programs at the Dalit Freedom Network, then as the executive director of India Transformed.

Debbie grew up in Little Rock, Arkansas. She graduated from Ouachita Baptist University (BME, MME) and has done graduate studies in social work at the University of Denver. She is a lifelong student of the Bible. Through this book, her desire is to present the Gospel in a way that piques the interest of nonbelievers and presents the biblical narrative in a fresh way to believers.

She and her husband live on a farm in Colorado with two dogs and a bunch of chickens.